Not Quite a
Cancer Vaccine

Not Quite a Cancer Vaccine

Selling HPV and Cervical Cancer

S. D. GOTTLIEB

Rutgers University Press

New Brunswick, Camden, and Newark, New Jersey, and London

Library of Congress Cataloging-in-Publication Data

Names: Gottlieb, S. D. (Samantha D.) author.
Title: Not quite a cancer vaccine : selling HPV and cervical cancer / S.D. Gottlieb.
Description: New Brunswick : Rutgers University Press, [2018] | Includes bibliographical references and index.
Identifiers: LCCN 2017015420 (print) | LCCN 2017021033 (ebook) | ISBN 9780813587790 (E-pub) | ISBN 9780813587806 (Web PDF) | ISBN 9780813587783 (cloth) | ISBN 9780813587776 (paperback) | ISBN 9780813587790 (epub)
Subjects: LCSH: Papillomavirus vaccines. | Cervix uteri—Cancer—Prevention. | BISAC: MEDICAL / Public Health. | SOCIAL SCIENCE / Disease & Health Issues. | HEALTH & FITNESS / Women's Health. | MEDICAL / Immunology. | HEALTH & FITNESS / Diseases / Cancer.
Classification: LCC QR189.5.P36 (ebook) | LCC QR189.5.P36 G69 2018 (print) | DDC 616.9/11—dc23
LC record available at https://lccn.loc.gov/2017015420

A British Cataloging-in-Publication record for this book is available from the British Library.

∞ The paper used in this publication meets the requirements of the American National Standard for Information Sciences—Permanence of Paper for Printed Library Materials, ANSI Z39.48-1992.

www.rutgersuniversitypress.org

Manufactured in the United States of America

For Boulette & Poodle

Contents

**Not Quite a
Cancer Vaccine**

1

Introduction

In the summer of 2016, Merck & Company, Inc., a pharmaceutical company, launched a new ad campaign that echoed ubiquitous "Tell Someone" commercials from a decade earlier. On a website titled "Know HPV," there are two versions of the ad in which the protagonists speak to the viewer in voice-overs.[1] In one, it is a young, dark-haired, ethnically ambiguous but probably white woman, and, in the other, it is a young blue-eyed and freckled white man. Both are in their mid-twenties. We see images and videos of the young adults from the past: as images and short video clips fade in and out, the narrator ages in reverse, while the older self, the man or woman, narrates his or her dismay that when he or she was a child, their parents didn't choose to vaccinate their child against the human papillomavirus (HPV). As the man explains, "I was infected with HPV. Maybe my parents didn't know how widespread HPV is. . . . Maybe they didn't know I would end up with cancer because of HPV. Maybe if they'd known there was a vaccine to help protect me when I was eleven or twelve. Maybe my parents just didn't know." If they had known, wouldn't they have given him the vaccine, which has been available since 2006? In the montage that accompanied the male narrative, a young boy, presumably the narrator's past self, asks the camera directly, "Right, mom? Right, dad?" The ad ends with a simple orange screen and the words "What will you say?" read by an invisible female narrator, who encourages parents not to wait, to talk to their children's doctor today. I watched it as I revised this book, finding myself unexpectedly affected by the emotional manipulations the nostalgic representations of childhood evoked, thinking of my own children, who are still under five years old. As with Merck's 2006 "Tell Someone" ads, their first HPV vaccine ads, the 2016 marketing pitch was perfect, eliciting a strong emotional reaction in viewers even as it avoided an explicit directive to use Gardasil, the primary HPV vaccine.[2]

Indeed, as with the "Tell Someone" ads, the 2016 advertisement never mentions a brand name. Instead, the advertisement ends with the female voiceover's exhortation to viewers to "learn more at HPV.com." The website says that readers should know that there is a vaccine for HPV, but as with the television commercial, it does not explicitly identify the brand name Gardasil. It is not until you click on the link titled "Learn what you can do now" that a text box allows you to choose between "Yes, I want to learn how to protect my child," or "No, thanks. I'd like to stay on this site." The "yes" decision links to the Gardasil9.com website.

This most recent Gardasil advertisement exemplifies a new regime of anticipation in which "histories of the future are replacing histories of the present."[3] Vincanne Adams, Michele Murphy, and Adele Clarke explain that in these emergent practices, "the future of now is that which not only gives meaning to the past, but conjures new temporalized domains, versions of the present as sites of contingent and malleable action."[4] The young adult who speaks to the viewer of the commercial exists simultaneously in the past, the present, and the future, anticipating his or her current diagnosis of cancer. The advertisement's protagonist also asks the viewer to concurrently occupy the time now, when action is possible, and to project who one's child will and could be. The adult child asks his parents of today if they knew or know now that a vaccine against cancer exists. The direct entreaty engages with a broad set of affective strategies of fear, hope, vulnerability to invoke a moral imperative, the questions, "Right, mom? Right, dad?" to which there ought to be only one answer. Yes, I want to learn how to protect my child. A failure to vaccinate thus becomes an abandonment of care. We, the viewers, are suspended in anticipation of an avoidable cancer as we are confronted with the uncertainty of future diagnosis and urged to shore up our children's bodies against a possible adverse outcome. Because an HPV infection may never progress to cancer and the risk of dying from HPV-related cancer is comparatively low for people living in the United

States, the fear-driven anticipation is overwrought. Yet anticipation creates a logic that is impossible to resist. As the debates about Gardasil during its first few years on the market in the United States revealed, nearly no one would outright condemn a vaccine for cancer. But although a cancer vaccine might seem like an unimpeachable good, Gardasil was not just a cancer vaccine. Robert Aronowitz has called the HPV vaccine "Janus faced;" it alternates between its function as a prophylactic to minimize the risk of HPV and its designation as a vaccine against cancer.[5]

Gardasil prevents infection from specific types of HPV, the most common sexually transmitted infection (STI). HPV is so ubiquitous that nearly anyone who is sexually active will be exposed to it at some point in his or her life. There are approximately forty types of HPV that are sexually transmitted, and researchers have identified over one hundred HPV types, including ones that are not sexually transmitted. Some HPV STIs cause genital warts, while other HPV STIs can, but *do not always*, develop into a variety of cancers of the reproductive or oral-pharyngeal tracts. Not all sexually transmitted HPVs are associated with cancer, and even those that are may clear up before progressing into cancer. There is no treatment for HPV, although warts can be removed if they are uncomfortable or aesthetically unpleasing. Not everyone infected with the virus will know they have it because many HPV types do not manifest visible symptoms. In fact, when someone is infected with the cancer-causing types of sexually transmitted HPV, she cannot know she has the virus without medical intervention and diagnosis. The Pap smear and the HPV test are two screening technologies used to identify cervical abnormalities (in the case of the former) or the presence of an HPV type (in the case of the latter). The HPV test allows clinicians to distinguish whether a person has the cancer-causing or non-cancer-causing type of the virus. Although both men and women get HPV and its related cancers, there is no standardized test for HPV in men. HPV-related cancers and precancerous abnormalities prompt complex triage strategies that further compound the confusion and ambiguities that make HPV infection difficult to educate people about or to manage.

Thus, infection with HPV introduces a host of uncertainties for individuals about what may or may not happen. Merck's Gardasil messaging embraced and even capitalized on these ambiguities. The "Know HPV" ad demands action of its viewer; there is no time like the present, the future self admonishes. The injunction to know a virus that perhaps we ought to all already know, yet cannot always know because of its invisibility without medical intervention, then heightens the urgency. The marketing of Gardasil, subsequent policy interventions, and public health campaigns that promoted the vaccine all engaged with a specific anticipatory logic, where "a future that may or may not arrive, is always uncertain and yet is necessarily coming and so therefore always demanding a response."[6] Know it, but also know that it is already everywhere. As the 2006 pre-licensure "Tell Someone" advertisements ominously warned women, "millions of people already have the types of HPV that can cause cervical cancer. . . . *You* could have HPV and *not even know it*."

The Holy Grail

In January 2007, six months after the U.S. Food and Drug Administration (FDA) approved Gardasil, physicians, public health officials, and pharmaceutical industry attended an immunization coalition meeting in southern California. The meeting took place in the sleek new building of a large health foundation, based in the soon-to-be gentrified downtown of a large metropolis in southern California. Those who attended grappled with how to promote a vaccine for adolescents that could prevent, as the advertisements claimed, "cancer caused by a virus." How would they effectively promote what one physician called the "holy grail" of immunizations? He exclaimed, "No vaccine in the past fifteen years has excited me more."

The panelists noted that adolescents are a difficult population to vaccinate because of their liminality: they are not quite children and not quite adults. Their liminality calls attention to the imagined potential of their future selves. Unlike infants and babies, who receive frequent checkups and are usually vaccinated according to a schedule pediatricians recommend, adolescents may not visit the physician as often or consistently. Added to the challenges of adolescent vaccination, cervical cancer, which Gardasil promised to prevent, is usually managed by adult women's gynecologists, not pediatricians. Gardasil required pediatricians and family physicians to promote a cervical cancer vaccine at early adolescence.

Two meeting attendees drew attention to other complexities Gardasil introduced. During the audience questions and discussion, the first to raise concerns was Lucy, a public health program manager. She worried that as the most expensive vaccine on the market, Gardasil would be a "boutique" vaccine that would be available only to families who could afford it. These concerns resonated for her, as Lucy told me later when we began to work together on a Centers for Disease Control (CDC) project, because one of the predominately African American[7] communities in the large metropolis had very high cervical cancer rates and high rates of STIs.[8] Her city public health department would spend the next few years surveying the receptiveness of this community to the new vaccine. Who was the imagined population, she asked of the meeting attendees, and how would those who needed it gain access to it?

Even as public health officials lauded the novelty and potential of the intervention, Gardasil troubled health management strategies and elicited provocative policies. Although the HPV vaccine was (and still is) the most expensive vaccine on the market, once the CDC's Advisory Committee on Immunization Practices (ACIP) recommended Gardasil, the agency's low-income vaccine program Vaccines for Children (VFC) began offering it at no cost to eligible children. This at least partly addressed Lucy's concerns, although families who did not qualify for VFC and could not afford health insurance would surely fall through the gaps. Gardasil also generated federal policies for immigrant women seeking U.S. citizenship, for whom there were no government vaccine subsidies. Almost immediately after the FDA approved Gardasil, state legislatures began debating whether vaccination should be a requirement for middle school girls. In each of these policies, the vaccine called attention to the bodies at risk, social expectations about government interventions, and the implications of population-level regulations.

In its first years on the market, Gardasil contributed to U.S. debates about women's access to health care and reproductive rights. Its target recipients—young females—and the vaccine's primary decision makers—parents, usually mothers—embodied potential and actual reproductive individuals. At the January 2007 adolescent vaccines meeting, a Planned Parenthood medical director stood up to ask the room of immunization advocates how Planned Parenthood could provide Gardasil to the young women seeking sexual health services at their clinics. She reminded attendees that under California state law, minors could not consent to vaccinations. Parental consent or even awareness that their children were seeking care at Planned Parenthood would impede the organization's goal to provide young women with safe, confidential access to sexual health services.

From the perspective of a sexual health care provider, Gardasil is a prophylactic tool that prevents the most common and most difficult to prevent STI. The medical director argued that like birth control pills or Pap smears, the vaccine would give young women a measure of control over their sexual health, a critical part of Planned Parenthood's mission. But the HPV vaccine's legal designation as a vaccine determined its policies and clinical delivery strategies, dominating public debates. Merck's corporate marketing and national public health institutions, like the CDC, cultivated a structured absence, downplaying the vaccine's sexual health benefits and focusing on its role in cancer prevention. Yet as the Planned Parenthood director made clear, for many medical practitioners, it was impossible to ignore Gardasil's target STI. The vaccine's "Janus-faced" quality shaped public debates that were simultaneously about young female sexualities and not about sexuality. However, despite Merck's hope that it could avoid parents' resistance to the vaccine because it prevents an STI, the company's emphasis on Gardasil as an immunization tapped into another cause of ongoing public anxieties: vaccines.

Vaccines are a contentious subject in the early twenty-first century, both in the United States and abroad.[9] Until very recently, U.S. vaccination policies, which use school-entry requirements to maximize immunization rates, controlled the spread of vaccine-preventable diseases. However, health officials have expressed concern that two recent measles outbreaks in the United States, in 2008 and 2015, reflect the growing numbers of parents who refuse to vaccinate their children. Newer vaccines lend insight into the nuances of these resistances. By looking at the motivations for developing Gardasil, the process of its FDA approval, and the political and policy efforts to disseminate it, we can understand broader sociocultural values about vaccination policies and practices. Gardasil also illuminates how powerful pharmaceutical companies market and distribute new vaccines.

Not Quite a Cancer Vaccine

This book analyzes how Merck and public health actors deployed a highly crafted framing of Gardasil as cancer prevention, in order to market and promote the vaccine. Merck's deliberate avoidance of the vaccine's benefit for the future sexually active person fostered distrust in parents, the people who needed to embrace the intervention. The focus on cancer is everywhere in HPV vaccination materials, from the first marketing strategies to a more recent push in late 2016 to increase vaccine uptake. Yet despite the cancer narrative that frames Gardasil's promotion, the specifics of HPV's relationship to cancer, the effectiveness of preventive cervical cancer screening, and the low rate of U.S. cervical cancer mortality were not part of the information advertisers or health educators emphasized to the public. Most notably, the marketing and legislative interventions failed to point out the high rates of HPV morbidity, a compelling and persuasive reason to vaccinate boys and girls. The HPV vaccine has the lowest rate of use among all the recommended standard childhood vaccines.[10] Why have less than 50 percent of eligible children received a vaccine that promises to prevent cancer? Public health officials and oncologists who seek to alter parents' tepid response to the vaccine underestimate a critical reason the HPV vaccine has not achieved broad acceptance.[11] As I conducted the research for this book, it became clear that the narrative of Gardasil as cancer prevention functions as misdirection. In order to deflect anxiety about Gardasil's primary role as a preventive for the most common STI, Merck and proponents of the vaccine avoided talking about sex. Because of this, the emphasis on Gardasil as a cancer vaccine and the deliberately evasive marketing strategy linked the product to U.S. debates about immunization and raised parents' suspicions about its primary purpose.

The concept of anticipatory regimes provides a lens through which to understand Merck's marketing campaigns. Anticipatory regimes describe the processes of this particular cultural and social moment that are not just temporal but also shape people's affective and moral states.[12] The impact of these anticipatory states have pervasive influence, shaping important phenomena such as health care practices. Health care research and direct services have been shaped by a process of medicalization, in which human life, including areas that were not previously of medical concern, now require medical management not only "masked as technical, scientific, and objective" goals but as a reflection of social desires about how individuals and populations ought to be.[13] Medicalization of individuals and populations has further evolved through technological and cultural shifts that Clarke, Shim, Mamo, Fosket, and Fishman call biomedicalization, an "increasingly complex, multisited, multidirectional, processes of medicalization."[14] Biomedical management provides a site for the expression of anticipatory regimes, and they subject individuals to affective and moral judgments.

The temporal, affective, and moral dimensions of Gardasil's promotion are particularly salient now, ten years after the vaccine's launch. Future bodies figured prominently in the "Know HPV" advertisements, demanding urgent and imminent action. However, the HPV vaccine has the lowest rate of coverage among recommended childhood vaccines in the United States.[15] Clinicians, particularly oncologists, argue that the vaccine's potential has not been fully realized.[16] Thus, the narrative that Merck crafted for Gardasil's value capitalizes on these complex judgments, seeking to drive demand for the vaccine.

Although Gardasil is now a vaccine for both boys and girls, the FDA initially approved it only for girls and young women ages 9–26. Soon after that, the ACIP issued a recommendation that encouraged vaccination of girls between ages eleven and twelve.[17] This made it a gendered intervention. Unlike other vaccines regulated by the FDA, which are universal immunizations, Gardasil's initial designation raised cultural anxieties about female, and especially young female, sexualities. Further, Gardasil joined a growing number of vaccines for populations after early childhood. The U.S. pediatric immunization schedule focuses on younger children, but Gardasil and other adolescent vaccines target populations who, although they may not yet be of the legal age of consent, have the ability to vocalize their preferences.[18] Merck's dissemination and promotion of Gardasil required a diverse set of actors who previously had not had to coordinate efforts across the lifespan of medical care. Because it is a vaccine for early adolescents, Merck required the cooperation of pediatricians to recommend and promote it. Cancer and STIs are usually part of gynecological and adult medicine and are less common in pediatric care; conversely, vaccines are incidental or rare in gynecological practice. Although health officials and pharmaceutical marketers tried to seam together resources to promote this potentially impactful intervention, the public discourse around Gardasil highlighted fissures and gaps in Merck's attempts to make it widely accepted.

Merck's emphasis on cervical cancer tapped into public anxieties about female vulnerability and revealed the kinds of bodies pharmaceutical companies see as appropriate and attempt to manage. Gardasil exemplifies "a twenty-first century story of big pharma, corporate disease awareness and direct-to-consumer (DTC) advertising, and 'patient activism' enrollment."[19] This book examines the strategies Merck, clinicians, and public health proponents used to promote the vaccine, the concerns raised by mothers whose children were the primary target market for Gardasil, and the patient advocates who believed the vaccine offered a solution all women should embrace. Although its proponents and its opponents understood the vaccine in disparate ways, the contentious debates Gardasil triggered shared an anticipatory outlook in which possible futures shaped conversations about the present, set moral standards, and shaped debates.

Ambiguous Yet Pervasive: The Epidemiology of HPV and Cervical Cancer

Existing medical, research, and social-cultural practices informed the trajectory and development of the HPV vaccine. Why were so few people aware of HPV, even though it affects most sexually active individuals at some point in their lives?[20] What sorts of bodies were imagined as at risk for HPV, and how might that have shaped the decisions about what interventions researchers believed were appropriate? Although HPV's relationship to cancers other than cervical cancer were not as well established in the late twentieth century, by the early twenty-first century, when Gardasil entered the market, epidemiologists and medical researchers knew that HPV can cause a variety of reproductive and oral-pharyngeal cancers.[21] This raises the question of why this vaccine was marketed exclusively as a vaccine for cervical cancer. The epidemiology of HPV and the history of reproductive and sexual health interventions for women informed the logic of the cervical cancer vaccine's development.

There are more than 100 types of human papillomavirus. Of these, about forty are sexually transmitted.[22] Some cause warts. Others can lead to cancer. We know that the sexually transmitted types affect the genital and anal regions, and recent research has confirmed that HPV causes some oral and throat cancers.[23] As with any sexually transmitted infection, a person can be infected the first time he or she engages in sex. In addition, unlike some STIs, HPV can be transmitted through skin-to-skin contact. HPV is a challenging STI to prevent, as condoms do not reliably prevent transmission. Thus, a person who has never had penetrative sexual intercourse can get infected.

Before Harald zur Hausen's research in the 1970s identified HPV as the cause of cervical cancer, scientists had long speculated that there was an association between cervical cancer and sexual activity; historically, cervical cancer rates were much higher among married women than among unmarried women.[24] In the mid-nineteenth century, Italian researcher Rigoni-Stern argued that nuns did not get "cancers of the womb," as uterine and cervical cancers were collectively called. He concluded that these cancers were related to marital status, which was a proxy, albeit a limited one, for sexual activity. Although Rigoni-Stern's work does not meet contemporary scientific standards due to its lack of rigor, and he did not distinguish between cancers of the uterus and cervix, he is a figure in the cervical cancer story because of his astute awareness that social context had something to do with these kinds of cancers.[25] Richard Shope, a pathologist who is known for demonstrating that influenza was caused by a virus and not a bacterium in the 1930s, first identified what would come to be known as papillomavirus after encountering a rabbit with "horns," an appearance that has contributed to the myth of the jackalope.[26] (The animal's horns were in fact warts.) Shope examined the horn-like material under a microscope and identified the warts as caused by a virus.[27] Forty years later the scientist Harald zur Hausen connected the human papillomavirus with genital cancers.[28] His findings eventually led to the development of the HPV vaccine.

Current studies identify fifteen types of high-risk HPV, which cause cancer, three types that are probably high risk, twelve types that are low risk, and three types that are unknown.[29] Not everyone who is infected with a high-risk HPV type will develop cancer. Infection with HPV may lead to cervical, oral, penile, vaginal, or anal cancer, but an HPV diagnosis does not tell the infected individual anything definitive. Instead, it introduces a clinical ambiguity that requires management and tracking of the patient. In addition, although younger women sometimes develop cervical cancer, cervical cancer usually affects women later in life because of the slow progression from viral infection to cancer. HPV is a necessary but not a sufficient condition for cervical cancer. In other words, cervical cancer usually cannot occur without a prior infection with HPV, but not all HPV will progress to cancer.[30] Unlike other papillomas, such as the warts-causing low risk HPV, high risk HPVs do not show signs or symptoms. In addition to being difficult to protect against, there is no way to tell if the person you are having sex with is infected with a type of HPV that can cause cancer. Most infections clear on their own; you may never know that you were infected, and even during infection there may be no identifiable signs.

Public health data on the rates of HPV infection usually note that the incidence of the disease is an estimate because of the difficulty in tracking cases and because HPV is so widespread that it is most likely an underreported condition. Of course, no data on infections are ever perfectly accurate. Not everyone infected with a disease will present to a doctor, and it's possible that not every incidence will be reported to an agency that tracks the data. But the data on HPV rates are nebulous because of the slow progression of the disease and the likelihood that many people who are infected will never see a doctor for their infection because they have no idea they are infected. Finally, the data on nationally representative HPV prevalence rates have historically been based on women, which means that the overall infection rate in the general population is also a projection, albeit a scientifically rigorous one.[31] The ambiguities related to the difficulty in tracking all infections, the difficulty individuals may have in knowing their infection status, the likelihood that infections will clear on their own without medical diagnosis or intervention, and the lack of consistent male HPV screening, which eliminates half the population from screening and surveillance data, may well have shaped the general population's ignorance about HPV at the time Gardasil became available.

Cancer and HPV

Globally, there are more than 450,000 cases of cervical cancer a year, and cervical cancer deaths are estimated at more than 230,000 annually.[32] It is one of the leading killers of women.[33] Nearly 90 percent of cervical cancer deaths worldwide occur in lower-income countries.[34] Reasons for this include economic, geographic, or other barriers to accessing care; cultural stigmas associated with gynecological interventions; and limited medical resources in some areas of the world. In the United States, about 12,000 cases of cervical cancer are diagnosed each year and around 4,000 women die.[35] Regular gynecological screenings have significantly reduced the number of deaths from cervical cancer, although not equally for all women.[36] Successful cervical cancer screening in the United States has reduced cervical cancer incidence so much that epidemiologists question the scope of the HPV vaccine's benefits.[37] Thus, in the United States, cervical cancer may not be a primary reason to vaccinate. The testing procedures for and the gaps in knowledge about the incidence of HPV in the general population reflect economic and medical expediency. Knowing that you have HPV does not tell you much about your future health; it only tells you that you might need more screening and surveillance. In addition, HPV data illustrate gendered divisions in medical care. There is no HPV test for men. Men do not get regular sexual health checkups as women do, so HPV management, surveillance, and interventions have disproportionately focused on female bodies.

Although the U.S. cervical cancer mortality rate has held steady for more than thirty years, these numbers obscure a troubling social justice disparity. Only recently have epidemiologists adjusted their incidence rates of cervical cancer to exclude women who have had a hysterectomy.[38] Adjusting the denominator to reflect only those capable of developing cervical cancer revealed the racial disparities of cervical cancer mortality, which are far more troubling than already notable discrepancies suggested.[39] The rates of cervical cancer mortality for black women in the United States, and for the oldest black women, in particular, are comparable to the very high rates of cervical cancer mortality in less industrialized countries.[40] The structural inequalities in the United States make it difficult to determine which factors—race, social class, or access to health care—are most responsible for this inequality.[41] As is the case with many other cancers, women of color are diagnosed later in the disease stage, partly due to provider biases about how women of color might participate in their health management and perhaps also due to women of color's hesitancy to seek care.[42] As a result of long-standing mistreatment by the medical profession, women of color may be hesitant to seek care from providers who do not take their concerns seriously or treat them with respect.[43] In the United States, cervical cancer is a disease that reflects social disparities, cultural barriers, and the consequences of racism. As the significant reduction in cervical cancer deaths in the United States has demonstrated, cervical cancer is preventable.[44] The newest data on cervical cancer disparities suggest that the level of racism in health care management in the United States has been significantly underdocumented.

Since not all HPV infections progress into cancer, HPV-related morbidities, including genital warts, are the primary burden of disease associated with HPV infections for U.S. women, not cancer. In addition, cervical cancer is not the only cancer HPV causes. HPV, can also cause anal, oral-pharyngeal, and genital cancers.[45] Precise HPV rates are difficult to come by because of HPV's etiology and the limits of data collection for the infection. Most of the current data focus on HPV-related cancers, as those are clearer, if retrospective, ways to count cases. Merck's marketing of Gardasil deliberately conveyed the urgent need to vaccinate because of the threat of cervical cancer, thus focusing their strategy on an intervention specifically for young female bodies.

In countries where women don't get regular gynecological care or have access to HPV tests, cervical cancer remains a leading cause of female mortality.[46] These women could benefit greatly from an HPV vaccine. No available HPV vaccine protects against all cancer-causing HPV types, and the prevalence of HPV types varies depending on geographic region. Two cancer-causing types of HPV, HPV 16 and 18, cause the majority of cervical cancer cases globally, but other common HPV types that cause cancer in countries outside the United States were not included in the original formulation of Gardasil.[47] Thus, the people who could most benefit from an HPV vaccine might not receive its protection. This epidemiological fact suggests that women in high-income countries like the United States are the imagined target population, making it a commodity first and a medical intervention second.[48] As the most expensive vaccine on the market, Gardasil was unlikely to be affordable to women in lower-income countries or lower-income communities in the United States.[49] In the United States, cervical cancer incidence affects women of color at a disproportionate rate.[50] Black women constitute the population that is most likely to die from cervical cancer.[51] Nothing about Gardasil's initial formulation suggests that these urgent disparities informed the development of the vaccine.

Vaccines are not neutral objects: they are medical interventions that are commodities. The development of an HPV vaccine and Gardasil's speedy approval in the United States reflect a public health and medical need, or at the very least, the claims of such a need. Medical interventions include political and economic priorities as much as (and sometimes more than) medical necessity. The motives of pharmaceutical companies to create new products are often about financial incentives rather than medical urgency. One need only look at the absence of treatments for conditions that afflict poorer countries, such as malaria or Ebola, to see that target markets inform pharmaceutical companies' refusal to develop products that may generate low economic returns. Thus, the story of Gardasil is also about geography, power, and the kinds of bodies Merck, the FDA, and public health officials deemed appropriate for this intervention.

Research Context

This book examines the emphasis Merck and health practitioners placed on Gardasil as a cervical cancer preventive in order to understand why its primary attribute, its ability to prevent some types of HPV, was underemphasized and downplayed in the United States. I also argue that the corporate interests that marketed Gardasil influenced the low acceptance rates of HPV vaccines. The U.S. institutions and actors with authority who promoted the vaccine deliberately shaped how the public came to understand the new vaccine. Thus, we must also ask what was lost by shifting the public's attention away from HPV. Merck's cancer-prevention marketing strategy raises social and cultural questions about what would have been at stake if the vaccine had been more accurately promoted as an HPV vaccine. How did the focus on cervical cancer stigmatize women who were no more at risk for the infection before Gardasil than they were after it was introduced? Since most of the discussions about HPV vaccination focused on female bodies, even though HPV affects men and women, how might we interpret the ongoing burden of prevention that Merck's advertising strategy placed on women?

These questions are directly related to how pharmaceutical corporations construct, what I call, an epidemic without a demand. I analyze the story of Gardasil's marketing through the words of those who make decisions about children's vaccines (usually mothers), public health officials, policymakers, and medical providers and how its advocates and its detractors positioned their claims. In the intersections of these diverse actors, we might come to better understand why Gardasil provoked strong reactions. My focus in this book is the creation of Gardasil's messaging and marketing and the responses of those who critiqued the vaccine rather than the perspectives of those who used it. Although I cannot make causal conclusions about the impact of these discourses, the rate of HPV vaccine uptake in the United States a decade later supports the data collected for this book.

I draw on ethnographic research conducted from 2006 to 2010. I collected most of my data in southern California, but I also analyze broader discussions at the national level. Although I had planned to study two HPV vaccines, Gardasil and Cervarix, GlaxoSmithKline's HPV vaccine, Cervarix did not receive FDA approval until late 2009 and was removed from the U.S. market due to low market demand in August 2016.[52] Although Cervarix was on the market during part of the research period, Gardasil is the HPV vaccine to which I refer in the book. The version of Gardasil available during the research period was a quadrivalent vaccine that protected against two types of HPV that cause genital warts, HPV 6 and 11, and two types, HPV 16 and 18, that may lead to cancer. My primary data collection ended just as the FDA approved the use of Gardasil in boys. Thus, I focus on Gardasil as a vaccine for girls and young women. The initial indication for girls-only has shaped assumptions about the vaccine; the discussions and debates about the newer HPV vaccine, which protects against nine types of HPV and is available for both girls and boys, continues to raise similar concerns that its earlier quadrivalent formulation provoked. In other words, the data and research conducted here, a decade ago, continue to be relevant to the newer HPV vaccine.

Unlike classic ethnographic projects, in which a specific community of people are the subjects, the subject of my research was Gardasil in the U.S. market, by which I mean that its movements informed my fieldwork sites and led me to those who were involved in its dissemination, promotion, or opposition. Who wanted to use the vaccine? Who refused it? Who advocated for it? As I conducted research among various communities, I heard competing discourses about the vaccine. These conversations often happened concurrently and demonstrated the conflicts in the marketed representations of the vaccine. My field research began on the East Coast in 2006, when I attended a continuing medical education session for clinicians at the American College of Colposcopy and Cervical Pathology and the May 2006 Gardasil Food and Drug Administration hearing. In 2007, I attended the first annual conference of the leading U.S. cervical cancer patient advocacy organization. I began conducting fieldwork in California in late 2007. While I was in the greater Los Angeles metropolitan area, I conducted research with physicians who administered Gardasil to their patients at a low-income clinic. I spent time with public health officials in sexual health, immunization, and women's health departments in southern California, all of whom promoted the vaccine. I spent eight months with mothers who attended a southern California natural health parents' group, many of whom were highly skeptical about any immunizations for their children. I attended the parents' group's monthly meetings, volunteered at their booth during a natural health event, and conducted hour-long interviews in the homes of members or in public places. At the request of the chapter leader, I became a dues-paying member and was added to their local and national e-mail listservs. Although I never participated in conversations, I received regular e-mails with discussions about members' national and local concerns. I volunteered with a cervical cancer patient advocacy organization, which I refer to as the Cervical Cancer Group (CCG), and a black women's health organization, which I call the Black Women's Health Group (BWHG). These two grassroots groups had very different perspectives on Gardasil and Merck. I focus predominantly on the advocacy group for cervical cancer and HPV survivors because their strategies aligned repeatedly with Merck's marketing slogans and interests. The members of this group often amplified the message of the pharmaceutical company in a way that seemed to undermine the organization's nonprofit status and had the unintended effect of delegitimizing their narratives. The CCG exemplified the intersection of public health, patient advocacy, and corporate marketing that dominated Gardasil's market launch and subsequent campaigns. In addition to the anthropological fieldwork I conducted with the CCG and BWHG, in 2008, I attended the annual CDC immunization conference in Atlanta, Georgia and collaborated on a CDC-funded research project with a southern California county public health department to understand physician promotion of the HPV vaccine. In this role, I observed the public health researchers' concerns about getting more people to use the HPV vaccine.[53] These voices and perspectives shape this story. From the early days of my research until the completion of this book in 2017, I continued to follow media, listservs, and policy conversations about the implementation and dissemination of the HPV vaccine.

I initially tried to conduct some fieldwork directly with Merck. I contacted Dr. Carlos Sattler, who was listed on Merck's website as the person in charge of Gardasil.[54] A month before the FDA hearing, I asked if I could set up an interview. Dr. Sattler forwarded my request to a different and more appropriate contact, Dr. Richard Haupt. When Dr. Haupt responded to me, he inadvertently included Dr. Sattler's e-mail to him expressing wariness about my intentions.[55] Their explicit distrust of my identity still makes me wonder who they feared I could really be. A muckraking journalist? A conservative anti-vaccine radical? Dr. Haupt's assistant agreed to set up an interview, but after a number of rescheduled phone appointments, I never received the phone call at the appointed time. I never spoke to anyone in the Merck offices, and thus I rely predominantly on the company's public materials to interpret how they framed their product and their involvement in broader debates about Gardasil's dissemination.

Many actors and institutions were involved in Gardasil's dissemination. Although I do not focus on southern California as a central actor in my research, there were times that its sprawl, its lack of centrality, and the required driving from disparate locations echoed the tangle I experienced as I tried to understand who was involved in vaccination practices, policies, and regulations. Like the highways that run through southern California, connecting diverse neighborhoods, one actor emerged as the most influential in shaping the vaccine's trajectory. The pharmaceutical company Merck, which had the greatest financial investment in its widespread use, crafted its position to fend off imagined imminent debates. As this book will demonstrate, the unanticipated reactions to Gardasil show how quickly a carefully crafted market position can fall apart. The Gardasil campaigns reveal lobbying strategies that are common practices within the pharmaceutical industry. With feedback from regulatory agencies such as the FDA, Merck designed the ideal user of this vaccine. Despite my inability to gain access to the pharmaceutical company, the content analysis of Merck's marketing makes it possible to unpack the company's projected imaginations of its target audiences.

Merck bears some responsibility for the low awareness of HPV at the time it launched Gardasil, how well the U.S. public understood the utility of Gardasil, and the contours of the policy discussions around Gardasil's dissemination. Of course, Merck is not solely responsible for educating potential users about its vaccine. Women's relative ignorance about HPV has much to do with how medical practice and research have imagined women's bodies, the history of scientific knowledge of HPV, and the fact that most women's bodies clear the virus without medical intervention.[56] Even though Merck invested heavily in HPV awareness campaigns in the months leading up to the market launch of Gardasil, in the opportunities lost, the marketing choices made, and the things not said, Gardasil ties together debates in the United States about the merits of vaccination, women's health politics, and the influences of corporate marketing.

The first half of the book considers how Merck transformed a ubiquitous health condition that few knew about into a marketed, packaged risk for cancer. Merck downplayed the positive impact of well-established cervical cancer screening interventions and the relatively low death rate from cervical cancer in the United States. Instead, through its ambiguous pre-licensure campaigns, its licensure application to the FDA, and its management of potential objectors to the vaccine, the company defined the problem for the public and heightened anxiety about the risks of cervical cancer. Chapter 2 explores the marketing messages Merck used to prepare its two target demographics: mothers, who would be making decisions about the vaccine for younger children, and young women. Merck took advantage of relative ignorance about the ubiquity of HPV and its relationship to cancer to set the terms of the vaccine's urgency. In Chapter 3, I show how Gardasil marketing gave cervical cancer patient advocates a legitimizing representation of their experience, which had previously been barely mentioned in public conversations. I examine the facility with which one advocacy organization appropriated Merck's slogans and what this tells us about how deliberately the pharmaceutical company crafted the vaccine's marketing messages. Chapter 4 examines how Merck framed the problem for clinicians. Although this tactic is unremarkable in contemporary pharmaceutical practices, Merck invested in educating physicians to prepare them to handle a potentially controversial vaccine by proactively managing the terms with which doctors presented the problem to their patients. The physicians I interviewed and observed in public settings reveal the impact of the messaging Merck crafted even before the FDA approved Gardasil. Chapter 5 looks at how Merck prepared the public to understand Gardasil as a cancer vaccine during its Food and Drug Administration Vaccines and Biologics Advisory Committee meeting. Starting with clinical trial research design and its interpretations of clinical trial data, Merck positioned the vaccine as a cervical cancer vaccine first rather than as an HPV vaccine. This categorization was more than a marketing strategy; it was essential if Gardasil were to receive a fast-track review. This strategy allowed Merck to present its data for review much earlier than it would have been able to if the vaccine had not qualified for such a designation. This chapter also explores the epidemiological knowledge about HPV and its relation to cervical cancer. Although this connection is well established, it is not without complications and contingencies that make an HPV vaccine less of a panacea than Merck would have liked the public to believe. Chapter 6 considers how after the FDA approved Gardasil, Merck lobbied for state-level legislation that would require the HPV vaccine for girls entering sixth and seventh grades. Its lobbying efforts quickly became public knowledge, and this ill-conceived strategy may have long-standing repercussions in the form of contemporary distrust of HPV vaccine policies.

The last two chapters examine how parents, patient advocates, and clinicians navigated the vaccine's promise. Once Gardasil was released into the health care market, much of the public's objections focused on it as a vaccine. Chapter 7 examines how Merck's language permeated the efforts of cervical cancer patient advocates; how one black women's health organization rejected the seemingly hollow promises of Gardasil and introduced important concerns about social justice, race, and inequality into an otherwise barely troubled conception of for whom Gardasil was intended; and the general population's confusion about the ambiguities of HPV that remained after Gardasil's market launch. Chapter 8 explores how some mothers distrusted vaccine safety and health officials' promotion of vaccines and why they did not find Gardasil's proponents persuasive. Merck's marketing strategies reverberated through women's understanding of their HPV diagnoses and reveal the impact of corporate influence on people's experiences of their own health.

The book concludes with a consideration of the current state of HPV vaccines today and the revitalized efforts to promote the vaccine after low rates of use by the majority of eligible individuals. In the summer of 2016, news stories lamented the notably low usage of the HPV vaccine in the United States. In response, clinicians and public health officials have proposed the strategy of emphasizing the vaccine's cancer-prevention benefits, a proposal that lacks novelty and fails to account for the vaccine's short, but complex history in the United States. Gardasil has never *not* been imagined as a vaccine for cancer, even though it has never really been a vaccine for cancer.

2

Imminent Vulnerability and Commodified Empowerment

The vague directives appeared in women's magazines; printed on full-page heavy weight paper, inserted in the middle of articles, these tear-out postcards encouraged readers to "Tell Someone" or "*Cuéntale a alguien*." In the spring of 2006, I began to notice the print teaser campaign, capitalizing on imagined social experiences of females in the United States: the postcards strategically placed in women's national magazines; and stacked in mounted display racks on the walls of restaurant bathrooms, sites imagined as where women might congregate.[1] Who would send these cards to a friend? What ought women tell? One image depicted a crudely drawn cartoon in which women of various ethnicities stand zombie-like with blank eyes, each woman tapping the shoulder of a woman in front of her. The last woman is awkwardly bent over an old-fashioned, corded telephone. Another card pictured rows of free-floating ovular face-like objects with slightly parted and lipsticked mouths but no other features, as if the artist didn't think an accurate representation of human faces were necessary. Indeed, there is no way to be sure they were supposed to be women, except for the lushly drawn mouths with painted lips.[2] They were neither realistically drawn women, nor fully embodied. Their corporeal incompleteness suggested that they did not yet know what there was to tell or perhaps even that they should tell at all. Other postcards targeted specific, segregated groups: on one, a trio of cartoon black women sat in a row in hair salon chairs, looking at magazines and seemingly in mid-conversation; on another, two young women's heavily made-up faces filled the postcard. On one side, one woman's face was only half represented, her face bisected by the edge of the postcard. The other woman gave a side glance, her face in three-quarters profile. The palms of their hands overlapped and merged in grainy imagery, forming a heart shape, their palms smeary, as though their hands were pressed up against a window. These young women were presumably Latinas, based on the Spanish version of the slogan, "*Cuéntale a alguien*." In describing these images, they sound odd and incoherent, but this is how they appear, disconcerting and chimeric.[3] Their femininity was clearly marked in each image, even as it seemed to reflect an artist's imagining of what made each character distinctly female. They were not women, but representational figures of an ideal consumer. Each card depicted cartoonish figures and implied social interaction between women. The women engaged in gendered activities such as getting their hair done or talking on the phone. Merck's marketing strategy drew upon the notion of shared intimacies to ensure one's friends would know what to do to protect themselves against HPV.

But there was also something vaguely sinister in these postcards, which did not divulge that they were marketing materials for a new product that did not yet have FDA approval. On the left-hand side on the back of the postcards, the text asked, "Think cervical cancer isn't an issue until you're much older? Millions of young women have a virus they don't even know about. It's called human papillomavirus (HPV), and certain types can cause cervical cancer. For most women, HPV clears on its own. But for some, cervical cancer can develop. Ask your doctor about the importance of Pap tests. Cervical cancer, caused by a virus." This text was followed with words that were set off from the other text in a cartoon word bubble: "Now that you know, Tell someone." At the bottom of the card was a website address (tell-someone.com), a phone number (1-877-NOW-TELL), and information that one could "send ecards at tell-someone.com." On the right side of the card, there was a place to write the address of a friend.

When I first saw one of these cards, my initial assumption was that the campaign was about domestic abuse campaign and that the message was

FIGURE 2.1 Sample postcard from the 2006 "Tell Someone" campaign. *Source*: Author's Collection.

that secret shames should not make you powerless. The nonspecific slogan could have been about telling all sorts of female secret experiences. What was the information that needed to be circulated, and how might it be empowering? The ambiguous message was repurposed a couple of months later, on a popular website called PostSecret. The site invited people to mail the website's creator postcards that divulged secrets they'd never told anyone. One person had edited one of the "Tell Someone" postcards. The anonymous poster interpreted the advertising campaign as a reference to a never-revealed violation, "I finally did Tell Someone what you did to me." The PostSecret repurposing highlights how emotionally laden it can be to reveal and to tell. Is telling liberation or a shameful disclosure? Merck's advertising slogan and the mailed in PostSecret implied disclosure as free-dom, and the Tell Someone PostSecret card alluded to the complexities of Merck's suggestion to tell.[4]

The postcards' authoritative declaration infantilized their audience and positioned them as vulnerable and susceptible to a nebulous threat. In a deft use of anticipatory discourse, the advertisements contributed to a particular way of knowing one's body—as at risk, vulnerable, and in need of urgent intervention. The bizarre representations of disembodied heads and cartoonish women called attention to bodies that were implicitly aberrant. Instead of more traditional pharmaceutical advertisements, which usually feature photographs of clear-eyed, wholesome individuals, even if they may suffer from the condition for which the company offers a solution, the Tell Someone representations exemplified what Deborah Lupton has called an "emotion-risk assemblage."[5] These assemblages are both material and non-material, and they are simultaneously collective and individual.[6] The pre-licensure advertisements cultivated a particular kind of knowledge of one's body that has deeply moral implications. The judgments coalesced around female bodies only; there were no postcards or television advertisements that encouraged boys and young men to "tell someone."

The use of female bodies in advertising campaigns is nothing new, of course. Sex sells. Women's bodies shill for more products, even nongendered ones, than male bodies do.[7] Women's bodies also represent fertility and reproduction. The Merck campaign implied that much was at stake for future producers of future citizens.[8] The emphasis on youthful females as imminently reproductive minimizes the male role in reproduction and focuses on women's risks as though they were self-created. Although Merck later sought FDA approval for males, the limited data it presented during the first review process and the gendered advertisements suggest that Merck strategically chose to target women's bodies. Prior to the FDA's market approval, Merck could not include the name of their product in its ads. Instead, they primed an audience to anticipate the answer to an obscure invitation. *What* to tell would be revealed shortly.

Pharmaceutical companies invest a lot of resources to sell their products. Merck's overall marketing budget has been shown to be twice what it spent on all of its research and development across its products.[9] Precise figures for Merck's early HPV vaccine campaign have been hard to find, but one article claimed that in the first year Gardasil was on the market, Merck spent $127 million in advertising over six months.[10] In the spring of 2006, primetime television commercials, one of the most expensive times to pay for advertising, featured women, looking directly at the camera, who announced eagerly, "I just want to tell someone, anyone!" They explained that they wanted to tell everyone about cancer caused by a virus. The 45-second advertisement revealed more than the postcards, educating viewers that "Millions of people already *have* the types of HPV that can cause cervical cancer," and "*You* could have HPV, and not even know it."[11]

The advertisements switched from an insistence on sharing information to the shock of HPV's ubiquity. "I was stunned at how many people have HPV. . . . Millions? That's insane."[12] The ad framed sharing knowledge as a moral duty. One woman emphatically stated, "I feel like my responsibility is just to tell everybody I know."

Vaccination as Empowerment

The "Tell someone" advertisements were similar to other pharmaceutical ads at the time. Direct-to-consumer pharmaceutical ads convey intimacy and familiarity in order to make the world of drugs and doctors friendlier. Pharmaceutical ads feature actors speaking directly to the camera, sharing knowledge, and educating the viewer. The pre-licensure advertisement featured women who were well dressed, polished, frank interlocutors. Some were mothers, standing with arms around their adolescent daughters. As Merck would later emphasize explicitly in its ads for Gardasil that featured a subsequent slogan "I Chose," the women were portrayed as responsible, engaged health consumers. The women's surprise about their previous ignorance about HPV conveyed that although they considered themselves to be otherwise well informed, somehow they had not known about the virus and its potential threat of cancer. But given the paucity of coverage of HPV in mainstream media or even general sex education about HPV, who could blame them?

Unlike future ads that would elaborate on the imagined liberation Gardasil offered, the Tell Someone ads emphasized dawning awareness. While previously cervical cancer may have seemed like an abstraction or a rare condition, suddenly it was tied to a very common yet invisible STI. I knew that the campaign foreshadowed the FDA approval of Gardasil; yet I still found that they were cleverly unsettling, well-honed messages for their target demographic, young, middle class, health-conscious, educated U.S. women, which could have included me. Despite the advertisements' emphasis on risk and vulnerability, the messaging became more complicated as the ads introduced a female health care provider, dressed in a white lab coat to convey her authority. She reassured viewers that most HPV clears up on its own. The message was mixed: you might be at risk for cervical cancer, *and* you will be fine.

In June 2006, the FDA licensed Gardasil. Several months later, Merck switched from the ambiguous "Tell Someone" message to the "One Less" campaign. In these television ads, girls riding horses, accomplishing athletic gymnastic routines, or cheerleading filled the screen. "I want to be one less statistic. One less!" In another One Less advertisement, a young woman expertly danced the flamenco and said, "*Una menos.*"[13] These girls were the ones who were saved. Not pictured: the girls who will be unprotected. The "Tell Someone" campaign featured women in their twenties or thirties and, occasionally, a woman who might be older standing next to her teenage daughter. The women who announced that they didn't know that "cancer [could be] caused by a virus" stated that they had learned something new. Similarly, in the "One Less" campaign, although mothers and daughters appeared together, the advertisements focused on the younger women and their activities. "One Less" invited viewers to join a larger resistance movement. In one of two versions of the advertisement, a young woman is shown jumping rope in a spare boxing gym. She shadow-boxes alone in a boxing ring, wearing hand wraps to protect her hands and to convey her commitment. As she throws a punch, the screen is filled, in capital letters, with the words "GET VACCINATED." The "One Less" campaign imparted a girl-power quality. Instead of "One Less" suggesting an absence, the slogan implied that Gardasil made the vaccinated girls important and distinctive. Choosing not to vaccinate would expose young women to HPV infection and, as the empowered activeness of these young women suggested, it could waste their potential. Merck's subsequent advertisement slogan, "I Chose," revisited the mother-daughter connection. In these ads, a mother helps braid her daughter's hair or paints her daughter's nails as they look at magazines together. "Choose to get vaccinated" makes the directive explicit. Later iterations of Gardasil brochures preserved the message that vaccination was a duty. In contrast to the ambiguous suggestion to "Tell Someone" or references to a risk category that few were aware of previously, after FDA approval, Merck boldly framed the vaccine in the language of choice and action.

The Gardasil advertisements echo a phenomenon in U.S. health care and public health interventions over the last half-century. Health has become an all-pervasive project in this country. Aspects of life that were not previously associated with health care interventions are now the target of individuals' health-oriented actions. The transformation of quotidian human experiences into problematic behaviors exemplifies a process social scientists have called medicalization. Medicalization is a cultural and social process that informs healthcare delivery and public health interventions, and it imposes moral and ethical judgments on behaviors.[14] These judgments position those who do not participate in optimal health-seeking activities as making the wrong choice. The consequence of such a process is the normalization of certain behaviors and outcomes; individuals who make alternate choices or do not intervene in the way that is prescribed then become aberrant or problematic. Implicit in these norms is the expectation of compliance. However, a medicalized logic excludes the economic, cultural, and structural reasons why people may not adopt particular behaviors. It also fails to sufficiently account for how people may make seemingly non-compliant choices based on different preferences. Pharmaceuticalization expands the medicalization of everyday existence further: its message is that health and life should be managed through pharmaceutical products.[15] The medicalization and pharmaceuticalization of risk "reconstitut[e] healthy women as risky subjects," making women's bodies universally problematic.[16] Although each Gardasil advertisement campaign was different, they all shared a tone of implied universality, risk, and the power of choice in health outcomes. From the "Tell Someone" campaign to its "I Chose" incarnation, Merck framed the vaccine as part of a shared female experience but also a shared female bond to protect against cervical cancer. In this way, pharmaceuticalization offers a manufactured intervention to solve a problem its audience did not previously know about. Terms like "commitment" and "connection" linked women together. By deploying a strategy of empathy, in which mothers might identify with their daughters' bodies, Merck imagined mothers as ready for persuasion.[17]

The economy of deliberate prevention pervaded the advertisements for Gardasil. How could you, a responsible parent (and more importantly, a mother, who knows what abnormal Pap smears might be like), not choose to protect your daughter from the prevalent and pervasive risk of cervical cancer? However, in contrast to the looming mortality and gendered vulnerability that a breast cancer diagnosis evokes (which Eve Sedgwick, playing on Audre Lorde's own confrontation of womanhood, articulated as, "shit, now I guess I really am a woman"), these advertisements invoke the intimacy of female companionship, intergenerational support, and a medicalized form of female empowerment. The language of the Merck advertisements plays on an inversion of mortality and gendered vulnerability.[18] In a highly marketed construction of gender, the vaccine inserts itself among other milestones of womanhood, contributing to an (imagined) shared bodily female experience.[19]

Pharmacology today promises potential liberation from the unseemly or unpleasant "side effects" of having a body, and the Merck ads asserted that any mother would want to spare her daughter from the potential downsides of having a female body, such as cervical cancer. But Gardasil does not eliminate the risk of cervical cancer completely. It prevented some types of sexually-transmitted, cancer causing HPV, but not all. Merck's claims in the early advertisements did not engage with the complexities of HPV infection, management, or risks of cervical cancer.

Oral contraceptives provide an example of how medicalized bodily processes such as menstruation, pharmaceutical companies can generate new markets. Although oral contraceptives and the HPV vaccine are not the same things, both products reveal how pharmaceutical companies obscure marketing decisions that are presented to consumers as self-evident benefits. In the last decade, birth control pills have been marketed as products that require only quarterly bleeding cycles or can eliminate menstruation altogether. Hormonal birth control pills disrupt the ovulation-menstruation cycle that occurs when an egg is not fertilized. Not only do women on the birth control pill not ovulate, and therefore cannot get pregnant, their bodies also do not shed the lining of the uterus, which is what happens every twenty-eight days to a woman who ovulates, is not on birth control, and is not pregnant. Thus, a woman on oral contraceptives who takes pills every day of the month and skips the packaged placebo week of pills by continuing with the non-placebo pills, will also avoid the bleeding cycle that was designed by the pill's developers to make the birth control pill seem more "natural."[20] The week of bleeding that women who use traditional birth control pills experience is quite literally a packaging decision: it mimics non-contracepting women's bodies but is not necessary when using hormonal contraception. The newer birth control pills that offer infrequent bleeding or bleeding-free formulation are a *marketing* strategy, not a medical innovation. It is how the pills are used, not a hormonal difference from earlier formulations, that prevent the breakthrough bleeding cycle. The repackaged birth control pills' four bleeding cycles a year, which eliminate the 28-day cycle of bleeding, has been marketed as "the same but different."[21]

The messaging of Gardasil, as with the newly packaged hormonal contraceptives, promises a form of liberation, suggesting it will eliminate the inconveniences of a female body and its vulnerabilities. The existence of hormonal birth control *has* changed women's lives, giving them the freedom to control their fertility. The new packaging with their quarterly bleeding cycle, in contrast, does not radically alter women's lives any more than hormonal contraception has already accomplished. Similarly, Gardasil did not introduce the liberating cultural and health shift that the "One Less" message seemed to promise. With its limited protection against the many types of HPV, the HPV vaccine does not alter the medical management of female bodies. The HPV vaccine did not and still does not change the fact that women will continue to need medical care to maintain the health of their cervix. Pap smears and HPV testing remain necessary because even after vaccination with Gardasil women can still get infected with HPV, will still need to have Pap smears, albeit less frequently, and can still develop cancer due to HPV types Gardasil does not protect against. Gardasil adds another (medically mediated) preventive step one *ought* to take to be a fully responsible individual and, more importantly, as a fully responsible reproductive female.

Gendered Bodies and Authentic Patients

Tools, devices, and medications reimagine "what a body is and where its significant boundaries are located."[22] Gardasil was no different. From the speculum of the mid-nineteenth century to hormonal contraceptives of the twentieth century, technologies construct the body by focusing on an anatomical part or purpose. As a manufactured technology, Gardasil did not need to be a vaccine specifically for cervical cancer, since HPV causes a variety of cancers in both men and women. Nor did it need to be a vaccine specifically for women, as its eventual approval for males plainly demonstrates. Western medicine approaches the female body as problematic and frames it as exceptional, even though female bodies are no more common or uncommon than male bodies. As Emily Martin has argued, the medical biases about women's bodies can be seen in scientific texts, which train doctors and scientists with purported objectivity; they describe female and male biological processes differently by using gendered terms for cellular processes, which cannot be culturally bound but are biological and beyond social-cultural influence.[23] Although justifications for medicine's focus on women's bodies have traditionally emphasized the female reproductive stages, from gynecological interventions before pregnancy to obstetrical oversight during pregnancy, male bodies are also potentially sexual and reproductive. Yet there is no standard screening test for HPV in men, even though the Pap test has been used in U.S. gynecological care to identify abnormalities in the cervix since the 1940s and became standard practice in the 1970s. The DNA-based HPV test has been available in the United States since 1999 for triage in ambiguous Pap results and was approved for screening in 2003.[24] A number of medical professional organizations recommend the use of a polymerase chain reaction (PCR) test for HPV as primary screening.[25] Screening men for anal or oral HPV is not standard of care in the United States, although some providers may do anal screening for men who have sex with men.

The absence of male standard of care for HPV highlights that HPV management is heteronormative and biased by gender. These gender-related biases persist throughout sexual and reproductive health care. Male hormonal birth control has yet to be commercialized, despite years of research into possible methods.[26] The differences in how medicine treats male and female bodies impacts how individuals experience and understand their own bodies. As Emily Martin notes, these material and practical distinctions reflect historical and cultural processes that have "tied 'women' to their bodies and to what are seen culturally as biological processes."[27] Our feminine or masculine qualities are not inevitable attributes due to our biologies; gender and others' assumptions about it are the result of complex social and cultural processes. Thus, the absence of HPV triage in men and the lack of routinized HPV-related cancer tests in men show us how women's bodies are made the sites of scrutiny for an STI and its related cancer that do not discriminate by sex.

The sex specificity of early Gardasil marketing perpetuated the asymmetry found elsewhere in reproductive health research.[28] Nothing about Gardasil's mechanism of action, purpose, or method of delivery required the vaccine to be a female-specific vaccine. From the time of its pre-approval launch, Merck focused on women's bodies and cervical cancer, revealing how the company prioritized regulatory criteria and marketing opportunities over the public's interests. Although public debates in the first few years after the FDA approved Gardasil did not explicitly address that concern, the media noted that some people objected to Gardasil because they feared it would encourage promiscuity by eliminating one of the health risks of sexual activity.[29] In a strangely contradictory stance, some conservative figures embraced the vaccine because of its ability to protect "innocent" young women from promiscuous and careless male partners.[30] Both positions imagined an impact on young women that vilified sexual activity and focused on female vulnerability. The vaccine's initial targeting of females and the discussions of young women's sexualities perpetuated the notion that women alone are responsible for their sexual health.

The response to Gardasil from the Cervical Cancer Group (CCG), an organization of women who had been diagnosed with HPV or cervical cancer, repeated cultural tropes of female vulnerability. CCG members articulated an acute awareness of the vaccine's female specificity. Even though the group's members were far more familiar with HPV than the average U.S. woman, they absorbed Merck's slogans and claims that the vaccine would empower women as though the language were their own. Representations of their experiences had not existed in the mainstream media before Gardasil was available. Drawing on framings by pharmaceutical companies and medical culture that have intertwined consumerism and citizenship as a form of patient empowerment, CCG members interpreted the marketing strategies of Gardasil as a legitimation of their cause.[31] As I will describe below, while most likely not deliberate, the CCG members' advocacy and testimonials transformed the Gardasil campaign slogans into personal and intimate proclamations. The CCG complemented Merck's marketing perfectly. As a patient-driven advocacy and support group, they offered an authentic voice for the vaccine's endorsement.

Gary, who owned a molecular/pathology laboratory but is not a doctor, established the non-profit CCG with his wife, Margie, about a decade before Gardasil debuted. On the CCG's website, Margie was described as a "DES daughter." The term refers to a woman born to a mother who took the drug diethylstilbestrol (DES) during her pregnancy. Until the carcinogenic harm to children born to women who had taken DES was identified, it was prescribed to women to reduce complications in pregnancy and to prevent miscarriages. It is now associated with cervical and vaginal cancers in females who were exposed in utero. When Gary and Margie founded the CCG, neither of them had cancer, but a couple of years later, Margie died of a noncervical cancer. The group's origin narrative evolved significantly over the years. On the version of the CCG website cached in the

Internet Archive, the organization described its creation in the late 1990s as a response to decreased insurance reimbursements for cytopathology labs. This narrative had changed by 2007, when the group framed its history as a support and advocacy organization for HPV-positive patients and cervical cancer patients and survivors.[32] Gary continued to run the organization and to expand its scope over time, invoking Margie's influence and commitment to the project whenever he talked about its founding. After Margie died, Gary met Larissa, a woman who identified herself in a major national news magazine as having "a very strong, persistent virus." Gary and Larissa ran the predominantly online-based organization out of their home in southern California while holding down full-time jobs. Gary was its public representative and executive director. I had hoped to get to know Larissa, who self-identified as an HPV survivor, beyond her public persona as Gary's fiancée, and eventual wife, but she deferred to Gary for most communications when I contacted them together. Gary was the spokesperson for the organization in the media, and Larissa's media presence usually downplayed her role in managing the group. In one article in the region's major newspaper, Larissa was quoted as person who worked for the CCG and who would choose to vaccinate her daughters, but the journalist focused on her identity as a mother rather than as a co-director. Although the group never addressed the issue directly, it surprised me that a man led a women's health organization.

The CCG's print newsletter, *Inspirational Tales*, featured survivors' intimate familiarity with cervical cancer. The spring 2007 newsletter included four pages of testimonials from nine women who had endured treatment for cervical cancer. The newsletter proclaimed: "Here are . . . our members' stories of struggle, determination survivorship and HOPE!" Each of the women mentioned their previous ignorance about cervical cancer and HPV. One testimonial invoked Gardasil's pre-licensure campaign: "Just like the commercial says, 'Tell Someone—Anyone who will listen.'" Another young woman stated, "I know I can't get the word out to very many people but if I can teach just one person more about this terrible thing then I feel that I have saved a life."

CCG members interpreted the vaccine as an emotionally laden intervention and appropriated Merck's anticipatory discourse. The members' deeply felt and future-oriented conception of their bodies echoed Merck's rhetoric. Their reiteration of phrases they had heard in Merck's paid for advertising is an example of how disseminating information may replace concrete action such as accessing treatment or encouraging further research about the disease. One member reinterpreted Merck's Tell Someone campaign: "Now I want to let every woman know cervical cancer is no longer a death sentence." But as epidemiological data have shown, cervical cancer is rarely a death sentence in the United States.[33] The fraught tone echoed the urgency conveyed by the Gardasil "Tell Someone" ads. The latest Gardasil ads that aired in the summer of 2016 revisited the ominous tone. Titled "Know HPV," these advertisements instill anxiety in parents who may not have chosen to use the vaccine to prevent future cancer in their children. Even though CCG members were aware that Gardasil does not prevent cancer, only its cause (HPV), their testimonials reiterated the story Merck sought to sell. The women did not promote more accurate descriptions of Gardasil as a vaccine that can reduce HPV-related complications and can prevent gynecological interventions associated with cervical cancer. Merck's taglines effaced the complexities of the diagnoses of and treatment for HPV and cervical cancer. Although I do not wish to minimize the suffering of CCG members, their narratives of HPV and cervical cancer echoed the marketing slogans for Gardasil; it is hard not to see how Merck's influence dominated the organization's materials. It is likely that Merck conducted extensive market research using focus groups and interviews to capture the experiences and language used by those with HPV abnormalities or cervical cancer so that the messages would resonate with their audiences.[34] There could be no better advocates for an HPV preventive than those who could only wish that they had had such an option. Though they did not identify themselves deliberately as spokespeople, CCG members exemplify the consumer-as-advocate persona that has become increasingly common with the rise of social networking sites that allow individuals to review or to endorse products and services.

The conflation of pharmaceutical marketing strategies and authentic patient voices had its clearest representation in a two-page public service announcement that the CCG paid for in the January 2008 issue of a major women's fashion and lifestyle magazine.[35] Both pages featured young white women not quite smiling at the viewer. On the first page, the text said, "Millions of people already have HPV." The words were identical to those in the "Tell Someone" advertisements and postcards. The text emphasized consumer empowerment language and mimicked Merck's claims that vaccination was the responsible choice, with phrases such as "learn the truth about HPV" and "educate yourself." The copy encouraged readers to move from acquiring knowledge ("learn the truth") to action ("help protect yourself"). The implication was that not vaccinating represented an abandonment of self-care. This suggestion of responsibility turned up among a variety of institutional actors: at the meetings of an immunization coalition that promoted vaccination; in CDC immunization materials and at the CDC's annual immunization conference; and among physicians I interviewed who were beginning to present the HPV vaccine to their patients as an uncomplicated choice. They shared the position that the right choice was to vaccinate and that choosing to leave one's cervical health to chance was irresponsible.

The CCG sought to minimize the stigma associated with HPV. On the middle of the second page of the public service announcement call-out text reminded readers, "There is *no stigma* associated with HPV or cervical cancer" [their italics]. Itemizing how to "Help Protect Yourself" with different "Strategies for Preventing HPV," the fourth item in the list suggested readers "communicate with loved ones." After restating that "there is no stigma associated with HPV or cervical cancer," the recommendation continued, "and talking with loved ones and others will go a long way in changing perceptions about this important issue. With the high natural prevalence of HPV, it is important to note that any woman could acquire HPV or develop cervical cancer." The group's intention to reassure women that HPV is both pervasive and not shameful called attention to potential judgments to the contrary. The public service announcement's reference to stigma is not about whether or not one ought to be ashamed, but rather about mitigating others' biases and the assumption of others' perceptions of one's behaviors. The statement's deliberate assertion that there was no stigma in fact suggested that one *ought* to worry about others' judgment. CCG's mention of the topic of stigma suggested that because HPV is an STI and because it is an underdiscussed health concern, it might be shameful.

Merck's double-sided advertisement for Gardasil bisected the CCG's two-page public service announcement. "Calling Gardasil a cervical cancer vaccine is only the beginning of the story," the Gardasil advertisement stated. On the reverse side of the page, facing the rest of CCG's content, were the standard warnings and side effects, printed in small font to compress a litany of disclosures that companies must include in any pharmaceutical advertisement. The placement of the Merck ad blurred the distinction between itself and the advocacy organization. On the first page of CCG's public service announcement, under CCG's dictate to "learn the truth," the organization had included copy that said "Brought to you by the [CCG] and Merck & Co., Inc." Gary told me that the CCG accepted money from Merck in order to get their "message out there." The CCG did not endorse a particular vaccine but instead sought to promote the availability and use of an HPV vaccine for women. However, Merck co-opted the public service announcement with its sponsorship. Because GlaxoSmithKline delayed its submission of Cervarix, its HPV vaccine, to the FDA, those who promoted an HPV vaccine before 2009 were tacitly, if not explicitly, endorsing one pharmaceutical company (Merck) and one vaccine (Gardasil).[36] Thus, advocating for HPV vaccination as an essential health behavior also meant promoting Gardasil.

An Opportunity Based in Ignorance

In the United States, where medications are manufactured by private corporations and access to health care depends on how much you can afford to pay (or the insurance company plan you can afford), responsible health behavior cannot be separated from consumer behavior. The dominant theme of choice in Gardasil's early advertisements obscured the fact that Gardasil was the *only* option at the time. These advertisements reinforced potential stigma by implying that a failure to vaccinate indicated irresponsible behavior. Doing nothing implied carelessness.

Merck's Gardasil marketing strategies in the vaccine's first few years on the market expose the company's concerns about public acceptance of the vaccine and the ideas Merck believed would need deliberate framing. The widespread public ignorance about HPV gave Merck an open field as it worked to create a market for Gardasil. Their framing of a new topic could have guided the conversation in a variety of directions. Merck had a clear opportunity to focus its message on HPV-related cancers beyond cervical cancer. Ten years after Merck's marketing campaign began, it acknowledged that people still did not fully understand the link between HPV and cancer.[37] This continued lack of awareness demonstrates that Merck could have done a better job educating the public about the benefits that its vaccine offered. But in 2006, as Merck tried to prepare the public for the little-understood relationship between cancer and HPV, the company drew on well-established imaginaries of female vulnerabilities and stigmas instead of constructive and informative education. Merck's push to set the terms of the debate extended well past marketing: the company deliberately crafted its message driven by marketing, not medical, priorities. The FDA review process offers further insight into Merck's imagined target audience. Even though the "Tell Someone" ads never included boys or men, Merck presented its data to the FDA with the hope that boys would also be eligible for Gardasil. The absence of male bodies in the pre-licensure advertisements, however, offers evidence of Merck's doubts that they would receive FDA approval for boys. Creating a market for Gardasil did not just rely on creating patient demand. The FDA approval process helped determine who Gardasil's recipients would be. Advertising was only one of the strategies Merck used to generate a culturally bound narrative to sell its vaccine.

3

The Pap Smear, Racist Histories, and "Cervix" Cancer

At the first annual conference of the Cervical Cancer Group (CCG) in the fall of 2007, fifteen months after the FDA approved Gardasil, Marina, a singer-songwriter in her mid-30s who had survived cervical cancer, began an evening reception with a musical performance and handed out small pin buttons proclaiming "Save the [Cooch]," a euphemism for vagina.[1] The round pins featured a cartoonlike cervix with a face. The use of the word "cooch" to refer to the cervix didn't make much sense, since the cervix is not the vagina and cervical cancer is not a problem of the vagina per se, but the provocative declaration made many women smile. Marina told us that before she was diagnosed with cancer at the age of 31, she didn't know where her cervix was. The hidden physiology of the cervix may contribute to the lack of understanding about cervical cancer. In contrast to the symbolic visibility of breasts, the cervix is not visible without special equipment. Yet the cervix is an integral part of the female reproductive system, and the frequency with which women expressed ignorance about its existence or vulnerability surprised me. Many conference attendees echoed Marina's admission of ignorance over the next few days. Over and over women stated that they didn't know much about the cervix before they were diagnosed with HPV or cervical cancer. Their narratives of revelation resembled the "Tell Someone" advertisements. Their confessions of shock, ignorance, and dismay at never having been taught about HPV or its relation to cervical cancer suggested that Merck had conducted successful market research to capture women's perspectives on HPV and cervical cancer.[2]

The conference participants' excitement about meeting other women diagnosed with conditions that had been long treated as unmentionable was palpable. The organization hosted a "meet and greet" event with cocktails and hors d'oeuvres, giving attendees a chance to socialize before the next day's more structured schedule. On display were three handmade quilts with writing on each square, most with a woman's name and a statement. The quilt and the squares evoked the AIDS quilts that offer a visual representation of lives lost to AIDS, with each of the more than 48,000 squares representing a person who has died.[3] Although the CCG quilts appropriated the concept of representation, unlike the AIDS quilts, they did not specifically represent lives lost, nor did the squares offer mementos of an individual, as the AIDS quilt does. The nearly identical quilt squares had comments handwritten in marker that celebrated Gardasil: "'Thank god for the vaccine. Now my daughter doesn't have to go through what I went through'—Nancy, Omaha, NE." One woman wrote, "'I was told HPV caused my cancer. Sex @ an early age may be the reason. What will people think.'—Shirley, Oxnard, CA." This particular anxiety about youthful sexual activity's relationship to cancer demonstrated a lack of scientifically precise information. Younger women are more susceptible to HPV because their cervices do not fight the infection as effectively as those of older women. Although some evidence suggests that a combination of an earlier sexual debut and a higher number of sexual partners may put individuals at higher risk for *developing* cervical cancer, the *progression* of HPV to cancer is not directly correlated with age at sexual debut.[4] Thus, Shirley's correlation of "sex [at] an early age" with cervical cancer redistributed the blame from the infection to the behavior. All the evidence suggests that almost anyone who has been sexually active risks getting infected with HPV at some point in his or her life. In light of the scientific facts about the etiology of HPV infection, Shirley's self-recrimination was unduly harsh.

An oft-repeated CCG proclamation featured in the three middle squares of one quilt: "Early—Detection—Saves Lives," an allusion to the importance of regular Pap smears. However, those who uttered this reminder rarely spoke explicitly about what detection required. The clinical process of the Pap smear and HPV triage can hardly be summarized in pithy slogans. Whenever Gary spoke publicly, he would repeat these words, and the mantra appeared prominently throughout the public materials the CCG produced. In December 2007, the group's website described the quilts as putting "a personal face on the battle against cervical cancer," but because the quilt squares were aesthetically identical, they had the effect of homogenizing rather than individualizing women's experiences. In a synthesis of marketing and real life, Merck's "One Less" commercial included a teenager quilting with a woman who appeared to be her grandmother. The girl first cross-stitches "One Less" onto a single piece of fabric, and shortly after, she holds up the finished quilt with the words in red in the middle. For both the CCG and Merck, the quilts represented intimate testimonials and a nonthreatening dissemination of a message. The CCG quilts proclaiming that "early detection saves lives" lacked individual details or personal mementos. The Gardasil ad and the CCG quilts seemed to be hollow symbols, quaint, but hardly representative of the women at the CCG conference or of Gardasil's target demographic.

Gynecological Histories and Contemporary Practices

Throughout my research, the women and mothers whom I met spoke openly about how ignorant they were about cervix health prior to their diagnoses. The lack of awareness of their physiology among women today draws attention to the loss of knowledge since the 1970s movement of embodied female empowerment. Second-wave feminist health collectives taught women to view their own cervix with the aid of a speculum and a mirror.[5] The vaginal self-exam offered a form of objectivity, allowing women to reclaim authority from gynecologists, to know their own bodies, and it reflected the "new moral economy of health care" that called for "the well-educated, well-informed, self-knowing patient to be prepared to advocate for herself as a consumer."[6] In the 1970s, knowing about and viewing one's own cervix was a form of liberation.[7] Forty years later, gynecological self-knowledge, as Merck and CCG members presented the idea, required women to know only that they had a cervix or that it might be vulnerable. This model of disease prevention, whether through vaccination or though detecting abnormalities, gets managed by a clinician. Merck's conceptions of empowerment, which the company defined as engagement with medical institutions, sampled the discourse without fully engaging with the emphasis on autonomy and reclamation that second-wave feminists invoked.

Women's ignorance of female physiology reflects historical attitudes toward women's bodies as uncharted terrain. The purported mysteries of the female body have, in turn, informed the kinds of medical devices and interventions researchers and clinicians have developed. How do women lose the knowledge of their own anatomies? The feminist health collectives were a radical, nonmainstream reclamation of women's control over their bodies. In mainstream discourse, all that remains of that ideology is the language of empowerment. The practices associated with "empowerment" no longer resemble anything like earlier forms of women's health activism.

In the United States, the rate of mortality from cervical cancer decreased significantly between 1947 and 1984, largely through the incorporation of Pap smears into regular gynecological care.[8] The standardization of the practice means that most U.S. women get the intervention and thus the disconnect between a standard medical practice and ignorance about its purpose is striking. The screening technology that has radically improved cervical cancer survival over the last fifty years in the United States, the Papanicolaou (Pap) smear, depends on a tool with a troubling history, the speculum.[9] The speculum allows health care providers to view and to access an otherwise inaccessible interior. The speculum helped to make sense of female anatomy, which anatomists had only begun to understand as different from the male body in the beginning of the nineteenth century. Until the eighteenth century, doctors and scientists believed that male and female bodies were structurally similar and imagined women's reproductive organs as inverted male organs.[10] By the nineteenth century, physicians and scientists distinguished between male and female bodies and perceived their distinct properties as belonging to separate social spheres (the public and the private); doctors interpreted women's physiological processes, such as menstruation, as disorders and pathological.[11] Although versions of the speculum existed centuries before J. Marion Sims refined its functionality in the mid-nineteenth century, Sims referred to the newfound visibility of female interiors as "new and important territory."[12] Female bodily interiors were hardly new, as women's bodies have existed as long as humans have, but Sims's proprietary attitude toward women's bodies defined his research. It was not just any women's bodies with which Sims worked. His work required the availability of commodified bodies that U.S. slavery facilitated. Sims used enslaved black women, with the consent of their enslavers, but not the women's own consent, as resources for his research.[13]

Sims's speculum research, and thus modern gynecological knowledge, drew upon specious, racist distinctions between white and black female bodies. In the nineteenth century, legal and medical categories defined slave women's bodies as uncivilized and impervious to pain, an attitude that dehumanized them.[14] Despite the legal and medical distinctions judges and doctors made between white women and black women in the nineteenth century, "the frailty and nervousness of one group [white women] provided the *raison d'être* of obstetrics and gynecology, while the insensate hardiness of the other [black women] offered the grounds on which they became the experimental 'material' that defined its progress."[15]

The modern speculum, now considered an essential tool in contemporary gynecology, exists because of the availability and commodification of slave women's bodies. The women on whom Sims operated suffered from vesico-vaginal fistulas, fissures in the vaginal wall that allow urine to leak through, usually caused by difficulties in labor.[16] Slave women with fistulas were no longer considered appropriate presences in kitchens and dining rooms because of the smell of urine nor were they sexually desirable.[17] Sims performed repeated surgeries—without anesthesia—on the slaves Anarcha and Betsey to repair this condition. He even made some of his surgeries public performances so he could share his "discoveries." The modern incarnation of the speculum is thus part of the nation's history of racist abuse and oppression. However, the horror of Sims's work is largely overshadowed by celebrations of the medical advances the speculum made possible. It has been compared to "what the printing press is to civilization, what the compass is to the mariner . . . what the telescope is to astronomy."[18] The speculum made the Pap smear possible.

The process by which the Pap smear became the "'right tool' for the job" reveals the assemblages and contingencies of how users integrate a tool into everyday practices.[19] The Pap smear's eventual entrenchment as a screening tool in women's health care depended on the convergence of multiple disciplines and fields.[20] The Pap smear did not start out as a tool for screening cervical health nor was it initially used in human females. In 1917, George Papanicolaou published a paper on estrous cycles in guinea pigs, describing how he used their cervical cells to measure their hormonal fluctuations.

Curious about whether these smears might have utility in humans, he swabbed women's cervices to capture cells. Although the field of reproductive endocrinology integrated the practice into standard research, gynecologists and pathologists did not receive Papanicolaou's research well.[21] It was not until the late 1930s and early 1940s that Papanicolaou began to use the smear as a method for detecting cancer. In the mid-1940s, the practice of screening the cervix with the Pap smear became part of the American Cancer Society's (ACS) push to expand cancer research.[22] Its relative simplicity and low cost appealed to the ACS.[23] Yet even in the context of a seemingly well-intentioned commitment to cancer screening, racial prejudices motivated the use of the Pap smear. The ACS contributed to the racialization of cervical cancer interventions by portraying cervical cancer as a problem of upper-class white women.[24] It prioritized white women as the recipients of resources and interventions that could improve their health outcomes. The consequences of these racist medical practices reverberate today.[25]

The cervix's relative accessibility and as a site of early stages of cancer make it ideal for intervention.[26] The method used to collect cells from the cervix has not changed much since Papanicolaou developed the cervical scrape in 1917. The Pap smear permits a relatively low-tech and low-cost method to catch early abnormalities. Although the practice of the smear has not changed much in its first hundred years, the classification schemes for reading the cellular data have changed multiple times since their creation in the 1920s and retain ambiguities in what constitutes cancerous and precancerous cells.[27] The classificatory schemes that clinicians use to interpret the results of Pap smears provide guidance in terms of triage; however, they do not provide patients definitive knowledge about their cervical health. Today, clinicians use more categories than in the past to interpret results, including categories that indicate precancerous states.[28] How pathologists classify abnormal results contributes to patients' uncertainty about their diagnoses of HPV and cervical cancer.[29]

Until 2014, the standard guideline for diagnosing HPV was with the Pap smear, which screens for cervical cancer. After a gynecologist swabs the woman's cervix, pathologists read the cell slides to identify abnormalities among hundreds of cells. Abnormalities indicate the presence of HPV, although they may alternatively indicate human error in reading or collecting the cells. There are many possible issues with the seemingly simple practice of swabbing the cervix.[30] One reason a swab may not capture abnormal cells is because of the limits of swabbing a localized area. Although the area the gynecologist swabbed may not have any abnormal cells, there may be abnormalities elsewhere in the cervix. It is one thing for someone to look at a single slide and attend to the possible interpretations of hazy cells, but pathologists read hundreds of slides every day. When a pathology report comes back with an inaccurate reading, it is called either a false negative or a false positive. A false negative means that the pathologist missed abnormalities that could eventually progress into cancer. A false positive also has its consequences. The woman may undergo unnecessary stressful and painful procedures. Neither outcome is desirable.

When the Pap smear became the standard screening protocol in gynecological practice, cervical and uterine cancers were the number one killer of women.[31] In the period 1947 to 1984, screening for cervical cancer reduced deaths by 80 percent.[32] Although cervical cancer mortality has dropped, the incidence of genital warts among women in the United States rose 450 percent in the period 1966 to 1984.[33] Scientists theorize that the increase in genital warts reveals a shift in sexual behavior among the population. The decrease in U.S. cervical cancer deaths suggests that there are significant opportunities to reduce cervical cancer mortality for women in countries with high rates of cervical cancer deaths. Although public health officials and gynecologists have celebrated the Pap smear as a miraculously simple intervention, the screening practice has relatively high rates of false negatives, the process of analyzing cervical slides is labor intensive, and interpretive classifications remain ambiguous, even after several iterations and reclassification schemes. These limitations suggest that the Pap smear is not the panacea that its 70-plus years of use might imply.[34]

Despite its limitations, the smear's integration into standard women's health practice reveals how actors normalize tools because they fit particular goals.[35] This normalization may shape how individuals perceive or experience their bodies. The Pap smear transforms the boundaries of the body and delineates pathological or normal bodies. The Pap smear quite literally transforms behaviors into material artifacts, with slides to examine and cells that reveal evidence of sexual activity. An abnormal Pap smear may denote the presence of HPV, but it may also indicate human error in cell capture or interpretation. Through the Pap smear, the gynecological exam invokes a moral discourse of potential stigma. It is easy to imagine these concerns as abstract or academic, but as the CCG members articulated, their diagnoses elicited feelings of stigma and shame. The many steps involved in managing cervical health sometimes confound clinicians, as two physicians recently argued. "The optimal strategy for cervical cancer screening is unknown, involving a complex interaction among multiple variables such as test performance, colposcopy accuracy, screening setting, patient acceptability, and costs." They point out that "current screening strategies are believed to confer similar benefits ... and harms ... but little attention has been paid to other important screening outcomes: the effect of extended surveillance, adverse treatment effects, and economic implications."[36] Managing an abnormal Pap smear may require colposcopies, biopsies, or the even more invasive loop electrosurgical excision procedure (LEEP).[37] Gardasil reduces women's HPV infections, which in turn reduces the emotional and economic burden of these interventions. However, the vaccine provides only partial disruption of these practices, as women may still be infected with HPV types that Gardasil does not prevent.

Biosocial Camaraderie

Merck's marketing of Gardasil generated public discussions about HPV and cervical cancer that did not exist prior to their campaigns. After Gardasil, CCG members no longer represented an invisible condition. They built their community around their experiences as bearers of the disease, knowledgeable about the extensive treatments for cervical abnormalities and the uncertainties about their future cervical health. The group's annual conferences and online forums provided opportunities for participants to express what Nikolas Rose and Carlos Novas refer to as "biological citizenship."[38] The bonds formed through an embodied condition exemplify biosociality. Biosociality is the social processes and the emotions that "bind ... individuals together" through shared biological attributes.[39] When the doctors and researchers who spoke at the CCG's conference panels were unable to answer audience questions about why some women's diagnoses were handled poorly or why researchers still do not completely understand the etiology of HPV, CCG members demanded accountability. They sought better explanations for their ambiguous diagnoses or prognoses and challenged the "professional expertise ... [with] very distinct experience-based knowledge."[40] This expression of embodied knowledge reclaims authority and rejects experts as alienating and abstract.[41]

A variety of patient-led cervical cancer awareness organizations, including the CCG, have replicated the strategies of breast cancer awareness campaigns. They offer encouragement to seek out knowledge, they use a colored ribbon as a symbolic reminder of those affected by a disease, and they repeat slogans about empowerment. At the first evening of the CCG's annual conference, singer-songwriter Marina told the attendees about her awareness-oriented cervical cancer organization. On her website, she describes her group's mission as "about being empowered, being informed, and connecting with others." The seven cervical cancer organizations I either observed in person or followed online shared a similar mission to promote cervical cancer *awareness*. This awareness advocacy brought women together because HPV or cervical cancer affected them personally, but none of these awareness campaigns offered concrete guidance about what happens after women gain knowledge. For example, once aware how common HPV is, women might have advocated for more choices about the kinds of interventions they would receive. Knowledge does not itself lead to empowerment, and none of the awareness strategies provided concrete suggestions about how to engage with the newfound information. Although the Gardasil vaccine provided a deliberate action that transformed knowledge into purported empowerment, it did very little to help women to better understand or to navigate the triage and management of cervical abnormalities for the women who were not eligible for the vaccine because of HPV or cervical cancer diagnoses or because of their age.

In the case of breast cancer, raising awareness might lead to the concrete action of breast self-examination, something an individual can do in the privacy of her home without immediate medical or professional involvement. It does not work quite the same way for HPV or cervical cancer. Even if every young woman were armed with a speculum, à la Annie Sprinkle's "Public Cervix Announcement" or the 1970s feminist health empowerment groups, HPV diagnosis and cervical abnormalities require medical intervention and management.[42] If nothing else, the increased awareness that Gardasil fostered ought to have led to a vocal rejection of how clinicians present cervical abnormalities in threatening, pathological terms. An abnormal Pap smear is a common occurrence, and most abnormalities turn out to be benign or resolve themselves even when no interventions are made.

Yet the cervical cancer patient-led support groups emphasized awareness as the primary goal rather than access to care, improved medical technologies, or improvements in racist medical practices. The first annual CCG conference promoted awareness as a fundamental goal, and post-conference discussions on e-mail and on online forums shared this focus. Many women had created or wanted to start their own awareness campaign. One woman, Cheryl, who was diagnosed with cervical cancer at twenty-six, presented herself during the first CCG annual conference as a poster child for cervical cancer as a younger woman's disease. Cheryl had published a memoir about her experiences with cervical cancer and a radical hysterectomy at age 30. She promoted her book to the conference attendees and offered a sympathetic ear and presented herself as a vociferous advocate for increased HPV awareness. On her personal webpage, she provided links to other cervical cancer awareness organizations, some of which are now defunct. I was curious about why the awareness strategy seemed to lead back to another organization that also promoted awareness and why neither group demanded concrete political action or changes in gynecological research or practice.

At the conference reception, women milled around, a few accompanied by male partners, discussing their health statuses and listening intently as new acquaintances described their medical histories. Like Larissa, Gary's fiancée, most of the attendees referred to themselves as "survivors" of persistent HPV or cervical cancer. Like the millions of U.S. women who have experienced HPV infection or its related cancers, most of whom survive, these women were not eligible for the vaccine. Nevertheless, they were all staunch advocates. Throughout the two days of the conference, women discussed how they could collaborate to spread the message of HPV's ubiquity and to encourage women to get Pap smears. Even though they had never met each other before and came from disparate parts of the country, the women quickly revealed personal details that would not normally be shared during first encounters. Although their sex certainly determined their experiences with the clinical management of their bodies, their bonds depended not only on their biological status as women but also on their shared experiences of gynecological interventions and scrutiny.

Cervical cancer disproportionately affects older women, but many of the women attending the conference were under the age of 30. This was the first time most of them had encountered other young women with cervical cancer. A number of the younger conference attendees spoke to me about their experiences with HPV and cervical cancer.[43] One woman, who was a few years out of college and had recently completed her master's degree in public health, said she had been in the Merck Gardasil trials. She was never told she had HPV, and the trial did not provide her with treatment. She eventually developed cervical cancer. The younger women who were HPV-positive or who had had cervical cancer were particularly enthusiastic about Gardasil. They told me how relieved they were to see messages about cervical cancer for women their age. The Gardasil advertisements featuring younger women resonated with them as they confronted concerns about their future reproductive potential and had to navigate telling partners about their infection.

The morning of the conference, as women filled the rows of tables facing a projector screen, I picked up the registration materials and various free products from a table at the back of the room. On the table along with the registration packets were informational materials and pharmaceutical companies' branded literature about cancer (general and cervical), HPV, and STIs. Surprisingly, there was nothing on the table from Merck. However, Merck's competitor, GlaxoSmithKline, which had not yet received FDA approval for its HPV vaccine, contributed an educational booklet about cervical cancer. The cloth tote bag that contained registration materials was beige with lavender straps, a color that CCG claimed for cervical cancer awareness.[44] Reminding me of the Victorian tradition of transitioning from black to lavender in later stages of mourning, the color may have sought to represent a collective femininity that breast cancer's pink ribbon has come to suggest, but it also evoked the color of dyed Easter eggs. The pastel hue felt unfinished and wan. The bag also included a hodgepodge of objects that were only tangentially relevant to the conference: in addition to a thick binder with the conference schedule and speakers' biographies, there was a hardcover book about a woman's struggle with cancer (not cervical) that had space in the back to journal about one's own cancer experience, a flyer for the Lance Armstrong Cancer Foundation, a pink enamel key fob that doubled as a purse hanger, a Luna Bar (an energy/snack bar marketed to women), and a pink razor. I wondered how these objects came to be part of the conference materials and why the companies had decided this was a good place to offer free products.

Information as Liberation

Gary opened the conference proclaiming, "Today is the day you've asked for, and what you've asked for is information." Throughout the next two days, he stressed participants' ownership of the conference, focusing on how the event prioritized their entitlement to information. Gary encouraged the attendees (almost all of whom were women) to destigmatize cervical cancer. He also proposed changing the name from "cervical" cancer to "cervix cancer." He thought the word "cervical" misrepresented the body part at risk. The adjective cervical, he suggested, perpetuated the invisibility of the cancer. The use of "cervix cancer" explicitly renamed the body part in question. Invoking war metaphors, he argued that cancer research required a broad attack and that cancer eradication efforts "need[ed] to have a prevention arm [and] the detection arm." Even though there has been progress, he reminded the audience that research still has far to go. Alluding to the previous eighteen months of public debate about the availability of Gardasil and whether it should be required for younger girls, he set the tone of the conference. "You're here, you're an example that it's [cancer reduction] not good enough. Imagine being able to stop the cancer before it starts . . . We have a situation [the HPV vaccine] where we can make that the case. We can stop the cancer before it occurs. There seems to be politics associated with that. I don't want to get into politics on any of that . . . but we can stop the cancer, and that's everything." Gary deliberately deflected discussion of the contentious debates that were taking place that year in a number of state legislatures about school policies to require girls to have the vaccine. He need not have done so, as the attendees were avid supporters of the vaccine, although none of them was eligible for it.

Gary's strategy for the organization drew upon an "everyday" activism of awareness rather than a politically motivated activism.[45] His primary strategies focused on promoting Gardasil and encouraging cervical cancer detection. "Early detection saves lives. Early detection saves lives," he intoned repeatedly. He believed that consciousness-raising "advocacy work matters." By rejecting politics and emphasizing awareness, Gary's exhortations highlighted the biosocial camaraderie produced by women's shared experiences of gynecological interventions. He beseeched everyone to "communicate the message and get it out there," and incited the group to yell out, "Cancer sucks!" When the crowd's response was not sufficiently enthusiastic, he made the women do it again with more gusto. Despite Gary's (and thus the CCG's) deflection of politics, awareness advocacy rhetoric cannot be decoupled from the unavoidably political realities of women's health in which Gardasil, HPV, and cervical cancer are implicated.

Gary invoked war metaphors that are often associated with fighting cancer.[46] Denise, another speaker, reminded the audience that it "takes an army" to increase the public's understanding of what HPV and cervical cancer are, although she never explained what the army needed to do or what it might accomplish in terms of public awareness. Gary assured the audience that since Richard Nixon first declared a "war on cancer," science had made significant advances, partly through the National Cancer Institute's research efforts, but he said that government agencies had started to cut funding and research.[47] He recognized that not everyone likes the term war to refer to cancer, but he believed it was apt. He compared the annual number of deaths in the United States due to all cancers as the equivalent of two large jets crashing into the ground every day. "Talk about a war," he said. His battle-cry language served to enhance the message of empowerment, suggesting that there was a call to action even as the actions people should take remained ambiguous. Moving back and forth between general cancer concerns and cervical cancer rates, he apologetically noted that he "hate[d] giving out numbers. We're not numbers." He acknowledged that the detection arm, the institutionalization of the Pap smear, had dramatically changed cervical cancer rates. He argued that even though "it's not a hundred percent, we know it's not a hundred percent, . . . since the 1960s, rates of cervix cancer have been reduced." He pushed the group to expect more from their health care: despite improved cervical cancer survival, they all deserved a world without cancer. For Gary, this meant embracing Gardasil as the solution to political and funding obstacles. Gardasil represented an alternative step to precede the group's long-standing mantra, "Early detection saves lives." Now women, although not these women, no longer needed to rely solely on Pap tests; the vaccine offered a compelling alternative health strategy in Gary's discourse. In every CCG presentation I observed, Gary reminded everyone to "vaccinate early!" along with the other reminders from before the vaccine era: "Pap test regularly" and "HPV test when recommended." The CCG strategy was one of accretion instead of disrupting or unsettling current gynecological practices. Gary did not question the imperfect pathology readings that can lead to false negatives and false positives, he did not mention the imprecision of swabbing the cervix to screen for abnormalities, and he did not argue that male screening might shift the burden of HPV management. Instead, he envisioned an arsenal of women's health strategies, layered one on top of the other.

At the conference, Gary made clear that CCG's missions were to empower cervical cancer patients and to minimize the shame its members articulated in confessional testimonials. Destigmatization involved changing the characterization of HPV and cervical cancer as taboo. Participants celebrated their survivor identity, having endured invasive tests and treatments for their HPV and cervical cancer treatments. Denise, a journalist and television producer in her early thirties, led the first session at the 2007 conference, setting the tone for the next two days with her inspirational talk. Her busy travel schedule allowed little time for doctors' appointments. She described how she received a cancer diagnosis in her mid-twenties while she was on the road for her job. She encouraged the audience to reject the stigmas associated with HPV and cervical cancer. Denise said the scar from her hysterectomy was a daily reminder to "never be ashamed of this cancer again." To spread this message, she had created a grassroots organization for cervical cancer survivors, an organization that still exists today. She also had established a separate organization in collaboration with Marina, the singer who had performed the night before. All three organizations focused on knowledge awareness. Denise's organization, which used to be named after her but whose rebranded name plays on the word cervix, includes a website that features a woman in silhouette raising her arms in victory and proclamations such as "No more fear" and "No more shame." At the end of her animated talk, Denise called on her "cervix-less sisters" to join her in rejecting the stigma of their disease. The audience gave her a standing ovation.

Denise's explicit refusal of stigma was a theme of the conference among speakers and participants alike, although not everyone could replicate Denise's assertive refusal of it. Audience members would preface their questions to panelists by identifying their diagnosis and describe their experiences with the medical profession before asking their questions. Following Gary's revivalist tone, attendees presented confessional testimonials that identified their previous ignorance of HPV and their subsequent awakening that they could be someone who got the disease. Cheryl, the memoirist diagnosed with cervical cancer at the age of twenty-six, had written an article titled "That Girl" for a magazine that targeted women with cancer. In the article, she suggested that she might be perceived as promiscuous after being diagnosed with a cancer caused by sexual activity. The article focuses on her previous ignorance that sex could lead to cancer and her regret over her youthful skepticism that sex was risky. She ends her narrative with her and her husband's "hope," which is embodied by her "seven frozen embryos." Cheryl's marriage and the support of her husband framed her struggle and provided her redemption from her painful medical experiences. In various online and in-person contexts, CCG members revealed the conflict they experienced between two identities: the empowered woman who rejects how others categorize her and the woman who had underlying anxieties about who or what HPV and cervical cancer made them.

Cheryl participated in many of the discussions at the conference and was a very visible presence. Yet she never acknowledged that using condoms would not prevent HPV. Although sex without condoms can expose an individual to various diseases, condoms do not reliably protect against HPV. As she explained in her essay, "When I was younger, my friends were having sex; it seemed like the cool thing to do. I told myself I didn't like the way the condom felt and allowed that to justify my poor judgment. Now I know better." This language suggests that Cheryl believed that she had failed to protect herself against her cervical cancer. The inaccuracy is troubling, as it reveals a flawed logic that muddles an important safer sex message: HPV can be transmitted with or without condoms. Cheryl blames herself for youthful resistance to condoms, and she portrays her refusal to practice safer sex as the reason for her subsequent cancer. She implies that she deserved her cancer instead of acknowledging the high likelihood of HPV infection for all adults at some point in their sexually active lives. Couched in the language of awareness and advocacy, Cheryl's self-blame reproduces a classic narrative of a fallen woman whose disease must be a consequence of sex outside the confines of marriage.

Even though audience members emphasized the ubiquity of HPV and asserted that there was no shame in an HPV diagnosis, they often qualified their questions before asking them: "I'm not overweight," "I'm not a smoker," "I have a perfect bill of health." The statements implied that some women deserved an invasive illness, that they brought their troubles upon themselves. These speakers contradicted themselves, at one moment rejecting the stigma they feared others attributed to their disease and in the next moment distinguishing themselves from other women who must have made risky choices.

New Risks

The availability of Gardasil changed how clinicians, health care profession-als, and advocacy organizations, such as the CCG, framed proactive man-agement of gynecological health. The CCG website warned that "a woman who does not have her three shot prevention vaccine and her regular Pap test screen and HPV test when recommended, significantly increases her chances of developing cervical cancer."[48] CCG messaging implied that not receiving the vaccine is the same as putting oneself at risk for cervical can-cer, as though one might not still be at risk for cervical cancer after receiv-ing the vaccine, as is indeed the case, particularly with Gardasil's original quadrivalent formulation.[49] Thus, conflating *not* vaccinating with an increased risk of cervical cancer positions women as consumers who ought to *choose* to participate in responsible health management. This framing extends the language of stigma; it positions women who have not been vac-cinated as insufficiently proactive.

The CCG's admonitions reframed stigma: women who do not vacci-nate are to blame for their cancer (risk). This is not entirely accurate. Not vaccinating does not increase the odds of developing cervical cancer. Such a claim implies that not vaccinating might increase one's risk for cervical cancer, just as smoking significantly increases the risk of lung cancer. It is true that compared to vaccinated women, unvaccinated women are much more likely to develop cervical cancer. But the implied logic of these state-ments matter: the misrepresentation of risk induces fear instead of produc-tively educating women about the various methods of mitigating the risk of cervical cancer. Further, the notable absence of comprehensive women's health education highlights flaws in the marketing of Gardasil. The vaccine contributes to a comprehensive women's health strategy to reduce risks of cervical cancer and HPV morbidity, but it alone is not sufficient. Yet this was not the message that Merck's advertisements conveyed. Its market-ing of Gardasil, which is echoed in the CCG's vaccine advocacy, defined healthy behaviors through a pharmaceutical lens.

An infection with an oncogenic type of HPV does not necessarily mean cervical cancer. In turn, a diagnosis of cervical cancer does not usually mean death in the United States. And although it is important to know one's HPV status in order to seek treatment that prevents progression to cervical cancer, the knowledge generates a host of other uncertainties.[50] In contrast to the concrete advancements in our understanding of the disease and the development of treatment research that other advocacy efforts, such as the HIV/AIDS movements, have accomplished, there is much that needs to change in women's gynecological care. Yet those who advocated for cervical cancer awareness during the early days of Gardasil's availability did not question the limitations of gynecological management of HPV or cervical cancer, many of which were invasive and emotionally distressing practices that would not change with the advent of Gardasil. Instead, CCG built on its pre-Gardasil invocation of "Pap Test Often," adding "Vaccinate Early," to its slogans. Gardasil's promise as a preventive measure then represented a mechanism of empowerment. Vaccination is indeed an action one can take to gain control of one's future health, but it also preserves the gynecological practices that existed before Gardasil. Instead of a replacement for regular screenings and clinical management of women's bodies, Gardasil added to the tasks a responsible woman *ought* to do. The lack of objections from CCG members to the flaws associated with gynecological care is notable.

The CCG's focus on awareness avoided a deeper engagement with the reasons why cervical cancer continues to affect women in the United States. The number of annual deaths, which for the past four decades has hovered around 4,000 a year, ought to elicit curiosity about why it has been so difficult to change this number. During my time with CCG members, no one ever asked that question. Data collected in the period 2008–2012 show that the rate of HPV infections dropped after Gardasil came on the market, despite U.S. parents' tepid acceptance of the vaccine.[51] It is likely that vaccination may protect some women who would otherwise have died from cervical cancer due to missed abnormalities, failure to access care or to seek care, or cultural discomfort with gynecological interventions, but Gardasil does not explicitly address the main reasons why U.S. women continue to die from cervical cancer: entrenched racist practices in screening.[52]

As a medical tool, a "crucial mediator" in the process of embodiment, Gardasil marked women's bodies as female.[53] For even though HPV-related cancers affect people, regardless of biological sex, Merck's research and marketing strategies targeted adolescent girls. The various tactics CCG members used to promote women's awareness of cervical health sought to empower women and to encourage them to reject the stigma associated with cervical cancer. Despite their rhetoric of empowerment and autonomy, the CCG members, in fact, emphasized the vulnerabilities of their imagined audience. It is difficult to distinguish which terms of empowerment were Merck's and which were the CCG's. At the conferences I attended in 2007 and 2008, I never heard a call for subsidized vaccines. No one asked when there would be free Pap smears or HPV testing for all. There were no demands for concrete policy changes that would ensure wider access to gynecological care or discussion of social injustices in women's healthcare delivery. Thus, a conference that prioritized the dissemination of information shored up and even produced the appropriate bodies for the vaccine by imagining the vaccine as the *ne plus ultra* for women's health. Yet the CCG's leaders and participants did not engage with their relative privilege: attendees were women who had resources to attend a conference out of town and who felt empowered to question their medical care. They did not advocate for improved access for those who continued to die from cervical cancer and they did not mention that women at greater risk of dying from cervical cancer might not have had the same power to challenge clinical interventions. In contrast to the feminist health movements of the 1970s, which sought to offer "new practices for interacting with, caring about, and managing reproduction—to seize the means of reproduction," the CCG's public platform and its members absorbed Merck's highly marketed and produced model of femininity and consumer engagement with health.[54] The appropriation of Merck's marketing language into the CCG's awareness activism complicates the advocacy efforts of the group.

These modes of engagement with Merck's slogans matter. Although the CCG attempted to renounce stigma associated with cervical cancer, its members remained deeply entangled with shame and uncertainty. Because Merck's advertisements avoided an explicit discussion of HPV as an STI and because the Gardasil advertisements alluded to but barely addressed that sex is the cause of HPV, and therefore the cause of HPV-related cancers, Merck perpetuated the culture of silence around HPV. By refusing a more political and critical challenge to public perceptions of cervical cancer, CCG members furthered Merck's narrative of HPV and its related cancers. In Gary's efforts to reclaim cervical cancer as cervix cancer and in his avoidance of a national political debate about Gardasil school-entry policies, he eschewed politics. Echoing the CCG's members' pre-diagnosis ignorance about their cervices, his implicit refusal of the feminist slogan "the personal is political" crafted the intimate bodily experiences of CCG members into something more marketable and (purportedly) universal. This model strayed far from the 1970s model of feminist empowerment.

4

Educate the Educators

Seven years before the FDA approved Gardasil, Dr. Jerome Groopman, a physician who writes about the intersections of medical phenomena and social life, wrote an article that detailed the experiences of Jenny, a college-aged woman, with abnormal Pap smears and her diagnosis with an STI that posed the potential threat of cancer. Groopman's article provides a glimpse of the public awareness of and attitudes toward HPV in the years before Merck or its competitor GlaxoSmithKline developed their vaccines. I tore the article out of the magazine and kept it in a file box for years. At the time, although I helped lead a student-run sexual health information group at my college, this was not a virus we had heard about during our extensive training, and this was the first time I had heard about HPV. The article provided a candid consideration of the consequences of a ubiquitous yet unfamiliar infection. Jenny told Dr. Groopman that her previous doctor had "made [her] feel as if [she] must be promiscuous,"[1] Groopman argued that those infected with HPV should not be stigmatized and that women who received an HPV diagnosis could do little but wait and see. He noted that two companies, MedImmune and Merck, were in the early stages of developing preventive vaccines, but most of the article addressed the recent development of technology that made possible the DNA typing of HPV and the benefits that DNA testing conferred over the Pap test. Groopman pointed out the lack of precision involved in Pap smear procedures and recounted how his patients with abnormal Pap smears were confused about what a diagnosis of HPV meant for their immediate and long-term health. He explained how relatively unknown yet extremely common HPV was at the time of his writing, as it still is today, almost twenty years later.

As Groopman acknowledged, an HPV diagnosis introduces a host of ambiguities and contingencies for the patient. In 2007, shortly after Gardasil was approved, Sophie, a 30-year-old woman, told me how she had repeatedly been given vague gynecological diagnoses after a Pap smear that was categorized as an abnormal smear of clinically undetermined significance (ASCUS). She described being in an exam room with multiple physicians gathered around her at the local teaching hospital. Added to the stress of having to return for follow-up care and her inability to get clear information about what the ASCUS diagnosis implied for cancer, her insurance company started charging her for procedures she had not had and refused to reimburse her for the routine Pap test, a screening that is considered part of standard preventive care by most insurance companies and medical professionals. Not only was Sophie caught up in the convoluted process of monitoring for potential cervical cancer, she was also fighting to make sure she wouldn't pay out of pocket for what Casper and Clarke call "the most widely used and entrenched cancer-screening technology in the world."[2]

I went with Sophie to one of her appointments and sat in the waiting room while she had her exam. The office scheduled colposcopies, the follow-up technique for viewing the cervix after abnormal Pap screening tests, on specific days. As was the case at other clinics I observed in Maryland and California, the waiting room had a television that broadcast *Accent Health*, a CNN-sponsored program that provides health stories, which the show calls news, and commercials from pharmaceutical companies.[3] Sophie said the television infuriated her with its constant barrage of HPV vaccine promotions while she waited, uncertainly, in the featureless waiting room. It was as though the commercials taunted her for failing to receive the vaccine, and any colposcopy clinic patient had a looped reminder that she was ineligible for the preventive treatment now that she was infected with HPV. The vaccine's promise was too late for those who were already in the process of screening, diagnosis, and management.

Sophie interpreted Gardasil's marketing as judgmental. She understood it as a critique, even though the vaccine was not available when she might have been able to benefit from it.

Those who advocate preventive medicine seek to teach people to lead healthier lifestyles, change their behaviors, and understand the long-term consequences of certain habits. But even women who manage their health compliant with medical authorities' suggestions, as the patients Groopman describes appeared to do and as Sophie did with her diligent follow-up, almost nothing can prevent an HPV infection, besides total abstinence. A sympathetic clinician, Groopman explained how little patients understood HPV. Prior to the availability of Gardasil, there is extensive literature that demonstrated how unaware young adults and parents, two key target audiences for the vaccine, were of HPV's prevalence, of HPV's relationship to cervical cancer, or of the role of the Pap smear in identifying HPV-related abnormalities.[4] This is a strange conundrum. It is difficult to think of other examples of an infection that more than three-quarters of the population gets but that so few people know about. One of the biggest obstacles that Merck and other Gardasil's proponents needed to contend with was the public's lack of awareness. Thus, there were multiple challenges to achieving public acceptance of the vaccine. Merck saw this as a marketing opportunity: it deliberately exploited the public's lack of awareness of HPV and its relation to cervical cancer.

HPV and Gardasil introduced a twist on the phenomenon of "disease mongering," a well-established practice in the pharmaceutical world that contributes to the medicalization and pharmaceuticalization of human life.[5] In this tactic, a new diagnostic category transforms physiological processes into a problem that requires pharmaceutical intervention, which in turn justifies selling new pharmaceutical products to treat the new syndrome/disease/condition.[6] Yet Gardasil did not fit into traditional disease-mongering tactics by which pharmaceutical companies identify a new "problem."

Priming the Educators

Merck faced the challenge of getting the public to understand a widespread and common virus that few knew about. It needed to generate a demand for a vaccine that few people appreciated as an important tool for HPV prevention. The narrative Merck constructed depended on the ignorance of young girls and the parents who would make decisions about their gynecological care. As Vincanne Adams, Michelle Murphy, and Adele E. Clarke have pointed out, "Anticipation is a mode of both creating markets and responding to projected needs, whether or not such crises are yet born out in the public sphere."[7] Merck adopted this anticipatory logic, arguing that all young girls were at risk of contracting HPV infection. This in turn produced a market of vulnerable bodies, an anticipatory focus on the intrinsic value of girls' bodies, perceived as "a crucial site for the creation of 'human capital.'"[8] Cancer was imagined as posing a threat to girls' reproductive potential. But this strategy also rendered invisible the gynecological interventions that existed at the time Gardasil became available. Merck's marketing campaign did not mention alternatives to Gardasil, such as improved screening technologies or access to care.

In the months leading up to the FDA's licensure meeting for Gardasil and the subsequent market launch, Merck's campaign focused on educating doctors.[9] Targeting clinicians increased the possibility of the "shared decision making" that expands interest in new pharmaceuticals beyond direct-to-consumer advertisements.[10] At the May 2006 annual meeting of the American Society for Colposcopy and Cervical Pathology in Washington, D.C., Merck sponsored an "Educate the Educators" session. As is common at many medical conferences, this session offered medical professionals continuing medical education (CME) credits, which are part of requirements for licensing and ongoing clinical training. The Accreditation Council for Continuing Medical Education oversees CME courses in an attempt to ensure that an appropriate division exists between education and the marketing efforts of pharmaceutical companies. Despite distinguishing between the divisions, education sessions may still serve the financial interests of pharmaceutical companies. The "Educate the Educators" session trained practitioners to become speakers who would educate both medical professionals and patients about the soon-to-be available HPV vaccine.

To pre-empt criticisms that CME programs might be glorified advertising, the educational programs usually address a broader health issue for which the companies make the newest treatment, and they rarely mention the product's brand name explicitly. On the registration form for the event, a disclosure noted that "Educate the Educators: HPV and the New HPV Vaccines Program is supported by unrestricted educational grants from

Merck & Company, Digene Corporation, Roche Molecular Systems, and GlaxoSmithKline."[11] Roche and Digene make diagnostic HPV tests, and GlaxoSmithKline would soon be seeking FDA approval for its HPV vaccine, Cervarix. As critics of pharmaceutical companies have argued, when these companies fund education opportunities for physicians, doctors may not be objective about the drugs they choose to prescribe.[12] One physician who wrote a confessional about this topic in 2007 titled his piece "Dr. Drug Rep."[13] Since Gardasil was the only HPV vaccine ready for licensing review, Merck's role in HPV education was impossible to ignore. The indirect marketing strategy of medical education reflects the transition from lenient regulation of pharmaceutical subsidies to physicians to increasingly restrictive laws about how much money a pharmaceutical company and its sales reps may spend on courting physicians. The "Educate the Educators" event exemplified this fine line between marketing and educational content.

The introductory speaker, Dr. Leonard,[14] a well-respected physician who had worked at my university's hospital in the past, told the room, "You are the people most suited for educating. . . . [You are] critically placed to provide the vaccine. . . . You are the HPV experts." Although Dr. Leonard asserted that the people in the room were uniquely prepared to be authoritative spokespeople for the new vaccine, the next hour of the session involved extensive education on the sequelae and evolution of HPV, the phylogenetic differences among HPV (sexually transmitted versus non-sexually transmitted, high risk versus low risk), how HPV is necessary but not sufficient for cervical cancer, and the "Natural History of HPV." These basic details of the infection seemed to me as though they ought to be well understood and familiar to the highly specialized audience of gynecologists and pathologists. Dr. Leonard started with a slide, contrasting the odds ratio that a person with HPV would develop cervical cancer to the odds ratio that a person who smokes will get lung cancer. Odds ratios provide a measure of how exposures affect outcomes. Smoking and lung cancer have an odds ratio of eight, which means there are very high odds that a smoker will develop lung cancer. HPV 16 and cervical cancer have an odds ratio of 434. This ratio exemplifies how "the association between HPV and cervical cancer [is] among the strongest statistical relations ever identified in cancer epidemiology."[15] To further impress on the audience the association between HPV and cervical cancer, Dr. Leonard launched into the "Natural History of HPV," citing a study in which young women at a college contracted HPV shortly after their first sexual encounter.[16] Jokingly, he said, "It's enough to make you not want to send your daughter to college." The audience laughed at this. There was no mention of infection prevalence among males or of the fact that women must necessarily get infected by their partners, male or female. The joke struck me as glib and laden with judgment for young female patients who received care from these providers. "Lock up your daughters and don't educate them because they might get STIs" was a strange leap in logic for a room full of highly educated practitioners.

Near the end of the two-hour presentation, Dr. Leonard showed a slide titled "The Burden of HPV—Globally and in the U.S." As an introduction, he asked the audience whether we "really *need* a vaccine." Dr. Leonard shared a slide with CDC figures for HPV that claimed that 15 percent of the U.S. population is positive for HPV at any given time and that a third of STI dollars are spent on genital warts, which are caused by HPV. He listed the economic costs of HPV without acknowledging the potential emotional or physical burden on women. He answered his own question ("Do we need a vaccine?") by demonstrating the efficacy of historic vaccines. Citing diphtheria and poliomyelitis, he argued that the World Health Organization (WHO) prevents three million deaths annually with vaccines. Although Merck had not yet received approval from the FDA, as Leonard pointed out, the HPV vaccine's high rate of efficacy and effectiveness made it a significant achievement and one worth promoting.

Although "Educate the Educators" was not specifically about the HPV vaccine, it prepared the practitioners to respond to a growing awareness of how widespread HPV is and the anticipated parents' demands for the new vaccine after they learned about HPV. The content of the presentation and the proactive framing of the clinical narrative suggested that providers were not in fact knowledgeable about HPV or the coming vaccine. One might argue that it is not reasonable to expect health care providers to be walking encyclopedias for an unfamiliar infection. However, HPV is not an uncommon infection; the session was held for practitioners who were gynecologists and pathologists; and the meeting took place at the annual conference for colposcopy and cervical pathology. These providers are precisely the population one would expect to need little education about HPV and cervical cancer etiology. The abundance of long-established facts about HPV at this session might have simply represented the criteria for CME accreditation. But if the session was a CME accreditation course disseminating already well-known knowledge about HPV's etiology, which would mean that its attendees were not learning new information about HPV, then it was a thinly veiled opportunity to convey the novelty and utility of Gardasil. This suggests that the Educate the Educators CME was a guise for Merck's launch of Gardasil. It certainly set the tone of urgency, fear, and hope that messages about the vaccine would foster.

Regardless of whether the session had to meet a minimum educational content or whether Merck knew that providers were ill-prepared to promote Gardasil, the session illuminated the underlying assumption that providers would not be equipped to discuss the HPV vaccine with their patients. Indeed, data from the last decade of the vaccine's availability suggest that providers do not feel prepared to recommend the HPV vaccine.[17] The educational materials provided during the CME event reflected a problem I observed repeatedly during research: knowledge about HPV is sparse among people in many communities, including those who ought to be most informed. Ignorance within the community that provides care to women suggests that the ambiguities and uncertainties produced in abnormal Pap smears and knowledge of HPV are replicated over and over in the exam room, in cytopathology laboratories, and in providers' interactions with patients. Jenny's and Sophie's experiences with their diagnoses point to women's confusions about their own bodies, which clinicians may perpetuate when they fail to explain HPV's etiology or they fail to support patients' autonomy.

When clinicians cannot or do not ensure that patients fully understand what HPV and its related morbidities mean, they strip their patients of the ability to make informed decisions. The low rate of awareness of HPV prior to the launch of Gardasil does not make sense given the high rate of HPV infections in the United States. It reveals a larger problem with how physicians educate patients to understand the purpose of a Pap smear, what HPV is, and how widespread it is. Abnormal Pap test results positioned Jenny and Sophie as women whose bodies required extensive oversight and engaged them in protracted negotiations. Yet in their *normal*[18] abnormalities, we can see how female bodies are bodies to track, regulate, and censure and how even compliant women require more surveillance.

Although we cannot definitively tie the knowledge presented in a professional CME course to what happens in the exam room, the carefully crafted session suggests that at the moment when the HPV vaccine became available, even the providers were not well equipped to address

HPV with their patients. This inconsistency in knowledge appeared across the disparate communities with whom I worked, from mothers who told me that they would teach their daughters to recognize the "signs" of HPV (although when HPV is cancerous, it has no visible symptoms) to providers who were hesitant to acknowledge that the HPV vaccine is an STI vaccine. Although Merck invested a lot of time and money in "educating" people—public health officials and providers in particular—about HPV and cervical cancer, a more comprehensive focus on cervical health might undermine the urgent need for the vaccine; its educational materials emphasized HPV's prevalence and the challenges in preventing its spread. Merck's education materials said little about the *treatability* of cervical cancer or the medical profession's rate of success at preventing HPV from progressing to cancer. Those aspects of gynecological care did not fit into the Gardasil tale.

The Connection to Make

I met Dr. Gonzalez at the January 2008 Southern California Immunization Coalition meeting about pre-teen vaccine week. He generously invited me to come to a staff meeting at his clinic so I could recruit staff for interviews. Based in a predominantly Latino neighborhood, the clinic was located on a busy street with low buildings and random shops set in strip malls. Across the street from the entrance to the clinic was a large junkyard. There were few chain stores, and most of the stores had signs in Spanish. As soon as I entered the clinic, I noticed *AccentHealth* on the television. It was the same service I had seen at Sophie's colposcopy clinic and the same one that was at the phlebotomy lab where I had gone to get my blood drawn a few weeks before. Mimicking television news shows, it featured "reporters" providing health education and information in short segments. Its broadcast was all in English, something that I would later ask one of the clinic's physicians about, since the majority of the clinic's patients spoke Spanish. He agreed that it was strange, but he didn't explain why they showed the broadcast in their clinic.

The waiting room was full, mostly of women and small children speaking in Spanish. The few men waiting were noticeably older than the female patients. People stared blankly at the *AccentHealth* programming on the television as mothers wrangled their squirming toddlers. The receptionists sat behind glass windows like bank tellers, at a strange remove from the patients. After the receptionist confirmed my appointment with Dr. Gonzalez's secretary, she buzzed me in and walked me back to the staff room, taking me past the examination rooms and the in-house pharmacy window. I had arrived fifteen minutes before the start of the meeting, and only a few of the doctors were in the staff room. Dr. Gonzalez showed up and told me he would introduce me before the meeting started, but I should help myself to food available in disposable foiled-covered aluminum trays.

An ethnically diverse group of men and women drifted in, some wearing lab coats, some wearing business casual attire. While the clinic staff entered the room, Dr. Grayson, one of the younger doctors, his hair bleached platinum and styled with gel to make it stand up, began uncovering the foil trays. He told me that he had experience with food presentation from a past life as a caterer. He would later reveal himself to be an unusual physician, the only clinician who told me that he advocated for Gardasil's use in males more than a year before Merck would submit it for approval in boys and men. As I had observed at the immunization coalition meetings, a pharmaceutical company provided lunch for the doctors, and one of the company's representatives attended the staff meeting to give out samples of her company's products. Once everyone had gone through the food line, Dr. Gonzalez introduced the pharmaceutical representative, Sherri, who was there to promote her company's insulin pens for diabetics. A petite woman, she wore a beige skirt suit and had a Lance Armstrong "Livestrong" yellow rubber bracelet around her slim ankle. It was an incongruous flash of yellow in an otherwise conservative self-presentation. The doctors and medical staff sat at tables that had been set up to form a U in front of a projector screen, eating their free lunch as they glanced up occasionally. Sherri, standing in front of the staff, announced that she was going to provide the doctors with samples, but they would have to write prescriptions for the fine needles the pens required. A number of the doctors thanked her for the "nice lunch and for your product." Sherri smiled, moved to the back of the room, and left shortly after. Dr. Gonzalez invited me to come to the front of the room next.

Standing in the light of the projector, I announced that I wanted to conduct interviews with the staff about the HPV vaccine. One of the older doctors asked me if I were working on Gardasil, Merck's vaccine. I replied that as it was the only FDA-approved HPV vaccine, it was the focus of my research. He then asked if I had received funding through Merck. I said, no, I have no financial ties to them. I explained that my grants came from the National Science Foundation and Wenner-Gren, a foundation that funds anthropology research. He mumbled that these funding bodies usually don't provide a lot of money and that it was probably not enough for an honorarium. He did not sign up to be interviewed. The interaction stayed with me for a long time, reminding me of how deeply ingrained the pharmaceutical subsidiaries are for many providers, especially for older physicians who practiced during the less-regulated 1980s and 1990s.[19] Six staff members signed up for interviews, although only three responded to my follow-up emails.[20]

The three doctors, Dr. Gonzalez, Dr. Santana, and the youthful Dr. Grayson, who was an osteopath, met me at the clinic for interviews on different days. When I arrived at the clinic for the interview with Dr. Grayson, he asked me to come to his office so he could finish some paperwork before lunch. He shared the small office with another doctor. Dr. Grayson's corner was decorated with family photos of small children and a classic poster of a Norman Rockwell image—the family doctor treating a young child. He suggested that we go out to eat and asked me to drive as his car was stuck behind another car in the clinic's narrow parking lot. On our way to the restaurant, he, like other doctors I would observe at the clinic and elsewhere, emphasized that he persuades parents to get the vaccine for their daughters by framing it as a cancer vaccine rather than a vaccine for an STI. "I emphasize that this is a cancer vaccine. It doesn't protect against all cancers. . . . It's not that I avoid discussing about information, it's just how I present it. . . . We're not doing it to prevent a virus, we're doing it to prevent a cancer caused by a virus." He repeated more than once that people need a "tangible" reason to accept the vaccine. He said, "some of the preoccupation is that it's a new vaccine. . . . I convince most people to get it." He implied that his patients and his patients' parents don't actually know what is good for them.

During our conversation at a local Mexican restaurant, Dr. Grayson told me he had received the first of the three shots for the HPV vaccine off label, paying out of pocket since insurance didn't cover it because the vaccine still had not been approved for men. He quickly asked me if it was okay that he had revealed this to me, as though I were going to criticize his use or report him to someone. He pointed out that Gardasil had received approval for males in other countries and that as a younger doctor, he was open to less orthodox uses of the vaccine. His personal use of the vaccine made me curious about why he didn't have more forthright conversations with parents. He understood the prevalence of HPV and the value of the vaccine for males. Yet he, too, hewed close to the more established messaging, promoting it as a cancer vaccine, even as he had a much less orthodox approach to his own health.

Mothers had told me that they doubted the medical authority of physicians and resented the attitudes of doctors that they knew best. The clinicians I interviewed or heard speak on panels about vaccines, and panels specifically about the HPV vaccine, corroborated these parents' suspicions. At an October 2009 panel at the San Francisco Commonwealth Club on the HPV vaccine, "HPV: The Silent Killer—Prevention, Treatment, Controversy," Dean Blumberg,[21] a physician identified as a "non-paid speaker for Merck," stressed that there was *no* need to explain to parents the connection between the STI and cancer. Perhaps unintentionally echoing Merck's "Make the Connection" campaign, he even called it "the wrong connection to make." Dr. Blumberg's dismissal of his patients' and their parents' comprehension of the association between HPV and cancer is an extreme example, but it is not dissimilar from the language and attitudes clinicians continue to express. In the journal *Pediatrics*, Douglas Diekema reflected on parental refusal of immunizations. "Although decision-making involving the health care of children should be shared between physicians and parents, *parental permission* must be sought before children receive medical interventions, including immunizations."[22] Physicians do have a responsibility to care for children's welfare, but it is not clear that parents perceive decision-making as what Diekema calls a "shared" process. In spite of recognizing that parents must provide direction for physicians, Diekema demonstrates the tension between parents and providers when it comes to the health of minors. Many of these doctors suggest that they are obliged to, *but would prefer not to*, let parents direct the health care of their children. The paternalism latent in these statements is more obvious to parents than providers may realize.

The doctors I interviewed also interpreted their roles this way. Physicians tried to manage parents' concerns by avoiding the discussion of Gardasil as an STI vaccine, but this paternalistic refusal to address the comprehensive benefits provided by the vaccine usurps parents' autonomy. When physicians do not give parents the full information, they damage the relationship between them. The mothers I interviewed were aware of physicians' attempts to persuade them to do what the doctor wanted rather than what the parents preferred, and this elicited distrust of their children's providers. Thus, the current recommendations that physicians emphasize Gardasil's cancer benefits and deliberately steer parents away from understanding that HPV is sexually transmitted may well perpetuate parents' refusal of the vaccine.

Years before the current recommendations to emphasize Gardasil as a cancer vaccine, the doctors I interviewed uniformly told me that they described the vaccine to parents as a cancer vaccine. Dr. Grayson was passionate about his strategy for motivating parents to vaccinate.

> When I present it, I don't talk about how people get the virus. I don't even go there. I just say, "This is a vaccine that kills cancer. No matter what you hear in the media, it kills cancer, a hundred percent of the time." And I say, "There may have been some controversy [about] . . . how people get the virus, but the fact remains that it is morally wrong for me not to offer a vaccine that can prevent cancer, when it's the sixth highest cause of death in women in the world." There's no reason for a woman in this country to die of cervical cancer. . . . This virus is why we do Paps. . . . It's not that I avoid discussing information, it's just how I present it. . . . We're not doing it to prevent a virus, we're doing it to prevent the cancer caused by the virus.

Physicians' willingness to slip a little with the details, such as Dr. Grayson's claim that Gardasil "kills cancer a hundred percent of the time," is not meant to be dishonest nor did he perceive himself as dissembling. Rather, it reflects his commitment to protecting and persuading patients. Grayson compared it to implementing population-wide screening for HIV, which he said he does routinely with all his patients, throwing it in with a battery of tests he tells his patients they need to have. He explained that this practice helps reduce "barriers to care." He said, "I test everyone, I don't care about risk factors. We just screen the whole population." Dr. Gonzalez also equated the HPV vaccine with standard care, comparing it to the effects of the chicken pox vaccine. He had not seen a case of chicken pox in two years, and though he had had the illness as a child, and though for most people it is not a severe disease, he believed that the reduction of disease was worthwhile.[23] He endorsed vaccines because they are "such an easy, basic measure that we can do to prevent disease . . . because we live in a post-immunization era. What I mean by that is we have not seen a lot of the ravages of disease. . . . It is easy for folks to emphasize that nothing is perfect, nothing is a hundred percent safe. . . . Sometimes we forget that."

At the end of my interview with Dr. Gonzalez, after I had turned off the digital audio recorder, he smiled at me and said, "I'm talking about faith." He paused, looking at me directly before elaborating "faith in science." Invoking the language of religion rather than the language of science, he suggested that there was a need for implicit trust in medicine. Yet scientific inquiry requires doubt and skepticism, the opposite of faith. Without skepticism, research could not move forward. Gonzalez's interpretation of medicine as a practice built on trust and faith rather than critical inquiry came to exemplify for me the incongruity between parents who are skeptical about vaccines and health care providers. The convictions of physicians and public health officials that the HPV vaccine is an unambiguous right choice, without exploring the nuances of the vaccine's limitations or the complexities of HPV, may explain some of the reasons why parents distrust Gardasil. Although Dr. Gonzalez invoked faith in medicine more broadly, doctors who claim medical practice as dogma and who are resistant to questions from patients make vaccine critics more persuasive to skeptical parents. A recent review of the literature on parents' attitudes about vaccines finds that "it is not vaccines per se that are mistrusted, rather it is the institutions (through which information about vaccines is delivered) that are mistrusted."[24] The rigidity of the pediatric vaccine schedule feeds into parents' unease with the *institutionalization* of immunizations. Parents I interviewed did not feel that standardized care reflected their needs.

It is not just the dogma that may exacerbate skepticism about vaccines. In my observations at Dr. Gonzalez's clinic and at two other southern California clinics, the process of administering vaccines and physicians' explanations of routinized vaccinations fostered parents' distrust. Children were escorted to a separate room, where medical assistants, rather than the physician, injected the vaccine. Before passing the patient to the medical assistant, doctors might explain to the parent what vaccines a child would receive. This ought to have been a moment for parents to ask questions, but as both Dr. Santana and Dr. Grayson told me, few parents did. The disconnect between the care provided and the ability to interrogate its delivery may enhance the alienation parents feel during their children's medical care and their perception that physicians do not want to engage with parental skepticism. The vaccination process, like the schedule that guides it, is anonymized and standardized, making it difficult for parents to raise questions about their children's needs.

Dr. Santana, who saw patients at both the low-income clinic and at a private practice for more affluent families, explained that the parents at the affluent clinic were less likely to be compliant with doctors' recommendations than his patient population at the lower-income clinic. Indeed, vaccine resistance primarily comes from more affluent communities.[25] Or, as Dr. Grayson explained, the clients at his clinic tended to be "more trusting of the doctors: 'Well, the doctors said so, so we should do it.'" The populations these doctors saw were different from the mothers I interviewed, who felt entitled to challenge the expertise of doctors. All three doctors saw their opportunity to convey authority as a preferred method of navigating the potentially contentious discussion about HPV.

Choosing to Know One's Own Body

Although every year millions of people are infected with HPV and tens of thousands of women are affected by cervical cancer, HPV has never motivated mass marches or demands for a cure from women's health advocates.[26] Thus, Merck had to persuade women that their daughters needed the vaccine. A variety of patient education strategies sought to generate patient demand for Gardasil by highlighting women's ignorance and their unrealized need for enlightenment. Approved in 2003 for use in conjunction with the Pap test, Digene's Hybrid Capture 2 High-Risk HPV DNA Test offers another example of health-seeking behavior framed as a choice, even though the absence of alternative products constrained patients' choices. In 2009, the FDA approved a second HPV test developed by Hologic, Inc., but for six years, Digene had a monopoly on the market.[27] In a strange parallel to Merck's "Tell Someone" ads, Digene launched its "Choose to Know" campaign in 2005.[28] The similar language and patient-empowerment recommendations demonstrate how pharmaceutical and diagnostics companies envision their audiences. In one print advertisement, five multiethnic women dressed as professionals face forward, looking at the viewer with defiant and confident expressions. Almost literally white-collar, all but one is in a button-down collared shirt; one woman wears glasses, presumably to connote her intelligence. Flanked by the other four women, the woman in the center wears a dark V-neck blouse and has crossed her arms. The text reads, "If you're a gambling woman, then getting just a Pap test is fine," implying that the routine cancer screening method alone will not provide adequate information. These women do not appear to be risk takers. Instead, their clothes and their stances convey that they are ambitious, confident, and responsible women who would neither take the chance on less than the best in health care nor waste time with imperfect knowledge when something better is available.

Digene's campaign included an orange rubber bracelet with the words "Choose to Know" etched into the band, reminiscent of the popular LiveStrong cancer bracelets the Lance Armstrong Foundation promoted. The yellow rubber bracelets gained popularity in 2004 after Lance Armstrong, a cyclist who won the Tour de France seven times and survived testicular cancer, launched his LiveStrong campaign to raise awareness for cancer survivors. The Digene and LiveStrong bracelets identified a particular cancer with a particular color in the same way that AIDS awareness campaigns used red ribbons and some breast cancer survivors adopted pink ribbons as their symbol. Cervical cancer survivors have also adopted the powerful iconography of color, ribbons, and bracelets. The CCG produced a purple bracelet, for example. And before the FDA approval of Gardasil, Merck launched a "Make the Commitment" bracelet kit that promised to donate one dollar to the Cancer Research and Prevention Foundation for each free kit ordered. Confusingly, the campaign was called "Make the Connection," and the website domain was maketheconnection.org, rather than consistently following the "make the commitment" title of the bracelet kit.

Make the Connection was associated with the Cancer Research and Prevention Foundation and the StepUp Women's Network, although the funding for the initiative came from Merck. I tried to order a bracelet kit in August 2006, but the website no longer offered the kit and the campaign had been discontinued. Along with its slogan, "Make the connection between HPV and cervical cancer," the site explained how the bracelet kit would further awareness. "By ordering a free *Make the Connection* bracelet kit, you will be helping to advance cervical cancer education and outreach. For every pair of bracelet kits ordered, Merck will donate one dollar to Cancer Research and Prevention Foundation, up to $100,000, for cervical cancer awareness and screening programs among medically underserved women."[29] The photos of the bracelet-making kit reminded me of the friendship bracelets preteen girls make at summer camp. It included plastic cylindrical and spherical beads and a small charm with crude icons of three people. The smaller middle person might have represented a girl, but the figures looked like rounded Xs with a dot in the middle to stand for a head. When I revisited the www.maketheconnection.org site in 2011, I found that the domain had expired. The site listed the contact information for the owner of the domain, the Edelman public relations firm. The site's newly transparent origin, a public relations firm, and the disappearance of the site after the marketing push had dissipated further discredited the idea that Merck was invested in raising patient awareness.

The site's expiration notice calls attention to the many strands of Merck's opportunistic marketing strategies, some of which were celebrated in an *AdWeek* story about Bev Lybrand, the woman behind the initial Gardasil campaign.[30] Both the Digene and Merck campaigns played on women's fears that they might be insufficiently responsible, suggesting that only those who don't care would fail to seek out information about their health. Implicit in the instruction to "make the connection" or to "choose to know" is the notion that failing to do so is irresponsible and negligent. However, in this case, the knowledge women could gain was in direct service of commodities offered by pharmaceutical companies such as a diagnostic test or a vaccine.

5

Merck and the FDA

Prior to the Food and Drug Administration's review of Gardasil, progressive media worried that the vaccine might not receive legitimate consideration by the U.S. regulatory body. Katha Pollitt, an outspoken progressive, warned that pressure from conservatives would force women to choose, as she dramatically proposed, "between virginity and death!"[1] In early 2006, journalist Michael Specter suggested that FDA approval of Gardasil might be in jeopardy because of policy measures during George W. Bush's administration that undermined women's and families' access to health care. Specter proposed that politics, not science, would inform the FDA's deliberation process.[2] Comparing Gardasil to Plan B, an emergency contraceptive pill whose delayed approval was driven by conservatives' anxieties about giving women more control of their bodies, Specter noted that the HPV vaccine might also tap into conservative politicians' and other moralists' disapproval of young women's sexual activity.[3] In preparation for these imagined resistances, women's health advocates celebrated the vaccine as a feminist cause, providing women with a preventive sexual health measure that did not require their partners' participation. Fears that the FDA review would stall because of anxieties that the vaccine condoned adolescent sexual activity, however, failed to anticipate

Merck's counter-strategy, which was presaged in the "Tell Someone" advertisements, reminding viewers this was a "cancer caused by a virus."

In May 2006, I attended the meeting of the FDA's Vaccines and Related Biological Products Advisory Committee (VRBPAC) in Gaithersburg, Maryland.[4] As I drove to Gaithersburg from Baltimore, I listened to a National Public Radio (NPR) news broadcast about the upcoming meeting to review Gardasil. The journalist noted briefly that most family-values organizations were not opposed to Gardasil's approval, although they were concerned about the prospect of the government *requiring* the vaccine for pre-adolescent and adolescent children. A physician spokesperson for the Medical Institute for Sexual Health, which NPR identified as an organization that "advises conservative groups," explained, "We believe this is going to be very important in terms of prevention. . . . The possibility of HPV infection remains from sexual assault, from date rape, and there's always the possibility that young people may marry someone who was previously exposed and is still carrying the virus."[5] Although this physician claimed that the Medical Institute for Sexual Health supported a "cancer vaccine," his language both ignored the ubiquity of teenage sexual behavior and focused only on the extreme (and even violent) forms of exposure to the prevalent virus. His point that young girls were at risk of infection from "assault, date rape" or a non-abstinent future spouse suggested that girls do not have sexual agency. His statement trod a fine line. The Medical Institute for Sexual Health's support for Gardasil sidestepped the anticipated opposition of the vaccine as articulated in Pollitt's and Specter's concerns. However, the description of young women as sexually vulnerable and in need of protection made clear that the organization would not endorse the vaccine completely. The Medical Institute's acceptance of Gardasil as a cancer vaccine would become a common position among socially conservative organizations, moral judgments couched in tolerance. For example, a representative of the Family Research Council met repeatedly with Merck "to address concerns that the vaccine might encourage promiscuous behavior by providing a false sense of protection against sexually transmitted disease."[6] The council's representative reported that Merck told them that "they have not found that effect," adding that "we are monitoring this."[7] Although these groups did not object to a cancer vaccine, they planned to refuse any HPV vaccine policies for their children. The unexpected position of various conservative groups illustrates Merck's initial success to frame Gardasil. The company deflected focus on HPV's sexual transmission and elicited support for a cancer vaccine.

The spring 2006 meeting of the VRBPAC, where Merck presented Gardasil for FDA approval, revealed the structure of Merck's foundational strategy for selling its cancer vaccine. The FDA is a gatekeeper for products that affect consumer health, such as food, cosmetics, and medical devices and drug products. The agency purports to offer an objective evaluation of safety based on scientific assessments; however, committees evaluate prospective products using materials and presentations given by the companies that seek approval. U.S. regulation structure does not involve independently run clinical trials or evaluation of products but instead depends on the companies to police their own processes. Pharmaceutical companies must demonstrate that their product provides a meaningful benefit to the target population. Built into these trials is a series of choices about which populations to study, the drugs to which the company will compare the experimental drug's efficacy (if appropriate, since novel drugs do not have comparable products), and the positioning of the problem for which the drug will present a solution. Thus, the lens through which the FDA reviews the materials comes from the pharmaceutical company's research design and the argument the company has developed to justify the value of its product. However, the research pharmaceutical companies' conduct may also be informed by conversations with regulatory officials; these give companies insight into what sorts of strategies will be most likely to persuade government officials.

The 2006 FDA meeting to review Gardasil evolved from nearly a decade of research and iterative conversations between Merck and the FDA. These conversations between institutional actors informed who the recipients for the vaccine would be and carefully positioned the problem that Gardasil might solve. As Merck's representatives explained at the 2006 Gardasil review meeting, the FDA's advisory committees informed Merck's decision to develop a vaccine for HPV, rather than a vaccine for its related cancer. Like Merck's advertisements before and after FDA approval, which encouraged women to perceive their bodies as risky and vulnerable, the FDA review meeting focused on females' risk for cancer. Gardasil's benefit for the millions of U.S. patients who got HPV infections each year received significantly less attention during the FDA review than its cervical cancer promise. These choices would have significant policy implications. The FDA regulatory process was both a lynchpin for the problem Merck sought to sell and a fertile ground for Merck to hone its message of the vaccine for cancer.

Research Priorities

The morning session of Gardasil's FDA review focused on Merck's description of the burden of HPV, the history of developing Gardasil, and how the vaccine would address an "unmet medical need."[8] The hearing was open to the public and took place in a large hotel. During the FDA review, two Merck directors, Drs. Patrick Brill-Edwards and Eliav Barr, carefully framed the medical relevance of the vaccine. Both acknowledged the successes of cervical cancer screening and stressed the often-cited figure that 3,700 women would die from cervical cancer in the United States each year, or as Brill-Edwards reframed the numbers, "10 American women will die each day from [cervical] cancer."[9] Brill-Edwards, Merck's director of worldwide vaccine regulatory affairs, explained to VRBPAC members that "an Advisory Committee, very similar to today's procedure, was convened in 2001 to consider the clinical endpoints that would serve as the basis for licensure.... At that time, Merck proposed that studying cancer itself isn't feasible, because it takes too long and it disadvantages too many women."[10] Brill-Edwards justified Merck's decision to target HPV and to make precancerous cervical intraepithelial neoplasias (CIN) the endpoint for the vaccine by noting the potential harm to women had Merck developed a vaccine that targeted cancer prevention.[11] Dr. Barr said that most precancerous HPV infections "regress," which means that most HPV infections clear on their own and do not progress to pre-cancerous stages. Merck researchers decided to make CIN (pronounced "sin") the target endpoint for their clinical trial research because CIN has a "direct link to cancer." He noted that 25 percent of HPV infections may progress to CIN, leading to more than 300,000 cases of later stages of CIN, known as CIN 2/3, annually.[12] The emphasis the Merck research team placed on precancerous stages of cervical cancer indicates that Gardasil is a vaccine for HPV, not cancer.

The scientific logic that guided Merck's clinical trials illustrates how Merck's marketing obscured the complexities of HPV and cervical cancer management. There are ethical and scientific reasons to prioritize CIN 2/3 rather than cancer. It would have been unethical for the pharmaceutical company to allow women in their study to develop cancer without treatment so researchers could assess whether the vaccine prevented cancer. Epidemiologically, CIN 1, the earlier stage of precancer, clears frequently without intervention. The company chose the precancerous state, CIN 2/3, that was on the "critical path to cancer."[13] The vaccine targeted only four of the nearly forty sexually transmitted types of HPV, and it demonstrated high efficacy and efficiency. In some studies, it conferred protection against the four types of HPV in almost 100 percent of women, although this required a highly controlled population that would be difficult to replicate in real-world settings. In summarizing the epidemiological data that supported Gardasil's approval, Dr. Barr stressed the prevalence of HPV: "HPV is a highly endemic infection and prophylactic vaccination is an excellent way to prevent highly endemic infectious diseases, and on the basis of that, Merck decided to develop a prophylactic HPV vaccine."[14] In other words, an infection with HPV precedes nearly all cervical and all HPV-related cancers, and thus the most effective way to prevent cervical and other HPV-related cancers is to prevent their cause, HPV.

It was not just Merck's strategies that imagined future vaccinated populations. A collaborative effort between Merck and earlier FDA committees defined which populations were appropriate for vaccination. As Dr. Brill-Edwards had described to the committee, Barr explained that the FDA's Advisory Committee's 2001 discussion had helped shape Merck's research priorities to focus on CIN as a proxy for cervical cancer.[15] Barr reminded the committee members at the 2006 Gardasil meeting that Merck's choice of research subjects in the Gardasil clinical trials reflected the VRBPAC's strong suggestion that women infected prior to vaccination ought to be included in the study population.[16] In the statement Barr gave to the review committee in 2006 that Merck had developed its vaccine in accordance with a preceding committee's expectations, we can see the FDA's influence, whether deliberate or not, in Merck's vaccine design: a vaccine that might deflect public concerns about a vaccine for an STI. Merck's discussions with the FDA informed the company's decisions about how the vaccine might be strategically positioned as a cancer vaccine.

An Unmet Need

Even though the clinical data collected on Gardasil focused on HPV and its precancerous stages, Merck presented the vaccine as a cancer vaccine during the review hearing. In fact, in order for the FDA to consider Gardasil under its fast-track review process, it had to meet certain criteria. The FDA fast tracks new drugs "based on whether [they] will have an impact on such factors as survival, day-to-day functioning, or the likelihood that the condition, if left untreated, will progress from a less severe condition to a more serious one."[17] The FDA deems drugs to treat AIDS, Alzheimer's, and cancer as appropriate for this accelerated review process. The disease that a new drug targets does not *necessarily* need to progress rapidly into severe illness, according to the fast-track requirement. HPV may never progress to cancer, or may progress to cancer slowly, over many years. Merck capitalized on the ambiguities of HPV to position its application for a license for Gardasil. The ambiguities meant the difference between a rapidly approved vaccine and a more deliberative review process.

The fast-track review would allow Merck to get its vaccine to market quickly. Although Gardasil had value as a life-saving tool, it certainly is not the only way to reduce mortality from the cancers HPV causes. The urgency of review that fast track implies, however, does not match HPV's risks for mortality. Relatively few U.S. women contract HPV *and* die or have HPV-related morbidity immediately. In contrast to HIV, another condition that justifies the fast-track process, without a fast-track review for new medications, HIV+ patients could face dire consequences if medications for the disease were not expedited. To withhold treatment if it were shown to be better than existing ones would be considered unethical. Effective HIV treatment can prevent declines in health and secondary opportunistic infections. Because cervical cancer progresses slowly, the promised benefit of Gardasil could have been temporarily addressed by a stronger push to screen women for cervical cancer or improvements in how pathologists read slides while the new vaccine underwent a more deliberative FDA review process. Gardasil met one FDA criteria for fast tracking: "the condition, if left untreated, will progress from a less severe condition to a more serious one." But, as the data show, there is no evidence that the majority of women infected with HPV will develop cervical cancer. During the FDA review hearing, Merck spent very little time explaining the most compelling reason to approve Gardasil—protection against the most common STI that is also one of the most difficult to prevent.

One hypothesis about Merck's push to get Gardasil to market relates to the company's painkiller, Vioxx. Beginning in 1999, Merck marketed Vioxx as a superior painkiller because it wouldn't cause as many gastrointestinal problems as other painkillers did. However, during the first year the product was on the market, evidence emerged that people who took Vioxx were at an increased risk of heart attacks and death, which scientists at Merck knew about before the market launch. In 2004, Merck withdrew Vioxx from the market. The company eventually settled the many lawsuits with injured patients related to the drug for a total of $4.85 billion in 2007.[18] In 2008, the *Journal of the American Medical Association* published evidence that Merck had written some of the Vioxx studies. Major medical journals had published these studies under the names of physicians as their original authors, without acknowledgment of Merck's role.[19] In 2011, Merck paid $950 million in a criminal settlement for its marketing and advertising of Vioxx.[20] In addition to issues with the drug's safety, there were also accusations that the company had illegally marketed Vioxx for conditions not approved by the FDA. Thus, the FDA's review of Gardasil took place at a time when Merck's public image was at a nadir. A new blockbuster product would both distract from the Vioxx debacle and generate revenue the company needed.

Bodies at Risk

Brill-Edwards began his presentation to the committee by evoking Sir Isaac Newton's humble recognition that his work depended greatly on the advances of his scientific predecessors. "In the health sciences, there is nothing more rewarding than being able to contribute to meeting an unmet medical need. . . . [Sir Isaac Newton stated,] if I have seen further, it's by standing on the shoulders of giants. Now, in our case, we are standing on the shoulders of the basic scientists whose observations about this virus led to the concept to the vaccine and to the many clinicians and scientists who developed and implemented the successful cervical cancer screening programs that we have today."[21] By alluding to past advances in research on cervical health, Brill-Edwards reminded the regulators of how far women's health management has come, but he also implied that these interventions were not enough. More than once, Brill-Edwards reminded the committee that the vaccine would "build on the success" of cervical cancer screening programs.[22] Barr presented the need for the vaccine as urgent: "In the absence of cervical cancer screening, the lifetime risk of cervical cancer is about one in 30. Pap testing and other means of screening have reduced the risk of cervical cancer in countries where screening is available from—by about 75 percent, so that's decreased the risk from about one in 30, to about one in 120. . . . It's worth noting that adenocarcinoma rates have been increasing in the United States over the past years because Pap testing doesn't detect this kind of cancer very well and HPV infection rates have been increasing in the population."[23] By providing the morbidity and mortality statistics associated with HPV and cervical cancer despite well-established screening protocols, Barr presented Merck's product as the unique solution. Barr and Brill-Edwards attempted to persuade the committee that the vaccine fulfilled a role for HPV prevention that nothing else possibly could.

The Merck research teams anticipated the concerns about HPV's connection to sexual behavior. The research for the Gardasil clinical trials included girls as young as 16, but through what is called immunogenicity bridging data, Merck sought approval for girls as young as 9. The decision to include these younger girls was informed by Merck's meeting with the 2001 Advisory Committee. Across multiple protocols, Merck allowed women into the study who demonstrated HPV infection at the time of the study or who might not adhere to the protocol, thus creating more "real-world" scenarios of how the vaccine would be used. "A critical feature of the program was that the vaccine enrolled women regardless of baseline HPV status and this was because we knew that this vaccine would be administered without prescreening and so, we wanted to get information in the general population. This was also[,] by the way, a recommendation of the VRBPAC of 2001, who felt very strongly that women who were infected at baseline should be included in the clinical trials to[,] at the very least, evaluate the safety of the vaccine in that population."[24] The bridge data permitted Merck to demonstrate the vaccine's safety in younger girls because, as the company's representatives at the FDA acknowledged, conducting clinical trials among prepubescent girls for a vaccine that protects against an STI might be challenging. Not only would it have been difficult to recruit test subjects, it could have been socially and culturally unacceptable to conduct gynecological testing or to discuss sexual behavior with younger girls. Barr pointed out, "[Gardasil] will be most effective when it's administered to populations prior to entry into the risk period, and that's the age group 15 and below. . . . we also knew that it was not feasible to do efficacy studies in this population because of limitations on discussions of sexuality and of HPV sampling in very young pre-adolescents."[25] Since

HPV is so common, anyone who has been sexually active is presumed to have been exposed to at least one type of the virus. Merck researchers reasoned that if the company marketed the vaccine as an STI prevention, parents and the media would ask why girls so young should receive a vaccine associated with sexual behavior. The efficacy data Merck presented to the FDA showed that Gardasil provided the best protection among those with no prior exposure to HPV. The ideal recipient of Gardasil was a never infected and never exposed body. Extrapolating from the current average age of sexual debut in the United States, evidence that some children are sexually active before puberty, and evidence that U.S. girls go through puberty at earlier ages than they did in the past, Merck sought approval for girls nine years old so as many girls as possible could be vaccinated before their first sexual activity. Vaccine opponents would come to interpret Gardasil as condoning sexual activity, but administering the vaccine to younger girls implied their *lack* of sexual activity. Merck's justification to the FDA for its emphasis on vaccinating girls who were not yet sexually active reveals how girlhood becomes what Vincanne Adams, Michelle Murphy, and Adele Clarke call an anticipatory site. They argue that girls' bodies reveal how their "human capital[,] [as] intrinsically an anticipatory form, call[s] for investment in the skills and health of humans for the sake of greater rates of return towards GDP in the future."[26] This narrative of the future has direct bearing on the present. The future bodies of girls required immediate intervention. However, to do so meant that parents would acknowledge the risk rife in girls' bodies and to compliantly take action by vaccinating girls against the risk.[27]

Sex and the Vaccine, or Sexing the Vaccine

After attending the FDA meeting in May 2006, I examined the meeting's transcript to see how often the word "sex" (or some variant of the term) occurred. It shows up thirty-one times in the 216-page document. This includes terms like "sexually active." The abbreviation "STD" for sexually transmitted diseases, the older terminology for STIs, occurs three times. The word "cancer" (not including related terms such as carcinoma) occurs two hundred twenty-one times, although a few are in the mentions of the names of organizations of the officials participating in the meeting. "Men" occurs thirty-two times and "boys" occurs twenty-two times. "Women" occurs 193 times. The word "girls" occurs only nine times, which perhaps tells us how carefully Merck wished to avoid incendiary discussion about the sexual activity of young women. The language chosen by Merck representatives at the hearing provides further evidence of the strategy the company used in all of its promotional tactics for the vaccine. Before market approval of Gardasil, during its FDA review, and in the campaigns that followed FDA approval, Merck never positioned the vaccine as a remedy for the most common STI. Merck's imagined market was clearly women, and the campaigns created a false looming threat of cervical cancer. Men and sex were not the priority, and Merck did not consider them critical for Gardasil's approval. In the first few years of Gardasil's market debut, the bodies deemed appropriate for Gardasil were always female.

The transmission of HPV and the eventual progression to cancer requires the sexual contact of at least two people, regardless of sex, and not just the women Merck positioned as always at risk. Merck pursued fast-track approval for Gardasil by emphasizing a cancer that only affects women, but the data it presented included research on men. Approval for men and women would have given the company a larger market share, and the vaccine's benefits would have been more wide reaching if both men and women were vaccinated against high-risk HPV. Barr argued for universal approval of Gardasil: "We are interested in facilitating the possibility of public health authorities considering vaccinations of males right from the beginning of the post-licensure period. . . . There is strong public health rationale for vaccinating boys and a cost to delaying the vaccination of boys. Vaccine coverage in girls is going to be incomplete. This is a hard age range to target. It's going to be some time until we get high coverage rates. We know that men transmit HPV to women and we know from previous experiences . . . [that] when you try to target vaccines to a particular population, you can't eradicate the disease very well, compared to universal vaccination."[28] Barr referred to the example of the rubella vaccine, which was designed to protect pregnant women from the disease because of its serious consequences to fetuses. He pointed out that before the rubella vaccine was given to both men and women, it was difficult to get enough people vaccinated to sufficiently protect pregnant women.[29] Instead of focusing on the potential cancer risks for men, which include oral and anal cancers, he emphasized vaccinating men as a more efficacious way to reduce cervical cancer rates. "And so—and we've also shown in our clinical—in modeling work that if you delay a vaccination in boys, you will reduce the overall population efficacy of the vaccine, you will delay the time until the maximum reduction in cervical cancer that you could expect."[30] Including males would improve the success of the vaccine as a prophylaxis for women's health outcomes. It could significantly reduce the anal, penile, and oral cancers that affect men, although Barr barely mentioned the direct benefit to men. Barr also described the scenario for men at risk as a heteronormative one. Men who have male sexual partners were completely absent from discussion during the review process, and Gardasil pamphlets distributed in pediatricians' offices to this day perpetuate heteronormative future imaginings of boys' sexual activity.

When pressed by the committee during the question-and-answer period, Barr acknowledged that the Gardasil safety data for males ages 16 to 26 would not be available until 2008, two years after the meeting.[31] An appropriate package insert for male vaccination in the older male population would not be available until 2009, three years after the initial review date. Merck offered data on younger boys so the committee might "maximally start the train towards reducing cervical cancer rates in the population by vaccinating boys and girls, versus girls alone."[32] Based on Merck's data for the FDA, which was skewed toward female subjects, and the presence of women and adolescent girls in their early ads, it seems likely that the company never expected to get approval for boys and young men during their 2006 review. The pre-licensure "Tell Someone" campaigns did not mention penile, oral, or anal cancers and there were no promotional materials that encouraged men to share the news of cancer caused by a virus. Monica Farley, the acting chair of the FDA review process for Gardasil, pointed out that "we have no efficacy data right now in males. . . . We also know that the efficacy study is ongoing at this point and an extension to males will be considered when we have that data available. We don't really have any safety data in males right now . . . over the age of 15."[33] Because pharmaceutical companies seek to capture the largest market share, Merck most likely presented its data to the FDA in a gamble that it would receive approval or would get clarity from the committee about what data it would need to have Gardasil licensed for boys too. The inclusion of the male data seems to be at best a gesture toward Gardasil's future use as a universal vaccine, and at worst an opportunistic test of the FDA's receptiveness to Gardasil in boys.

Women were the majority of the study population for a number of reasons. In the United States, women come to their providers somewhat regularly for Pap smears and other reproductive health needs. Most providers require a gynecological exam before they will give prescriptions for birth control pills. This practice may seem fairly normal to most women of reproductive age, but one of the reasons these prescriptions are tied to a gynecological exam is because women who use birth control pills are having sex without condoms. By engaging in unprotected sexual activity, they are at higher risk for exposure to disease, including HPV, even though condoms do not entirely protect against the transmission of HPV. A birth control prescription becomes an incentive for women to go to a doctor's office for preventive Pap smears. One intervention does not necessarily require the other, but medical professionals have deliberately connected the two in clinical practice. These and other institutionalized women's health practices make women a readily available study population.

Health care practice reflects the gendered assumptions about which bodies to manage and what sorts of technologies to design. One example is the male contraceptive pill. Although researchers have developed male hormonal contraception, men have not accepted its side effects.[34] While for women, the side effects of hormonal contraception may seem well worth the benefit of not worrying about pregnancy, men, who do not bear the physical or emotional burdens of an unintended pregnancy and child rearing as directly, have rejected the male pill for its unpleasant side effects.[35] Research on male contraceptives has progressed in fits and starts. One explanation that justifies the difficulty of developing a male hormonal intervention is that the male reproductive system is harder to manage. Women, on average, produce only one egg per month. The number of male sperm that contraception needs to impede confounds the current model of hormonal contraception; in addition, male bodies produce sperm all the time, not just at particular times. The idea that the male reproductive system is more complicated, however, reveals more about how we conceptualize the differences between male and female bodies than it does about any immutable fact about men or women.[36] Male and female reproductive systems present distinct challenges and require different solutions, but one is not inherently more complex than the other. Merck's less-than-robust research on Gardasil in boys perpetuated gendered biases in sexual health interventions.

During the lunch break between the morning and afternoon FDA sessions, the media interviewed officials and public relations representatives outside the hearing conference room. I watched as a representative of one of the family-values organizations assured the interviewer that the organization did not seek to block the vaccine's approval. The representative, echoing Merck's "Tell Someone" advertisements, pointed out that they would not object to protecting women against cancer but added that his organization did not believe the vaccine should be made, as he called it, "mandatory."[37] Influenced by Merck's public relations outreach, the family values organizations made clear that they were skeptics of government involvement in privacy issues, hence the frequent, but erroneous, use of "mandatory" when their representatives referred to vaccine requirements. For Merck, for public health proponents of the vaccine, and even for socially conservative organizations, the cervical cancer indication seemed to evade a contentious debate. Merck's cancer strategy failed to predict that once the vaccine became part of health policy discussions and state legislative dockets, the reactions would be as polarized as they might have been had the vaccine been explicitly positioned as an STI vaccine.

Less than a month after its review, on June 8, 2006, the FDA approved Gardasil as a treatment to prevent genital warts and cervical cancer in women. The approval did not generate as much media attention as the review process did. Journalist Nancy Gibbs pointed out, "Both sides [conservative and liberal] reflexively clenched their fists for a brawl, even when there wasn't much of a fundamental disagreement."[38] Gibbs anticipated accurately that the bigger debate would be whether the vaccine should be "mandatory." As we will see, no U.S. vaccine policies are legally mandatory; all state vaccine laws include certain acceptable reasons for exemptions.[39] The word "mandatory" implies government coercion and the absence of individual freedoms. Those who were critical of Gardasil focused on vaccine requirements as a violation of personal freedom, not on Gardasil specifically. Many of Gardasil's opponents claimed that they objected to *any* vaccine being made compulsory, but the STI prophylaxis surely had some role in the vaccine debates. Had Gardasil truly been a vaccine against cancer, it may well have quickly become a widely accepted vaccine. This is not what happened.

6

Vaccines and Politics

Pharmaceutical companies shape public conceptions of disease categories, generate demand for new products, and make health and illness "states of knowledge."[1] Through medicalization and "pharmaceuticalization," corporate interests directly influence our conception of our bodies and how we understand the risks we may face.[2] Unlike other examples of pharmaceuticalization that have produced a steady revenue stream for pharmaceutical corporations, with newly created chronic health conditions that merit a regular supply of drugs to manage, vaccines might seem distinct: they require discrete moments of inoculation to protect individuals from needing further medical intervention for a preventable disease. This prevention might also seem like it ought to remove people from medical surveillance and oversight, yet this is not how pharmaceuticalization works. There are always more opportunities for pharmaceutical markets to expand.

Traditionally, vaccines have focused on population-level interventions that are framed as an unqualified public good. Public health campaigns significantly increased global vaccine coverage in the 1980s.[3] An effective vaccine eliminates or mitigates the harm of a disease. Absence of disease is the hallmark of vaccine success. As one public health official commented at a 2008 immunization coalition meeting in southern California, "We tend to get complacent [about vaccinating] . . . because we no longer see the disease." I heard this concern repeatedly in the immunization advocacy community; a number of officials stated that when nothing happens, it is harder to persuade people of the vaccine's benefit. In the United States, vaccinating is part of all new parents' lives, whether they choose to vaccinate their child or not. It is a rite of passage for most U.S. parents, revealing beliefs about the intimate and domestic and broader community values about public and social responsibility. Public health and medical professionals consider vaccination to be one of the most successful public health interventions.[4] Vaccination practices reveal a society's beliefs about health and privilege, individual and population imaginations of the body, and they can be a tool of government control and an impetus for individual resistances.[5] Vaccines are part of global supply chains because vaccine-preventable diseases can impact national economies, and international political and strategic negotiations inform their dissemination and use.[6] Governments may make advance market commitments to the companies who develop the vaccines in order to ensure that new immunizations will be accessible and affordable, and international agencies, such as the World Health Organization, issue guidance on global vaccine strategies. Vaccines exemplify how "discourses on health are never just about health. . . . [They] function as repositories and mirrors of our ideas and beliefs about . . . what it means to be human, the kind of society we can imagine creating and how best to achieve it."[7] Further, because vaccines are usually given to children first, they are intrinsically anticipatory and future-oriented.

Unlike vaccine campaigns in other countries, in the United States immunization is tied to school entry requirements.[8] As a result, nearly all children who attend school in the United States receive their vaccines by the age of 5. One justification for mass vaccination is to achieve herd immunity, the concept that a high rate of vaccinated people in the general population will protect those who cannot be vaccinated because of counter-indicated health conditions. Public health advocates worry that herd immunity to many preventable diseases is always on the verge of disappearing. The ideal rate of vaccination for each preventable disease differs, and thus herd immunity levels are different for each vaccine.[9] CDC data from 2012 show that among children aged 19–35 months, only the hepatitis A and rotavirus vaccines have vaccination rates lower than 85 percent.[10] Less than 1 percent of U.S. children aged 19–35 months had received no vaccines at all in 2012.[11] These data are complex: they show that U.S. children had received at least one vaccine by the age of 3, for any given vaccine; however, they might not have completed the full series needed for immunity. It is difficult to increase the percent of children who have been vaccinated when the percentage already vaccinated are so high; those who have not been vaccinated may be the children of hard-to-budge vaccine refusers or of parents who are unaware of subsidies for vaccination.

After Gardasil was approved in the United States, more than half of the state legislatures debated policies that would require girls and young women to be vaccinated with Gardasil.[12] Direct-to-consumer advertising is permitted in the United States, unlike in other countries, but Gardasil is one of the few vaccines in the United States that featured a widespread direct-to-consumer campaign.[13] Merck generated public awareness of and interest in Gardasil through its marketing of the vaccine and lobbying legislators; paradoxically, Merck's paired tactics may have contributed to low rates of acceptance. In many ways, the pharmaceutical company's legislative advocacy was unremarkable, as pharmaceutical manufacturers frequently use lobbying tactics to get advantageous bills passed, but Merck's efforts to include Gardasil in state vaccine laws were remarkably ineffective.[14] More than half of U.S. states considered passing legislation that would require HPV vaccination for school attendance. Nearly all the proposed bills failed. In 2016, the only legislatures that had successfully passed such laws were Rhode Island, Virginia, and the District of Columbia.[15] Vaccination as a prerequisite for school attendance ought not to have garnered much notice, as school entry vaccine policies have a long history in the United States. However, because vaccination for school attendance has long been part of U.S. immunization dissemination, resistance to vaccination also has a well-established history in the United States.

A Vaccine Like Any Other

The initial media response to Gardasil may have also influenced public acceptance of the vaccine. A month after Gardasil was available to the public, news reports claimed that school clinics in the Los Angeles Unified School District (LAUSD) would be giving the HPV vaccine to students. The stories suggested that schools endorsed and even promoted the vaccine, but these inaccurate claims suggesting that schools would administer vaccines to children without parental knowledge or consent muddied the public's understanding of the role of schools in vaccine distribution. Some of the reports, like one in the *Los Angeles Times*, carefully pointed out that schools would provide the vaccine with parental consent and that Gardasil was available in LAUSD as part of the Vaccines for Children (VFC) program for low-income children.[16] However, the *Los Angeles Times* report also called the vaccine controversial and noted that Focus on the Family, like other "conservative organizations," accepted the vaccine only if it were paired with abstinence-only education.[17] Two years later, in October 2009, misinformation about the relationship school districts had with Gardasil persisted at a Commonwealth Club discussion about the HPV vaccine in San Francisco. One speaker at the event referred to the LAUSD's proactive "distribution" of the vaccine instead of describing it more accurately as one among many low-cost VFC vaccines that school clinics have available. Gardasil sparked public anxieties about its distribution, and these reactions would continue to inform how the public came to understand the vaccine's purpose.

In January 2007, I interviewed Dr. Kimberley Uyeda,[18] the LAUSD medical director, at her office in a trailer campus near a highway in central Los Angeles. The streets were desolate, but the sound of rushing cars filled the air; the on ramp for the interstate was just blocks away. Although the LAUSD trailers may have been intended as temporary structures, they appeared to have been there for a very long time. During our interview, Uyeda emphasized that the news reports about the HPV vaccine misrepresented the LAUSD's vaccine policies, since it was treated no differently than any other vaccine in the VFC program. The school clinics made VFC vaccines available to families to facilitate access and improve vaccination rates. She emphasized how important school-based clinics were because they provide vaccines to children whose parents might not realize they are eligible for low-income assistance. The VFC program, funded by state and federal dollars, distributed Gardasil throughout Los Angeles County clinics. Uyeda explained that schools would not *require* the vaccine until the state of California did. "Any immunization that comes out, if the county gives it to us and it's recommended by the ACIP [Advisory Committee on Immunization Practices] . . . more specifically if it's recommended by our California immunization law . . . the ones that we're more intense about are the ones required by [the time of] school entry. Those that are not required for school entry are all recommended and made available as the county gives it to us." Uyeda explained the chain of funding and distribution that accompanies any vaccines that the ACIP recommends: "We usually provide vaccines that are given to us by the county. We have a long-standing agreement to provide vaccines as they become available and as they are distributed to us. . . . We're just one of the many clinics that the county provides vaccines to." Uyeda sought to dispel any distinction between the HPV vaccine and all other vaccines the school clinics provided. She pointed out that schools were not directly immunizing students. "The vaccines are not given at school. . . . They're usually given at predetermined immunization clinics or school-based health clinics." The media depictions of children lined up to be inoculated against parents' preferences were baseless and unnecessarily controversial.

As Uyeda made clear, the HPV vaccine ought to be thought of as no different from other childhood vaccines. "This is a vaccine like every other vaccine. Kids are not vaccinated without the consent, the fully informed consent, of their parents. . . . This, like any other vaccine, is going to be treated the same way." Uyeda's emphasis on the fact that Gardasil was like every other vaccine reminded me of how public health policies have embedded their interventions in the U.S. education system. She cited the hepatitis B vaccine as setting a precedent for how the district implemented state policies for an STI vaccine. School clinics were not initiating rogue vaccination policies, she emphasized: "If it is part of the California immunization law, we do everything in our power to help kids" get the vaccine. The schools encouraged and even would enforce policies to ensure that children received vaccines. However, combining education and health requirements can lead to unintended consequences. Uyeda explained that schools had an incentive to promote immunization policies for vaccine-preventable diseases, since not enforcing them would be "essentially our problem once the students start to miss school."

Gardasil, which was promoted and disseminated as a routine vaccine intervention, did not fit neatly into established immunization promotion strategies, and Merck's emphasis on cancer prevention did not correspond to classic vaccination tactics.[19] The concept that Gardasil protected girls from a slow progressing disease (HPV) and a disease that they would not see until later in life (cervical cancer) made it difficult to persuade the public that vaccine legislation was necessary. Merck's deliberate maneuvers to position the vaccine as a standard childhood intervention failed to anticipate potent cultural anxieties about vaccines.[20]

During the first few years Gardasil was on the market, a number of states and federal agencies struggled with the public's reactions and resistances to Gardasil. Two cases set it apart from other childhood vaccines by focusing on vulnerable female bodies, imagined as those of future reproductive citizens:[21] the 2008 policy that required new immigrants to get the HPV vaccine in order to receive their green cards and the Texas governor's executive order requiring the vaccine for girls entering seventh grade. The failure of state legislatures to pass HPV vaccine laws and the low rate of HPV vaccine acceptance a decade after market launch reveal Gardasil's role in ongoing public debates about vaccines, women's bodies, and parents' resistances to government authority. Parents' rejection of school entry HPV vaccine policies contributed to the growing objections to state-required vaccines.

The Unintended Consequences of Regulation

Gardasil highlighted how the policy implications of a new product may take on an unexpected and unintended cast after the FDA approves it. After vaccines receive FDA approval, an advisory group, the Advisory Committee on Immunization Practices (ACIP), evaluates their importance for broader population health, and Gardasil was no different.[22] If ACIP deems the vaccine critical, its recommendations trigger a variety of policy and funding mechanisms that increase access to immunization for lower-income families. As Uyeda described to me, after ACIP recommended Gardasil for females aged 11 to 26 in June 2006, the vaccine was included in the Vaccines for Children program.[23] The ACIP recommendations did more than impact access to resources for those who already lived in the United States. Under the guidance of a 1996 requirement that immigrants to the United States receive all vaccines recommended by ACIP and the CDC, the U.S. Citizenship and Immigration Services added Gardasil to its criteria for anyone seeking permanent U.S. residency.[24] Vaccine policies hold those who use public resources, like schools, and those who seek residency, which can lead to access to citizenship, accountable for managing their health. Foreign women who refused or failed to follow the recommendations about Gardasil were excluded from access to certain U.S. resources; they could find a potential pathway to citizenship restricted.

ACIP does not mandate vaccination; it provides recommendations. The ACIP recommendations for U.S. citizens promote vaccination by triggering subsidies and providing guidance for insurance coverage standards. In contrast, the U.S. Citizenship and Immigration Services' immigration requirement imposed a significant burden on women seeking U.S. residency and, perhaps, future citizenship. In 2006, Gardasil was the most expensive vaccine on the market; the three-shot series cost $360.[25] Tying Gardasil to residency applications, already an expensive process, imposed a high financial burden on foreign women. Immigrant rights' advocates pointed out the policy was xenophobic; the requirement implied that female immigrants were suspect and needed to be inoculated in order to be entitled to U.S. residency. This interpretation rightly condemns long-standing biases against immigrants and strategies for managing populations that target women's bodies. The requirement for female immigrants includes an important legal reality: any child born to an immigrant on U.S. soil automatically receives U.S. citizenship. Thus, this policy implicitly focused on immigrant women's reproductive obligations to the government of their new home and defined which bodies were appropriate for producing future citizens. Native-born citizens were not required to vaccinate with Gardasil. Thus, the policy presented an unequal standard. But while the policy may have reflected cultural prejudices, it also revealed how the bureau in charge of citizenship and immigration applied guidelines set by a health advisory committee without attending to the logic of the committee's recommendations.

Females who wished to receive U.S. permanent residency could not refuse the vaccine, although no U.S. citizen and no male immigrant was compelled to vaccinate with Gardasil. However, the CDC removed Gardasil from its list of vaccines required for permanent residency after only a year in response to protests from immigrant rights' communities that pointed out the unequal standard it imposed. The revised criteria stipulated that immigrants needed to vaccinate against infections that could produce an outbreak, infections that have been eliminated in the U.S. population, and infections that are in the process of being eliminated in the United States.[26] Gardasil fits none of these criteria. By clarifying its disease management guidelines for immigrants, the CDC implicitly acknowledged that HPV did not match the criteria for vaccine-preventable infections.

The consequences of the application of ACIP guidelines to female immigrants captured the attention of relatively few, but it provides an important instance in which Gardasil-related policy impacted women disproportionately. The revised policy also demonstrates how poorly Gardasil fit into traditional vaccine policies; this difference contributed to vociferous public refusals of state laws to require Gardasil.

There is no doubt that Merck facilitated policy discussions and encouraged state legislators and those close to legislators to put bills on the dockets that would require the vaccine. Because of the public's low levels of comprehension and awareness of HPV, the Gardasil vaccine presented an opportunity for Merck to shape people's understanding of HPV and to motivate them to receive the vaccine. But promoting Gardasil as a vaccine through the channels traditionally used to generate vaccine uptake had the unintended consequence of drawing the attention of vaccine objectors, who had well-established networks. Despite Merck's careful framing of its new vaccine, the company found itself in the midst of unexpected debate and resistance.

Schools and Vaccines

Before Gardasil received its FDA approval, pro-HPV vaccine advocates assumed that objections to the new vaccine would focus on adolescent sexuality, but the public debate about HPV as a sexually transmitted infection did not emphasize this concern directly. Merck's strategic positioning of Gardasil as a cancer vaccine deflected abstinence-only debates and concerns about morality.[27]

In the nineteenth century, as compulsory education became common, public health initiatives enlisted schools to capture the greatest number of people who were eligible for vaccines. Massachusetts passed a law requiring vaccination for school attendance in 1855 and New York followed with a law in 1862. Indiana, Illinois, and Wisconsin passed similar laws in the 1880s.[28] In response to these requirements, one of the more famous Supreme Court vaccination lawsuits, *Jacobson v. Massachusetts* (1905), challenged whether states could compel individuals to get vaccinated. The case, which Massachusetts won, did not specifically address the relationship between school entry and the vaccine requirement for children, but it set a precedent that states *could* require health interventions for individuals in the interest of public health.[29] In 1922, in *Zucht v. King*, the Supreme Court upheld the constitutionality of state laws that required vaccination in order to attend school.[30]

Most U.S. children attend public or private schools. Only a small number of families choose to educate their children at home; thus, school entry provides a specific moment to catch children who might be undervaccinated or not vaccinated at all. For public health officials, schools present an ideal setting to implement public health measures, but schools have no explicit reason to prioritize public health interventions. Yet as Foucauldian critiques of institutional means of control have demonstrated, schools exemplify "multiple, automatic, and anonymous power; for although surveillance rests on individuals, its functioning is that of a network of relations from top to bottom, but also to a certain extent from bottom to top laterally. . . . It is the apparatus itself as a whole that produces 'power' and distributes individuals in this permanent and continuous field."[31] Vaccine opponents argue that schools are sites for education, not for enforcing public health laws or other laws unrelated to education. However, this argument ignores how governments manage populations and schools' role in social education. Jacques Donzelot argues that in the "entire political technology of life," institutions give "rise to infinitesimal surveillances, permanent controls, extremely meticulous orderings of space, indeterminate medical or psychological examinations, to an entire micropower concerned with the body . . . and interventions aimed at the entire social body."[32] Institutions such as schools and institutional processes such as applying to become a citizen, then, give governments and authorities opportunities to impose standards and control over individuals.

There are good reasons why schools might want to encourage high rates of vaccination—to avoid entire schools felled by a local epidemic, for example–but using school systems to implement a public health measure has some significant limitations. The school entry vaccination requirement makes individual institutions responsible for monitoring each child's vaccination record. This is an effective forcing mechanism. The standard pediatric immunization schedule gets supported by other institutional moments such as the beginning of the school year. School policies for vaccination require school districts to have medical directors and administrators who oversee children's entry records. Parents who oppose vaccines list multiple reasons for their resistance, such as concerns about vaccine safety or what one researcher refers to as the "libertarian health freedom perspective."[33] Parents who resist vaccine requirements often question the necessity of population-level vaccination as a prerequisite for school entry. They see public health policies as paternalistic. They argue that school-entry requirements use public health policy to achieve behavior change instead of trusting individuals to make choices on their own.

State legislatures and public health proponents proposed laws that would require sixth or seventh grade girls to receive Gardasil before they could start the school year almost immediately after its June 2006 FDA approval. In September 2006, Michigan was the first state to consider such a law.[34] As the media covered the FDA approval of the vaccine, conservative organizations explicitly objected to vaccination requirements for school entry as a form of unwanted government intervention. They argued that such policies would violate parents' rights to make decisions about their children's health and expressed concern that a vaccine for an STI would encourage promiscuity. Setting the terms of the debate, a number of conservative organizations publicly declared their support for a *cancer* vaccine, with certain caveats. When Linda Klepacki, an analyst for sexual health at Focus on the Family, described her group's position, she said it was an "awesome vaccine" but added that Focus on the Family was opposed to "making vaccination mandatory rather than leaving it up to parents to decide."[35] Klepacki presented the opposition of Focus on the Family using the language of parents' rights. Other Christian-based conservative organizations argued that because HPV is not an airborne disease and children ought not to be at risk of contracting it while at school, there was no persuasive reason why the vaccine should be tied to children's right to attend school. Whether or not to vaccinate, they argued, should remain a private decision.

Vaccinating to Preserve Life

In 2007, in an unusual moment of synergy between conservative pro-lifers and pro-vaccination advocates, Texas governor Rick Perry made national news when he issued an executive order that required the HPV vaccine. That February Texas legislators were debating a bill that would have mandated HPV vaccination as a requirement for school entry. Perry preempted their discussion:

Never before have we had an opportunity to prevent cancer with a simple vaccine. While I understand the concerns expressed by some, I stand firmly on the side of protecting life. The HPV vaccine does not promote sex, it protects women's health. In the past, young women who have abstained from sex until marriage have contracted HPV from their husbands and faced the difficult task of defeating cervical cancer. This vaccine prevents that from happening.

Providing the HPV vaccine doesn't promote sexual promiscuity anymore than providing the Hepatitis B vaccine promotes drug use. If the medical community developed a vaccine for lung cancer, would the same critics oppose it claiming it would encourage smoking?

Finally, parents need to know that they have the final decision about whether or not their daughter is vaccinated. I am a strong believer in protecting parental rights, which is why this executive order allows them to opt out.[36]

Perry framed his executive order through well-established language in order to navigate potentially resistant constituencies: he endorsed the vaccine's promise of female empowerment and at the same time assured his supporters that parents' rights were foremost in his mind. Referencing the hepatitis B vaccine, a once-controversial vaccine that is given to infants, he reminded his audience that vaccines received in childhood did not predict future behaviors. He emphasized that the vaccine protects women's health, deftly reassuring concerned parents that he valued preserving young women's virtue. However, unlike many feminists who advocated for the vaccine as a means of protecting the health of sexually active women, Perry emphasized that he believed in "protecting life," evoking the anti-abortion stance for which he was known. With these words, he allied himself with other conservatives who might perceive his intervention as overly permissive and promoting promiscuity. Despite Perry's attempt to position his endorsement as aligned with the views of his conservative constituents, his actions prompted three parents to sue him for overstepping his authority. Two days after Perry issued Executive Order RP65, Texas legislators submitted a bill to the House of Representatives that rejected any HPV vaccine requirements.[37] Within a month of the executive order, the state legislature had overturned it, obviating the parents' lawsuit.

Perry described the executive order as a women's health intervention and as evidence of his interest in women's well-being, but his other actions as governor cast doubt on this motivation. During his tenure as governor (2000–2014), the state of Texas restricted funds to Planned Parenthood.[38]

This action defunded programs that are central to Planned Parenthood's mission to improve women's health, including screenings for breast cancer and cervical cancer. It also made the state of Texas ineligible for federal funds that support preventive screenings, further hampering Texas women's access to affordable health care. Perry's statement about his motivation for the executive order rings hollow; he did not have women's health interests in mind. He was interested only in the health of girls who were not yet sexually active and women whose behavior conformed to his ideas of virtue.

One explanation for Perry's seemingly out-of-character support for Gardasil is that Mike Toomey, a Merck lobbyist who had been the governor's chief of staff from 2002 to 2004, may have influenced the governor's decision, although a spokesperson for the governor explicitly denied this.[39] The *New York Times* suggested that Merck's involvement in Texas was part of a larger lobbying effort across the country.[40] Less than three weeks after Perry issued RP65, Merck announced it would cease its national lobbying efforts due to concerns that the lobbying "could undermine adoption of the vaccine."[41] Merck's medical director, Dr. Richard Haupt, noted that the company stood behind its commitment to school requirements but worried that Merck's involvement in these policies was perceived (by the public) as "distraction to that goal."[42] The timing of the announcement suggests that the negative responses to Perry's actions contributed to Merck's decision to cease its lobbying.

In February 2007, partly in response to Rick Perry's executive order, Phil Gingrey, a physician and congressman from Georgia, introduced a bill in the U.S. House Committee on Energy and Commerce designed to undermine state policies that required HPV vaccines. The "Parental Right to Decide Protection Act" would have cut off federal funding "or other assistance for mandatory human papillomavirus (HPV) vaccination programs."[43] Gingrey's bill cited the ACIP decision to add HPV to its recommended childhood vaccination schedule as part of the motivation for his bill. It noted that neither the American College of Pediatricians nor the Association of American Physicians and Surgeons believed that the vaccine should be required because it would "exclud[e] children from school for refusal to be vaccinated for a disease spread only by intercourse" and was "a serious, precedent-setting action that trespasses on the right of parents to make medical decisions for their children as well as on the rights of the children to attend school."[44] Although Gingrey's bill failed to gain support in 2007, he reintroduced a new version in July 2009. The second version of the bill objected to Gardasil's risk for adverse events, citing concerns raised by the organization Judicial Watch about the vaccine's potential health harms. The Judicial Watch is not a medical organization but is a "conservative, non-partisan educational foundation" whose motto is "Because No One Is Above the Law." The 2009 bill also failed.

During Perry's 2011 campaign for president, he acknowledged that RP65 had been a mistake. He did not disavow the vaccine, but he focused on his failure to consider citizen involvement in health care policy: "The fact of the matter is that I didn't do my research well enough to understand that we needed to have a substantial conversation with our citizenry."[45] Perry framed the contentious order as a problem of public discourse. Perry has never engaged substantively with questions about the role Merck may have played in convincing him to issue the executive order.

Lobbying through Women Legislators

Merck targeted women serving in state legislatures in its lobbying efforts. One organization, Women in Government (WIG), offered Merck an opportunity to communicate with a group of female policymakers. Women in Government defines itself as a "non-profit, bi-partisan organization of women state legislators providing leadership opportunities, networking, expert forums, and educational resources to address and resolve complex public policy issues."[46] In 2004, WIG launched its Challenge to Eliminate Cervical Cancer.[47] The timeline of their interest in cervical cancer might suggest that pressure from Merck did not directly shape their priorities, but as the Center for Media and Democracy's *PRWatch* has demonstrated, both Merck and GlaxoSmithKline were listed as WIG's corporate sponsors from 2004 to 2006.[48] A map that WIG published in 2008 showed that their lobbying efforts had had early success: all fifty states had introduced some form of legislation about cervical cancer or HPV. On *PR Watch*, Judith Siers-Poisson described an interview with the WIG president, Susan Crosby, who acknowledged the organization received funds from Merck, among other corporations. Siers-Poisson also noted that Texas state representative Diana Delisi, the mother-in-law of Perry's chief of staff at the time, was the director of the Texas WIG.[49] This revelation further complicated public trust in Perry's executive order, RP65, and suggested that Merck had direct influence on government policies.

WIG allows corporate sponsors to have direct access to its members. As Siers-Poisson suggested, it is difficult to trust WIG's claim that it is invested in women's health and well-being when its corporate sponsors include Anheuser-Busch, a beer company, and Altria, a tobacco company, two companies that do not promote health-seeking behaviors. Although Crosby claimed that WIG offered unbiased information to its member legislators, Siers-Poisson justifiably criticized the corporately framed information that WIG disseminated to legislators. The source of information merits transparency, and corporate lobbying affects policy in meaningful ways.

In the California state legislature, Assemblyperson Sally Lieber introduced AB16, a bill that would have required HPV vaccination for girls entering the seventh grade. In January 2007, I traveled to Lieber's offices in Mountain View, California, to speak to her directly. When I got there, I was told she was still at a meeting off site. Her staff people eventually told me we could try to set up a telephone interview. The interview never happened. On the drive back to San Francisco, I heard on the radio that she had generated significant local news coverage that day with a bill that sought to criminalize parents who spanked their children. The anti-spanking bill received a flurry of media coverage, including in national newspapers, most of it mocking the absurdity of the law. Much like the public response to AB16, many people expressed outrage that a legislator felt entitled to tell parents how they could raise their children.[50]

Less than a month after the spanking-bill news storm, Lieber removed her name from the HPV bill as an author.[51] The bill was amended in February 2007 and Assembly member Ed Hernandez took over authorship of the bill. The revised bill stipulated that no vaccines would be required for school entry until five years after the ACIP recommended a new vaccine.[52] This was a response to parents' anxieties about vaccine safety. Governor Arnold Schwarzenegger vetoed the bill in September 2008, and California still does not have an HPV vaccine policy for school children. However, the California legislature is not hostile to all vaccines. After two measles outbreaks in the state, in 2008 and 2014–2015, the legislature passed a law to make it more difficult for parents to receive vaccine exemptions.[53]

The examples of California and Texas show that overeager legislators, whether influenced by Merck or not, failed to represent their constituents' interests. Most bills related to the HPV vaccine that legislatures have passed in the intervening years have emphasized improving the public's education about HPV, task forces to evaluate the feasibility of implementing school vaccine requirements, or funding mechanisms to increase access to an HPV vaccine. WIG's 2008 state legislation map,[54] which detailed different types of policies related to HPV and cervical cancer, showed how few states had enacted bills that the group categorized as Compulsory HPV Testing Insurance Reimbursement or Compulsory HPV Vaccine Insurance Reimbursement. In contrast, nearly half of the states had passed bills that WIG referred to as Statewide Cervical Cancer Elimination Task Force/Accountable Entity, and nearly all had passed legislation to ensure unrestricted Medicaid coverage of HPV testing. As of 2016, more than forty states had introduced legislation related to some aspect of the HPV vaccine, but not all of these included a requirement to vaccinate for school attendance.[55] Some of these proposed laws sought to educate students about the availability of a vaccine or to promote citizen education about HPV. In the first few years after Gardasil was approved, only the state of Virginia and the District of Columbia approved laws requiring the HPV vaccine for school entry.[56]

Framing the Vaccine

Ten years after Gardasil came onto the market, public health professionals and researchers were still struggling to persuade parents that the HPV vaccine is an important health intervention. The 2014 report of the President's Cancer Panel argued that the problem was insufficient efforts: "Despite strong recommendations from experts in the medical and public health fields, rates of U.S. HPV vaccination have fallen short of target levels. It will take concerted action by multiple individuals and organizations to increase HPV vaccine uptake. . . . The Panel presents high-priority goals and objectives that stakeholders should embrace to increase uptake of HPV vaccines. In many cases, these recommendations call for implementation of strategies shown to be effective for increasing uptake of other vaccines."[57] The reference to past effective interventions for other vaccines suggests that protocols for HPV vaccination are like those for any other vaccination and that the process of implementation ought to be familiar to those who disseminate vaccines. But the Task Force also subtly implied that physicians, public health advocates, and policymakers had not been as diligent as they should have been in efforts to promote HPV vaccines.

The Task Force's recommendations, however, do not differ from what had been happening across the country in the previous ten years. The reasons these efforts fell short of "target levels" in the United States are tied to complex social and cultural attitudes about vaccination that few have addressed when promoting Gardasil. Merck's strategy of emphasizing that Gardasil protected women against cervical cancer failed to account for the growing resistance to required vaccines in the United States.[58]

Evidence continues to mount that pharmaceutical companies influence regulatory bodies in myriad ways, so Merck's attempts to shape state policies to require HPV vaccination should hardly surprise us.[59] These interventions into legislation and recommendations that on the surface appear to be about individuals' well-being and healthier outcomes are far too embroiled in corporate interests to be trusted fully. In the case of Gardasil, the marketing strategies of a pharmaceutical company diminished the potential of a vaccine that offered effective prevention of HPV. In addition, Merck's efforts to include its vaccine in standard practices failed to produce the widespread use and acceptance the company intended. Perhaps this is evidence that pharmaceutical interventions are not always as insidious and pervasive as we might fear.

7

Complicity with Corporations

Cervical cancer patient advocacy has never achieved the kind of public visibility that activism for breast cancer has attracted, perhaps because of the taboo around women's bodies or perhaps because of its association with sex. Perhaps, also, because of the relatively few women in the United States who get cervical cancer and even fewer who die. Unlike the breast cancer activism of the 1980s, which included deliberately political demands by its participants, Merck's early campaigns for Gardasil and one cervical cancer patient group encouraged a distinctively nonpolitical advocacy to improve women's health.

Cervical cancer patient organizations existed long before the launch of Gardasil and before Merck's marketing campaigns, but their reach was limited. There had been no national discussion about cervical cancer, and unlike HIV, gonorrhea, or other STIs, for which there were highly publicized campaigns to raise awareness, HPV did not motivate public health campaigns. Merck addressed this silence in a number of ways. In addition to its direct-to-patient marketing campaigns for its vaccine, Merck subsidized projects to raise awareness of HPV and cervical cancer awareness. However, the corporation obscured its sponsorship. Merck's efforts in this regard were not unlike some magazines' practices of publishing "advertorials," in which print content that looks like an editorial or an educational piece turns out to be covert advertising. Merck funded pseudo-organizations with ambiguous names such as "Make the Connection" around the time it launched Gardasil.[1] In addition, it benefited from its relationship with the Cervical Cancer Group (CCG), which was not formally affiliated with Merck but accepted its money, thereby complicating its messaging.

The current health care model in the United States is shaped by private corporations and positions patients as consumers.[2] While the terms consumer and provider, which are used to refer to patients and doctors, may seem to be only linguistic distinctions, they "cast [the health care relationship] primarily in terms of a commercial transaction."[3] This use of language informs how patient advocates imagine their goals. In addition, it has facilitated corporate influence on health advocacy communities. When patients understand health care to be like other consumable goods, they are less likely to see their health as a practice of care and more like a commodity. Corporate interests often exert influence on patient activism by seeking out patients to serve as persuasive spokespeople for their products.[4] Patient narratives lend credibility to slick marketing materials and provide intimate, emotional counterpoints to corporate slogans, but patients' participation in corporate marketing strategies conflates activism with the companies' financial interests. A recent FDA report exposed how pharmaceutical companies operate behind the scenes to mobilize citizen petitions to the FDA in order to prevent competing products from receiving timely review.[5] While such petitions often do not raise objections that are scientifically valid, the FDA is required by law to review all of them. Thus, any citizen petition has the potential to delay a review of competitors' products, and, functionally, they protect the market share of the company that has initiated the petitions. The report found that in the period 2011–2015, pharmaceutical corporations filed 92 percent of "citizen" petitions.

In the months after the FDA approved Gardasil, a variety of advertising and magazines geared to the pharmaceutical industry touted the anticipated success of the potentially blockbuster product. One article, titled "Gardasil Campaign Taps Public Fear of Cancer," praised Merck's strategy of instilling anxiety in women. It also made explicit the company's commitment to developing relationships with advocacy groups and other nonprofits as part of its strategy for augmenting public education about

HPV and its association with cervical cancer: "Merck will continue to sponsor disease awareness programs by providing funds to local and national organizations—particularly those that reach out to underserved communities—that are bookmarked for HPV education."[6] But none of the articles said who these imagined underserved communities were. Corporate financial support rings hollow when its targets are described as faceless, homogenized, non-specific entities, despite the fact that the burdens of HPV and cervical cancer affect real people. Two women's health advocacy organizations with whom I worked interpreted Gardasil's promise of abated risk in diametrically opposed ways. The CCG, which had existed years before Merck launched Gardasil, embraced Merck's promise. In contrast, the Black Women's Health Group (BWHG) eyed the Merck ads warily. Their distinctive responses to the early ads for Gardasil and their reactions to Merck's attempts to buy their support highlight the racial, gendered, and economic assumptions that informed Merck's promotion of Gardasil.

"The Lovers of the Poor"

The BWHG, a small nonprofit organization in a predominantly black neighborhood of a large city in southern California, resisted what Harriet, the group's leader, called the "courting" of Merck. I learned of the BWHG during an interview with Mira, the medical director of the county's Office of Women's Health (OWH). Mira described the OWH's interest in the HPV vaccine as part of their investment in what she referred to as "post-reproductive women's health." Because cervical cancer is usually an older woman's disease, the OWH hoped the vaccine would reduce the incidence of cervical cancer, which is often diagnosed in women who are close to the age of menopause.[7] Mira told me that a Merck rep had been assigned to the OWH and had brought materials to the office but that the OWH couldn't use most of the materials because they were splashed with Merck logos. However, I noticed she was using a Gardasil-branded pen. Although I did not ask her about it, it stood out to me as exemplar of Merck's pervasive marketing tactics. Despite Mira's explicit rejection of Merck materials, the pen had somehow escaped her notice or was simply useful enough not to warrant its jettisoning. She described participating on a radio show with Harriet to discuss the HPV vaccine, of which Harriet was a vocal critic. Mira told me that after their encounter Harriet continued to forward e-mails to her from an anti-vaccine group that claimed to have data about adverse reactions to vaccines as evidence that vaccines cause harm. Harriet had asked Mira whether she had seen the most recent purported proof of the hazards of vaccines. Mira did not agree with Harriet's critiques of Gardasil, but she suggested that I speak with her. I was curious to meet Harriet because she clearly had left an impression on Mira and was one of the first health advocates I'd heard of who might offer a compelling critique of the vaccine.

Harriet and five other women had formed their grassroots group in the mid-1990s because of the need for better health education within their communities, which they defined as black women of all ages, and because they felt that providers were not giving them adequate information. Harriet was the only one of the six founders who was still involved with the group at the time I was doing my field research. At our first meeting, Harriet told me the history of the organization's founding. Harriet quoted a line from a Gwendolyn Brooks poem, "When the Lovers of the Poor Arrive," about outsiders "com[ing] in with white gloves" to a community and then leaving when things become distasteful.[8] The line resonated with me; it evoked the enthusiasm of public health researchers who enter communities to conduct research but do not continue to support these communities after they have collected data for the intervention evaluation.[9] Opposing the interventions of outsiders, the BWHG positioned itself as a response to broad political and social injustices from within its own communities. I use the plural here because the boundaries of their group were perhaps deliberately amorphous and aimed to be deliberately inclusive. While Harriet lived about ten miles northeast of the BWHG office, the group centered most of its outreach in the predominantly black neighborhood where its office was located. The small organization had a staff of two full-time people, Harriet and Lana, another middle-aged black woman who was originally from Ohio. Its primary activities focused on outreach and education. Lana provided sex education after school to kids at the local Boys and Girls Club and attended job fairs, where she distributed information about their organization. I volunteered at their offices for a month in March and April of 2008, mostly working with Lana in the office to develop materials for the sex education group. Harriet took care of the strategic planning and building relationships across like-minded organizations.

The BWHG took a holistic approach to black women's well-being. The organization hosted a career networking meeting each month. Its activities also included a group that discussed black women's reproductive health interests and conferences on reproductive health justice. One of the first BWHG projects, "Keep in Touch," focused on raising participants' understanding and awareness of breast cancer and cervical cancer. The original members formed the support meetings when one of the founders found a lump in her breast. Harriet told me that the women did their own research and found that there was a link between cancer and caffeine. Through diet, Harriet said, one member was able to "get rid of" the lump, although it was not clear to me if the woman had received an official cancer diagnosis. Their distrust of health care providers reflected their lived experiences and encounters with medical interventions and reflects larger social phenomena in the United States. Research has shown that black women, regardless of insurance coverage, receive delayed diagnoses and treatments for breast cancer.[10] Patients' experiences with these biases may affect whether women are willing to seek care when they have health concerns. Harriet pointed out her community knew these dynamics too well.[11] Harriet described the group's first conference, Birth Stories, as including "all the black midwives this side of the Mississippi." Their second conference, called "Kindred Sisters," centered on the relationship between African American women and African women. Harriet explained the conference theme as a response to U.S. health care research and delivery prejudices that assume "African women are guinea pigs" and treat black women as second in line for testing and exploitation.

Harriet argued that pharmaceutical companies are unreliable. Their track record shows that they prioritize "greed and profit [more] than the human condition and improving it," and she believed that they have no interest in "protecting the fertility of young women." Harriet said that she had noticed the "Tell Someone" ads when they first appeared and wondered what they were about. When she saw the "One Less" commercial, she thought that it was "cute, but we see through you." She believed that Merck had a reputation for not adequately testing its pharmaceuticals, but it was unclear whether she believed this was true for all pharmaceutical companies or was specific to Merck. She was skeptical about others' enthusiasm for the vaccine: "Let's be cautious about this." She believed that the cost of existing cervical cancer prevention for women was comparable to the cost of the vaccine, if not cheaper. The fact that women would still need preventive care even after they had received the vaccine confirmed her skepticism of the motives of pharmaceutical corporations. She believed this meant that Merck had designed the HPV vaccine to be a money maker.

She told me that pharmaceutical companies "come a-courting now." One of the companies had invited BWHG members to an "extremely expensive" lunch at a Beverly Hills restaurant. Harriet tried to invite as many members of her organization as possible so they could benefit from the company's largesse. The pharmaceutical representative asked them if they'd been to the fancy restaurant before, and Harriet said no, telling me this with a derisive tone, implying the representative had condescended to them. The representative ordered the tasting menu, which allowed them to try everything on the menu. When I asked her why she thought drug makers were coming to BWHG, she replied that they were trying to "soften" the community. However, she distrusted this sudden interest in black communities and believed that her group appealed to the company because of its grassroots approach. She did not want to provide tacit or explicit endorsement of their products. Harriet feared that being receptive to the pharmaceutical company's overtures would have repercussions in her work. She worried that her group would appear "compromised" by corporate influence if a pharmaceutical company were to market a new drug and the BWHG were to accepted funding from that company. Harriet didn't elaborate on what a compromise might entail, but after the lunch sponsored by the pharmaceutical company, the BWHG's members, her friends, and her co-workers asked her "Did you make any promises?" She assured them she hadn't.

Black communities in the United States have good reason to distrust medical research. The legacy of the Tuskegee Study of Untreated Syphilis in the Negro Male, which was conducted from 1932 to 1972, during which black men were intentionally infected with syphilis and denied treatment, and the forced sterilization of women of color are just two examples of black bodies being treated as expendable in the health sciences. The abuses are not just historical: mistreatment of black populations continues today.[12] Research practices are only part of a much more pervasive racism that is embedded in medical practices. For example, medical textbooks, which inculcate in new doctors the practices of the medical profession, have historically used black bodies to represent pathological bodies. The practice devalues people of color and perpetuates racist conceptions about whose bodies are deemed appropriate for viewing and experimentation.[13]

Health researchers persist in using variables that draw distinctions between people based solely on their skin color, even though anthropologists and other social scientists have discredited the assumption that race is an innate characteristic.[14] These categories also ignore geographical and ethnic diversity. The FDA's approval of a race-specific indication for a heart failure drug, BiDil, provides an example of how institutions and corporations perpetuate the conflation of biology with social, geographic, and cultural factors.[15] BiDil exemplifies how the fallacy of race gets perpetuated and codified in practices; it reveals how medical researchers, pharmaceutical corporations, and health care providers obscure human variability.[16] Health outcomes for people of color in the United States reveal that bias in treatment and access to care based on skin color persist. These disparities primarily reveal evidence of social, economic, and cultural inequalities rather than evidence of innate or biological characteristics. For example, a recent study of HPV-related cancers demonstrated that the rate of cervical cancer was higher among Latinos than among non-Latinos and was significantly higher among blacks than among whites.[17] Discrepancies in health outcomes illustrate how social and cultural practices are reproduced through institutions. As Charles H. Briggs argues, "Producing narratives of race, disease, and space involves the collaboration of biomedical professionals, public health officials, politicians, reporters, and, often, anthropologists."[18] Thus, institutionalized practices impact people in damaging ways. Racism has an embodied manifestation. These legacies informed Harriet's and the BWHG community's understandable distrust of medical and scientific research.[19] In drawing attention to how profit motives compound social and structural inequalities, Harriet's critique laid bare the complexity of racism in U.S. society.

Harriet perceived the problems and limitations of health care in the United States as a political phenomenon. When I asked her about her feelings about vaccines more generally, Harriet acknowledged that vaccines had reduced the rate of some diseases, but she was concerned about their reliability. She objected to the lack of universal health care in the United States and believed that the problem could be traced back to the "three big kids" who have a vested interest in access to health care. The three power brokers, she believed, were the "pharmaceutical companies, [the] AMA [American Medical Association], and health insurance [companies]," which all want to stay in business. She argued that their concern with "status, prestige, and money" shape current medical care and practice, pointing out that in the United States "healthcare is a privilege, not a right." For Harriet, endorsing a vaccine like Gardasil would ignore the consequences of a capitalist market for health care, something that Harriet could neither abide nor afford to ignore.

Harriet's critique of unequal access to health care and of corporate influence in the field of health care in the United States illuminates the privilege inherent in the willingness of the CCG to embrace Merck's messaging. The CCG's lack of engagement with the social and political disparities of cervical cancer and women's access to health care manifested in the group's deliberately apolitical call for awareness. The BWHG did not need a tepid call to awareness for women in their community to demand better care. Awareness implies an awakening to a problem that one did not previously know existed, and the BWHG and its communities did not have the luxury of such ignorance. In addition, the BWHG was not willing to compromise itself by accepting corporate subsidies.

Not Playing Politics

After I attended the first CCG conference on the East Coast, I moved to southern California to begin research in the fall of 2007. In December 2007, several months after the CCG's East Coast conference, I met with Gary at the home he shared with Larissa and their children from their previous marriages. Gary and Larissa ran the nonprofit out of their home in addition to holding down full-time paying jobs. Without a dedicated office space, the CCG existed mainly as an online presence, although the annual conference enabled its geographically disparate members to meet face to face. The members of the CCG lived throughout the United States and during the period of my research, the organization's online community expanded rapidly.

When I arrived at the gated entry to Gary and Larissa's home, I pressed a button on a call box to announce my presence. The gate opened automatically, revealing a broad driveway that was filled with five vehicles. Dressed in a buttoned-down shirt and neatly pressed pants, Gary greeted me at the front door and led me into the kitchen, where the housekeeper (to whom I was not introduced) and one of Larissa's daughters, Galit, were working. Sitting in the banquette breakfast nook, Galit was at her laptop computer, which had multiple stickers on the backside of the screen, including a

Planned Parenthood "Stand Up for Choice" sticker, a "Just wear it" sticker that advocated condom use, and a pro-Israel sticker. Gary and I sat down with Galit in the breakfast nook. Gary glowingly described Galit's successes at an elite West Coast university and her involvement in the CCG's work. Galit turned her attention back to her computer as Gary and I discussed how I could volunteer for the organization so that I could learn more about their efforts and help support their endeavors.

Because the CCG did not have dedicated office space, I developed the work I did for the CCG remotely. Except for the conferences and a few other in-person encounters, most of my interactions with Gary occurred through e-mail during my research. Gary generously supported my research, for example, by putting me in touch with a number of experts I would encounter when they spoke at CCG conferences, but those connections never materialized into research or conversations beyond a few e-mails. In addition to developing some of the CCG's materials, such as presentation slides about the vaccine, I told him about the quarterly meetings of the southern California county's immunization coalition, which I thought might be relevant to the CCG's work. I saw him at one of those meetings, where an upcoming pre-teen vaccine week was discussed. I culminated my primary research with the CCG by participating as a presenter at the second annual conference in the fall of 2008. I sometimes found it difficult to produce materials for them because our views on the vaccine differed significantly. The group embraced Gardasil unquestioningly, while I remained skeptical about its promise. When I would try to engage Gary with some of my ambivalences about the HPV vaccine, he would push back with well-worn slogans that he pronounced at various CCG events.

During our conversation in his kitchen, Gary told me about developing what he called a "parents educating parents" presentation about the HPV vaccine that he wanted to disseminate to parents' groups across the country. Gary saw this as part of what he called their "grassroots" movement. It was unclear to me how this functioned as grassroots, as it was not parents themselves who would generate the materials. Rather, he sought to generate interest among parents, which he explained might in turn lead to legislators paying attention to cervical cancer and the HPV vaccine. When I asked if his goal was to make the vaccine part of a required policy, he insisted that the CCG didn't "play politics." He smiled at me, as though I had tried to get him to say something incendiary. His reaction surprised me, as I had not intended to imply ulterior motives. I had mistakenly assumed that advocacy would include an explicitly political goal. Gary wanted to promote public awareness, which he thought would lead to private actions, an increase in vaccinations, and increased attention from legislators. What should come next remained ambiguous.

Gary expressly denied that the CCG's mission had any political component, both during our conversations and when he spoke to audiences at the group's conferences. I was never entirely clear about how he defined what constituted politics or political action. Women's health in the United States is inextricable from politics and policies, funding, and access. His rejection of politics during our conversation reminded me of a comment he had made at the annual conference a few months earlier. He began the conference alluding to the debates about legislating the HPV vaccine. He then said: "We can stop the cancer before it occurs. There seems to be politics associated with that. I don't want to get into politics on any of that." But as Harriet had aptly noted, political interests pervade U.S. health care, whether the issue is access to health care or the cost of pharmaceutical products. Choosing not to engage with politics does not prevent these concerns from affecting people's lives.

Gary's ambiguous language of a grassroots movement and his refusal to call his group's activities political confused me. Although Gary wanted to keep their work apolitical, it certainly had political implications, especially as he sought legislative change. His demurral denied the political debates about Gardasil of the previous eighteen months and the history of U.S. debates about women's sexual health. Gary's rejection of politics in the CCG's HPV and cervical cancer advocacy efforts seemed to exhibit a willful ignorance of how politicized U.S. health care is. The CCG's patient advocacy culture drew on deliberately political patient advocacy movements, such as patient activism for breast cancer and HIV/AIDS research and treatment. Despite the CCG's indirect benefits from earlier patient activism culture, the group's apolitical position reflected a recent change in modes of health activism. Some contemporary patient groups have veered away from explicitly political stances, adopting consumer practices to demonstrate their commitments to disease awareness.

One example of health care consumer advocacy is the pink ribbon campaign for breast cancer awareness, which has shifted the goals of past breast cancer activism away from demands for equal gender rights and investment in breast cancer research. However, decoupling health advocacy from politics may in fact impede patients' power to advocate for themselves.[20] One strategy of health activism has drawn on a rights discourse that positions advocates as citizens.[21] But instead of staking a claim in identity politics that might emphasize women's rights and access to care, the CCG's members represented a biosocial collective. In such collectives as Rebecca Dimond, Andrew Bartlett, and Jamie Lewis point out, individuals move "from patient to active citizen" and work to "influenc[e] the scientific agenda in collaboration or partnership with scientists and researchers." Although these collectives are "formed when individuals are brought together on the basis of shared biology, what binds them is not biological but social."[22] Actors who are affected by biopower's processes may not be wholly aware of how they shape them.[23] Gary's disavowal of politics does not eliminate the need to question the implications of apolitical patient activism.

The CCG's narrative of its founding evolved over time, but the digital record suggests that the group grappled with whether or not it identified as political as it evolved its mission.[24] In 2006, when I began following the organization's online presence and public activities, the CCG's website described its mission as a "grassroots nonprofit organization dedicated to serving women with, or at risk for, cervical cancer and HPV disease." However, according to the 2000 version of the website cached in the Internet Archive, the group described its founding as a response to decreased reimbursement for Pap smears.[25] The group worried that "reimbursement rates for the traditional Pap smear and the new FDA approved technologies, will be at levels that are BELOW COST to properly perform the cervical cancer screening procedure."[26] The text on this webpage focused on the complex problems with reimbursement and the concerns of cytopathologists who run the clinics that analyze Pap smears. The CCG argued that the changes in payments for cervical cancer screening put women at risk for cervical cancer. Because Gary owned a pathology lab, this reimbursement problem harmed his business interests. Despite Gary's description of the CCG's work as apolitical, its earlier positions were unavoidably political. The CCG initially framed the reimbursement gap as a political problem: "If the government and managed care companies do not raise reimbursement levels for the traditional Pap smear and new technologies, we believe some of these cervical cancer law suits we are seeing may end up naming the Federal and State government for reimbursing at levels that are below cost and causing a lower standard of care."[27] By 2006, however, the organization's website's description emphasized screening and access to care as its reasons for existence: "[The CCG] grew out of the need for quality cervical cancer screening for underserved uninsured women." However, I never observed any explicit activities to facilitate access to care for underserved or uninsured women.

The fact that the CCG was founded to address the concerns of cytopathologists in its initial goals makes it particularly strange that the advent of the vaccine did not foster more advocacy for improving existing cervical health management practices. As Michelle Murphy points out, the vaccine may well make some mass screening practices obsolete, which could harm cytopathologists' businesses.[28] This genealogy of the organization's priorities is not meant to discount the CCG's commitment to women's health. Instead, I want to highlight the inescapably political problems of women's health care, problems that even the CCG acknowledged in various media. The group's vacillation between an economic and political stance that challenged reimbursement rates for Pap smears and its apolitical resistance to "playing politics" follows the timing of the availability of Gardasil. It is notable that Gardasil's most ardent proponents, such as the CCG, rejected the slightest implication of political engagement, even though socioeconomic constraints and political debates shaped the dissemination of the vaccine.

Shortly after Gardasil became available, the CCG increased its public presence, echoing Merck's exhortation to "tell someone" as part of its promotion tactics. Positioning consumer choices as a form of advocacy and social identification, the CCG sent out frequent e-mails announcing new affiliations with a variety of online fund-raising and social networking sites. One indirect way to raise money on CCG's website encouraged its members to sign up for "eScrip," which offered "easy ways to earn for our [CCG] group." When people purchased products online through the link, CCG would get a small portion of the profits. In addition to the linking consumer habits to fund-raising, the CCG's website included links to social media sites such as Facebook, MySpace, and iGive. The strategy of using Internet activity as a way to raise funds has become increasingly common in the years since the CCG encouraged its members to engage with the "power of their purse."

Advocacy groups that accept funds from pharmaceutical corporations or tie their activism to corporate sponsorship become complicit in the manufacturers' strategies for cultivating consumer loyalty and marketing. Loyalty to pharmaceutical corporations is a strange blend of consumerism and health maintenance. As consumer goods, drugs are not the same as detergent or jeans. When pharmaceutical corporations fund patient advocate groups, they help define and shape health providers' notions of adequately compliant patient identities. As S. Lochlann Jain points out, "In these models of corporate care, everyone has their role and the scripts for these roles seem to be provided by, on the one hand, the caring corporation that allows us to play our roles through consumption . . . and, on the other hand, the role of 'survivor,' which seems to revel in narratives of the gift of cancer."[29] The CCG embraced the model of crafted survivorship and the corporately engaged patient. Consumerism and capitalism are deliberate parts of these relationships, as Jain notes: "The role of capital is incidental to none of this—neither the production of cancer, the models of treatment, nor the core centrality of the nuclear family as the consumptive unit."[30] CCG members embraced the identity of the survivor-cum-consumer advocate, a persona pharmaceutical companies have nurtured intentionally.[31] CCG members produced public narratives about cervical cancer and HPV. The narratives of their past uncertainties about their disease that could be resolved for others with the ease of Gardasil offered a more genuine endorsement than if Merck had enlisted celebrity spokespeople to promote the vaccine.

Corporate Messaging

Pharmaceutical companies lobby politicians, as Merck did in the first six months after the FDA approved Gardasil. Public policies related to health care have the potential to impact people in political, economic, and personal ways, as the policy that required female immigrants to have the HPV vaccine demonstrated.[32] Pharmaceutical companies have invested in a comprehensive strategy "of not only treatments and interventions but also information, education, health-promotion and prevention practices."[33] The CCG reproduced Merck's careful strategy of presenting Gardasil as necessary for women's health rather than a consumer product, and like Merck, the CCG sought to avoid the potentially contentious aspects of the vaccine. Gary's term "parents educating parents" unintentionally echoed the name of Merck's seminar "Educate the Educators" and similarly suggested a noninterventionist and self-directed engagement with the question of vaccination. Merck's most recent HPV advertisement, "Know HPV," makes this priority of knowing explicit. Gary framed parents educating parents as a benevolent project rather than as an opportunity for Merck to expand its market. His denial of political engagement was a privileged position that contrasted with Harriet's deliberate and necessary consideration of how racism and gender shape access to health care and outcomes. Gary's insistence that the CCG did not "play politics" replicated Merck's strategy of evading the most politically charged elements of the vaccine: its ability to protect against an STI. Merck's misdirection refused to address the socially fraught issues Gardasil might raise or the difficulties of garnering public support for widespread HPV vaccination. The act of promoting a pharmaceutical product has unavoidable political implications. Merck's silence and the absence of discussion about sexual health ought to have provided an opportunity for the CCG to engage more explicitly with U.S. politics related to sex, health care, and vaccines. Its failure to do so had its own implicit political meaning.

On CCG's online forum, women discussed whether physicians who endorsed Gardasil had ties to pharmaceutical companies and the significance of such relationships. One woman suggested that physicians who had spoken at the CCG annual conference might be compromised by their relationship to "Big Pharma." She provided a link to an article on *CNN Money* that quoted Merck's chief financial officer acknowledging that vaccines would be a "major contributor to [Merck's] top line growth."[34] Other women offered counterarguments. One asked others not to "beat up Big Pharma so fast." She argued that the companies helped educate people and raise awareness about cervical cancer, although, as the research for this book has shown, such efforts are sporadic, self-interested, and minimal at best. Her belief that pharmaceutical companies have the public interest in mind matches the image companies have worked hard to cultivate, but the data suggest that such companies invest much more in marketing than they do in research and development.[35]

On the day I visited Gary in his home, he told me that Merck would provide a financial contribution to the "educate the parents" project, although I never found out how much money was involved. Without any prompting from me, he said that it was not necessarily a bad thing that the CCG received money from Merck. He acknowledged that while some people believe that accepting money from pharmaceutical companies implied compromised efforts, the CCG did not think this was necessarily true. In January 2008, the CCG republished on its website marketing magazine's article that called Merck an "All-Stars Company of the Year." The article included this statement: "Gardasil, the HPV vaccine that turned Merck's corporate reputation from disgrace to that of life-saving innovator, has also provided a case study in the company's global marketing muscle."[36] By featuring this marketing narrative on its site, the CCG explicitly endorsed the hero narrative Merck sought to tell. Although the CCG's concern for women's health was legitimate, Gary's renunciation of politics and his willingness to accept money from Merck seemed contradictory. His position was similar to that of the president of Women in Government, who claimed that corporate sponsorship wouldn't sway the decisions legislators made. Whether or not legislators can truly be neutral after receiving financial support from major corporations, the general public distrusted the intertwined interests, as the failure of the push for HPV vaccine legislation suggests. Gary's acceptance of Merck's funding and the CCG's recapitulation of Merck's framing suggest that the synergy between Merck's rhetoric and that of the CCG were strategic by both actors. They each stood to gain from the other's material and social resources.

The CCG's enthusiasm about the vaccine made sense. Many of its members had been affected by a cancer that was now preventable, and all had experienced the uncertainties associated with an HPV diagnosis. What I found more difficult to understand was the organization's celebration of Merck rather than a celebration of the science that created the vaccine or the broader research priority of HPV prevention. I noticed that the organization never criticized any aspect of the vaccine, such as its cost or its limited protection against the four most prevalent types of HPV. The group's interest in the vaccine and their own health status did not necessarily lead them to become scientifically engaged activists. In fact, their failure to critique the vaccine on scientific grounds puzzled me throughout my research. No one questioned how little gynecological practices would change for women after the arrival of Gardasil, even though many CCG members expressed frustration and sadness about how painful or difficult their experiences with gynecologists had been. Women still need to receive Pap smears and the HPV test. Abnormalities still require follow-up and may lead to uncertain diagnoses. Much of what the CCG members articulated as particularly challenging—the ambiguities, the clinical uncertainty, and the feeling of vulnerability—would barely change with the advent of Gardasil.

A Tale of Two Organizations

The CCG's appropriation of Merck's message about what Gardasil promises failed to address one of the core reasons for continued cervical cancer deaths in the United States: lack of access to care and larger social inequalities.[37] Women's health and cancer raise critical social justice issues. Indeed, although Gardasil offers the benefit of reducing HPV morbidities and a reduced risk of cervical cancer, research on cervical cancer in the United States demonstrates that the women who die from the cancer are disproportionately women of color and are much more likely to be those who lack access to care.[38]

The CCG advocated an apolitical stance of self-awareness that embraced consumer identity as a form of empowerment. Harriet's cautiousness and distrust of pharmaceutical companies contrast starkly with Gary's willingness to participate in the bounty that pharmaceutical companies can extend to small nonprofits. While Harriet consciously refused to engage with pharmaceutical companies, Gary shaped the CCG's position to conform with the language Merck used. However, the ethical principles that guided Harriet's management of the organization had material costs. During the month I spent at the BWHG, it was clear that the lack of resources presented challenges to the advancement of the organization's mission.[39] When the group's Internet connection stopped working, which happened more than once, we had to wait for a friend of Harriet's to come over to provide technology support. On those days, we lost work time. Although the CCG did not have dedicated office space, Gary's business acumen and private wealth sustained the small organization and gave him confidence when negotiating resources to keep his nonprofit afloat.

The CCG's publicity matched Gary's enthusiasm for leveraging the opportunities Merck funding proffered. Skin color, professional experience, and perhaps even gender made it easier for the CCG to embrace the compromises Merck's support demanded. The leaders of the CCG were white, but perhaps more notably, the group's leader was male. Further, Gary's business-oriented thinking focused on quite different issues than those on which Harriet's grassroots commitments centered. The CCG honed and polished its public image through its presence on the Internet and its enthusiasm for Merck's messages. The CCG's comfort with the ambiguity that funding from a pharmaceutical company implied offered Merck a persuasive set of spokespeople to advocate for Gardasil.

The CCG and the BWHG had significantly different missions and constituencies, and their responses to Gardasil and to Merck's corporate largesse illustrate their respective complicity with and resistance to a marketed health care product. Michelle Mello, Sara Abiola and James Colgrove have shown that Merck provided a variety of unrestricted funds to interest groups.[40] I believe these investments have affected public perceptions of the vaccine: the low use of Gardasil in 2016 demonstrates that the lobbying and patient advocacy the company cultivated did little to motivate the general public to vaccinate. As corporations now frequently shape public discourse about health, individuals and organizations can participate in these conversations in disparate ways. These different engagements, however, reflect complex social hierarchies and privileges, as the BWHG and the CCG demonstrated. Members of the CCG represented those "positioned as self-regulating consumers, as targets of public health strategy, and as consumers of corporate growth markets," while the BWHG advocated for those who had been "missed by the complexities and challenges of health intervention and . . . [were] subject to the persistent power of structural vulnerabilities."[41] From public health messaging to the clinical discussions about Gardasil, Merck packaged and prepared the terms of these representations, but how race and class informed participation in corporate opportunities was less obvious. The pharmaceutical corporations' influence in these power dynamics cannot be overlooked.

8

Mothers and Gardasil

Public responses to proposed HPV vaccine policies demonstrated that it was impossible to understand how parents interpreted the newest vaccine on the market without exploring their opinions about vaccines more generally. Opponents of HPV vaccine policies for school entry articulated their refusals as objections to any government policies for their children's health. The anti-government stance may well have been disingenuous, since HPV vaccine opponents did not always mount the same refusals to other required childhood vaccines, such as the previously controversial measles, mumps, and rubella (MMR) vaccine. However, the alliance between social conservatives, who opposed the HPV vaccine, and non-vaccinating or slow vaccinating families, who argued that the HPV vaccine was another example of government interference in health care decisions about their children, gave the growing social movement of vaccine resisters an even wider audience.

The Gardasil advertisements called attention to mothers' desires to be well informed about their children's health care. Merck marketed Gardasil to emphasize a unique responsibility of mothers to protect their daughters, to draw on the older women's experiences of how medical practice manages and treats female bodies.[1] In the 2008 "Choose to Get Vaccinated" series of ads for Gardasil, mothers and daughters engage in various activities together, such as braiding hair and painting their finger-nails while looking at magazines. The images invoked shared social and cultural experiences of femininity. The mothers announced to the viewers "I chose to get my daughter vaccinated" as empowerment, but this form of empowerment is framed through a compliant medical lens. The mothers speak about a choice already made, although both versions of the adver-tisement end with the "Choose to Get Vaccinated" slogan. "I chose to get my daughter vaccinated because I wanted her to be one less woman with cervical cancer. . . . I chose to get my daughter vaccinated when her doctor told me the facts. Like other vaccinations, Gardasil is about prevention." A teenager, facing the viewer directly, announces, "I chose to get vaccinated after my doctor told me Gardasil does more than prevent cervical cancer." The young woman's grandmother acknowledges that it protects against other HPV-related diseases, but no one states explicitly that HPV is an STI. In the final voice-over, a different, invisible narrator says, "You have the power to choose. Ask your daughter's doctor about Gardasil." Or as the Gardasil website from the same time as the advertisement stated in its sec-tion for parents, "You do everything you can for your daughter, and if she is still at the age where you're making her healthcare decisions, this section is for you. It's not too early to be thinking about a vaccine for cervical can-cer for her."[2] The statements in these Merck ads were similar to the con-cerns mothers voiced during my research. It might well be that mothers learned from pharmaceutical company marketing that this is the language they could mobilize to assert their autonomy about health care decisions. The twist on liberation here, however, is that mothers' empowerment is actualized by following medical authority. Although the language and the framework of advertisements for Gardasil resonated with mothers' attitudes about the task of caring for their children, they did not persuade their target audiences. Mothers told me in interviews that pharmaceuti-cal companies, physicians, and other proponents of vaccination misunder-stand how mothers perceive their expertise.

Consumerism, Natural Lives, and Identity Politics

A prominent testimonial on the main page of the NaturalMoms website featured Leah, a member of the southern California chapter. Leah was a well-known child actress who as an adult received her PhD in a biology subdiscipline. Now, as the mother of two young children, she was restarting her acting career. Her photo and full name were published on the site next to an explanation for why she participated in the group.

> For those of us who parent against current trends, and for those of us who are parenting after educated compassionate decisions, to do so without support can be disheartening, discouraging, and often leads to straying from our instinct. [NaturalMoms] provides the support and education that we historically have gotten from close-knit communities. The way of life for the past hundreds of thousands of years informs my parenting on a daily basis. Even though I am not in a hunter-gatherer community, my parenting still needs to be encouraged and guided. By finding my tribe in [NaturalMoms], I have been able to reclaim some of that ancient wisdom that families used to share every day.

The NaturalMoms' website proclaimed its members' commitment to "natural or green living" and "alternative parenting." The website asked its readers if they felt they were "different" from other moms, and the community invited those who shared the "desire" to be the "best parents possible" to come together. Founded on the East Coast in the early 2000s, Natural-Moms expanded rapidly to multiple chapters nationally. Leah's testimonial evoked a group identification through motherhood that I observed among various communities that focused on mothering, both online and in person.[3] Who is your tribe? the group asked. How does participation in a group like NaturalMoms affirm your place in the world? Leah's reference to ancient practices implied that modern life gets in the way of ideal parenting practices. Yet as with many health fads that invoke prehistoric times, such as the "paleolithic diet," the NaturalMoms' website fails to acknowledge the very real benefits to human survival that interventions like vaccines, cooking food, and modern medicines have made possible. Leah's reference to the past romanticized it. The site did not advocate for a time when women could not vote, when tuberculosis and polio were rife, or before the availability of reliable birth control.

Motherhood is a powerful social identifier in the United States.[4] During the period of my research, websites devoted to photo-documentation and descriptions of mothering experiences have fostered online communities to reflect on the experience. Some document the joys of mothering adorable tots, others facilitate online discussions, and others promote products that have been "donated" by companies that want to tap into the readership women bloggers have cultivated.[5] In contrast to historical views of motherhood as full of potential collective political action, marketing messages have recast an ideal motherhood through consumer practices. The Internet has affirmed motherhood as a performative, and even lucrative, endeavor.[6] Organizations such as NaturalMoms present opportunities for face-to-face connections and, for women like Leah, offer legitimacy to women who do not feel supported by their local or other social communities.

At the first NaturalMoms meeting I attended, a former leader of the group who had moved to Georgia returned for a visit. She described trying to nurse her infant at the back of her church during a service. She recounted the insult of being asked to go behind a curtain so as not to offend the other churchgoers. The other women shared her outrage that the request implied breastfeeding should be covert or that it might be shameful to expose any part of the breast. Managing these types of public critiques was a common theme among the mothers I interviewed. They challenged others' judgments of their choices and asserted their right to evaluate what was best for their children. This "mothercraft" empowers mothers through "the embodied capacities of mothers to make informed and optimal decisions for herself and her family, to be a competent and responsible consumer."[7] The NaturalMoms' rejection of this church's notion of propriety echoes the stance of the 1970s feminist movement, which defended breastfeeding in public as a new version of women's liberation and demanded space for mothers to breastfeed without censure. When it came to the right to refuse vaccines, a topic that came up during many of the meetings I attended, the mothers adopted an anti-government stance of refusal. They did not believe that policymakers knew what was best for them and they asserted their authority as experts about their children's bodies.

The members of NaturalMoms who identified as vaccine resisters and others whom I encountered through listservs and family-values organizations argued that their personal preferences should prevail over social norms about the collective good or government policies. Statements made by a variety of family-values organizations at the time of the FDA review of Gardasil invoked the privacy logic that NaturalMoms articulated. For example, on the day the FDA reviewed Gardasil, the Medical Institute for Sexual Health took the position that they were not against what they called the "cancer vaccine;" they opposed government policies that mandated that their children receive the vaccine. The distinctions they identified between their position and opposing the vaccine, though small, were notable.[8] The seemingly disparate communities of social progressives (and many of the NaturalMoms placed themselves in this camp) and conservative institutions agreed about the right to privacy and to self-autonomy, even though their respective underlying principles were not the same. The family-values organizations insisted on the right to privacy to protect their religious and moral values, while parents who were slow to vaccinate their children or those who refused vaccines altogether claimed the right to privacy as a manifestation of consumer choice and empowerment. The NaturalMoms mothers articulated their preferences and desires by merging ideas about U.S. capitalism, democracy, individuality, and identity politics.[9] The marketing of pharmaceutical companies often invokes this language of consumer empowerment to sell their products, but the NaturalMoms transformed the language into a framework of refusal rather than consumption.

A few months into my research with NaturalMoms, Lucia, a regular attendee at the NaturalMoms chapter I observed for nine months in 2008, posted a question to the national and local listservs about how to engage with the media on the issue of refusing vaccines. She had agreed to do an interview with a local Fox News affiliated station for a segment on public health concerns about falling vaccination rates in southern California. Although I never interviewed Lucia, she attended all the NaturalMoms monthly meetings I observed. A cheerful woman in her late 20s with freckles and long straight hair, she looked more like an older teenager than a mother of two. Before having children, she had been a preschool teacher, and though I never heard her state it explicitly, her comments suggested she now stayed at home with her small kids. The language of "individual freedom" came up often in mothers' defense of their decisions not to vaccinate, but Lucia explicitly argued that the group could gain legitimacy by emphasizing this position. In her e-mail to the local NaturalMoms chapter, she reminded other mothers who might be interviewed at the monthly meeting to stay on topic. She pointed out that Fox News is a "conservative" network and would appreciate the "individual freedom argument" that emphasizes parents' right to choose vaccines. "This is the position i plan on taking," she wrote. She concluded her e-mail with the hope that "we can be the cool voice of non-vaxers."

As I arrived at the NaturalMoms meeting on the day of the Fox News filming, I saw Lucia holding one daughter in her arms and the other by the hand as she walked toward the meeting hall at the local library. The newscaster and her cameraman followed Lucia closely. Once they entered the building, Lucia and her daughters turned around and did it again. The repetition reminded me of the slowed-down repeat imagery often used on U.S. local news shows, and in fact, the final news clip showed Lucia approaching the library looped over and over again as though she were doing a perpetrator's walk. Inside, Lucia spoke to the journalist with the bright lights of the film crew shining on her face. She explained that she considered herself a "selective" and a "slow" vaccinator. She told how her pediatrician had coerced her to vaccinate her older daughter, Maria, who was now three years old. When Lucia was a child, both she and her brother had had mild reactions to vaccines. Concerned about Maria's fever and sores after her first series of vaccines, Lucia and her husband chose not to follow up with the rest of her vaccines. They had yet to vaccinate the younger daughter, who was almost two, and Lucia thought they probably wouldn't end up vaccinating her. She explained that she would vaccinate when the risk of the disease outweighed the risk of the vaccine. She did not elaborate about what sorts of risks those might be.

As mothers began to gather for the meeting, the news reporter moved among them, asking them about their choices. Dionne, a mother in her early 20s who was there with her toddler daughter, Tate, told the reporter about being forced to sign a waiver at the nursery school stating that she acknowledged that she was a negligent parent. The news reporter had asked to sit in on the meeting, and as was the custom at other meetings I attended, the mothers went around the circle, introducing themselves. They added a brief statement about their own experiences with vaccines for the reporter's benefit. Dionne said that she felt "raped" when she was forced to give Tate some vaccinations. Another mother mentioned that her pediatrician's office told her she might not be allowed to bring her child there because of the medical practice's concerns about insurance, although she did not elaborate on what that entailed. The group muttered their dismay and their skepticism about whether a provider could refuse care because of a perceived threat to their patients. After the television crew left, the meeting proceeded with its usual format, partly support-group and partly a gathering to share information; the topic that night was natural health care and products.

About a month later, the television segment was broadcast with the provocative title "War on Vaccines." The story opened with Lucia walking up the stairs in slow motion while the reporter said in voice-over, "To a lot of the medical establishment, [Lucia] and other moms like her are public enemy number one. They don't buy the government-mandated vaccine schedule." The footage featured images of the moms holding their cherubic-looking babies and toddlers romping around the room interspersed with testimonials from the group's members about why they did not vaccinate or chose to vaccinate slowly. Rebecca, the local chapter leader, cheerfully said, "I actually feel safer at this point forgoing the vaccines." Although the title of the story suggested that these mothers might be causing trouble, the report unexpectedly questioned the institutionalization of vaccination. As the cameras panned across the meeting room full of parents and children, Lucia's voice-over confidently stated, "We're not irresponsible. We're informed. And we're choosing to do it the natural, old-fashioned way." She described how her older daughter had had a rash after a combination vaccine. When her doctor refused to acknowledge that the vaccine could have been the cause, Lucia lost faith in his authority. Immediately after Lucia asserted what she argued was her deliberate and informed choice, a written statement from the American Association of Pediatrics flashed on the screen: "The consequences of a decline in immunization rates could be devastating to the health of our nation's children." The juxtaposition of the stark American Association of Pediatrics warning and the counter-arguments of the slow-vaccinating and non-vaccinating moms featured on the news story amplified the polemicism of the debate.

The news segment included an interview with Jay Gordon,[10] a prominent Santa Monica physician who is known for his criticism of the standard pediatric vaccination schedule. A statement on his website supports the position many of the NaturalMoms expressed: "No one knows your child better than you do."[11] Gordon claimed in the Fox News segment that "we give too many vaccines too early." He told the reporter that excessive vaccination means "taking chances you don't need to take," and he described it as a "toxic tipping point." The reporter also interviewed Jenny McCarthy, who often speaks about her belief that vaccines triggered her son's autism. McCarthy, an actor and former model, has used her celebrity to articulate her skepticism about vaccines. During her various media appearances, including for the Fox News NaturalMoms story, McCarthy insisted that "parents are terrified to vaccinate" because autism remains unexplainable. She asserted to various media outlets that she was not anti-vaccine, but rather anti-toxin. McCarthy's message consistently focused on the dangers of vaccines and never proposed other sources of potential toxins. As she said on Larry King's television show in April 2008, "Too many [vaccines], too soon.... We need an alternate schedule. We need to get rid of the toxins.... Thirty-six shots given [to infants].... Isn't it ironic in 1983 there were ten shots, and now there's thirty-six?"[12]

McCarthy and her partner, at the time, actor Jim Carrey, published a statement on CNN.com's website, in which they describe McCarthy's son's "recovery" from autism. In the statement, they conflate their concerns with the vaccine schedule and the number of vaccines: "Vaccines are not the only environmental trigger [of autism], but we do think they play a major role.... We need to consider changing the vaccine schedule, reducing the number of shots given and removing certain ingredients that could be toxic to some children."[13] The Fox News segment's inclusion of McCarthy as a vaccine resister muddled the message of the mothers interviewed for the story. The Natural Moms did not explicitly discuss a fear of vaccines' association with autism; they expressed more ambiguous concerns about vaccine safety. McCarthy's statements opposing the vaccine schedule and the number of vaccines children receive, however, was not unlike the ambiguity apparent in the positions taken by the diverse HPV vaccine opponents. There was nuance in the different arguments vaccine opponents presented, but in both cases, the refusers unified in their opposition despite their distinct logics of resistance.

On the NaturalMoms news segment, McCarthy said that what she referred to as the unreliability of vaccines would result in this "group of mothers not vaccinating ris[ing] higher and higher and higher; because, let me tell you, it's *going* to." She added, "They need to do something about that [pediatric vaccine] schedule." Lucia explained to the interviewer that "every child is different, and to have a schedule that's the same for every child, that can be dangerous." McCarthy is an important figure in national conversations about vaccines because of her celebrity. Public health officials malign her and vaccine-resisting parents laud her. Rebecca told me, "I think she [McCarthy] is awesome.... She is very strong.... She is very vocal about her opinions.... I love that about her. She will confront some of these doctors and ... get in their face about the issues.... I think she says and does what a lot of us are thinking, but she just says it and does it. She is very bold." Rebecca, who worked as a doula and was the mother of a young daughter, critiqued the failure of doctors and public health officials to hear mothers' concerns. Inspired by McCarthy's confidence, Rebecca and other mothers in the NaturalMoms group tried to question standard medical practices with varying success.

A key part of McCarthy's argument, as made in other settings, such as a Larry King evening news show and on a now-infamous *Oprah* episode, focuses on the fact that children receive more vaccines now than ever before, which she believes corresponds with a rise in autism rates. However, as scientists and others who reject fallacious inferences point out, correlation is not causation. The Fox television journalist explained to viewers that McCarthy believed that the power balance between physicians and patients needs to shift; physicians need to listen to patients. Thus, although the report cast the mothers' distrust of vaccines as the primary reason for their refusals, the news story made clear that many slow vaccinating and non-vaccinating parents perceived physicians to be unreliable and coercive.

McCarthy has become a spokesperson for autism awareness and has published popular books about motherhood and her son's diagnosis with autism.[14] Public health officials have held her partly responsible for encouraging vaccine resistances. Until 2010, she promoted an organization called Talk About Curing Autism, and she later became the president of Generation Rescue. On Generation Rescue's website, the organization identifies vaccines as a potential cause of autism, attributing behavior changes and less long-lasting side effects to vaccines.[15] One website titled "Jenny McCarthy Body Count," created by an individual who is unaffiliated with any public health institutions, presented a harsh critique.[16] Although it has since been renamed "Anti-Vaccine Body Count," its web address retains the original site's name. Its creator blames the number of vaccine-preventable deaths in the United States on McCarthy's questioning of vaccine safety. At the CDC's annual immunization conference I attended in Atlanta, Georgia, in 2008, Dr. Paul Offit, a prominent vaccine researcher and proponent, and a female employee in the CDC's Communications Department held a special session dedicated to rebutting McCarthy's claims. Unlike most of the conference sessions, which focused on presenting research data and evaluating health intervention programs, this session focused on the personal. The CDC employee portrayed herself as receptive to McCarthy's message. She described her own vaccine hesitancy. She had seen McCarthy speaking to Oprah at the time that she was preparing to take her second child to the pediatrician for his two-month vaccine series. She told the audience that she understood why parents had moments of anxiety about bringing their children to the doctor's office to be vaccinated. Yet she concluded that

McCarthy's words were harmful to the important mission of vaccinating U.S. children.

The Fox news story also juxtaposed the intimate and emotional aspects of parents' decisions with public health concerns. After images of McCarthy cuddling with her 5-year-old son, the news segment featured the local county public health director, an older, white, male, who wore a suit and tie. Even the video image had a grainy quality, as though he were a historical subject, not a contemporary to the mothers represented in the segment. He sat at his desk, typing on a computer, the business attire and setting presumably legitimating his authority. He objected to parents "substituting [their] judgment . . . [for that of] the whole scientific community" and said that to do so could cause "some risk to your child's health." His statement failed to address the concerns McCarthy and the NaturalMoms raised, focusing instead on an abstract imagined public. He missed an opportunity to convey to parents why vaccination is important to individuals and instead perpetuated the image of the rigid and indifferent public health official that many parents told me they found distasteful.

In fact, the portrayal of the health professional interspersed with images of mothers playing with their children echoed the concerns of one mother, who had three children and had agreed to participate in a media interview in her home state of Florida. In response to Lucia's post on the Natural-Moms national e-mail listserv asking for suggestions on how to present herself to the journalist in a sympathetic light, the mother from Florida wrote that she regretted doing a recent interview about vaccination because she feared that she and a medical professional would be represented very differently. She described how she had spoken to a journalist while she watched her children at a park, and she imagined that the interview with a medical professional would have him or her seated in an office with no distractions, fully able to focus. In contrast, she had found it difficult to finish a sentence during her interview because her children were constantly interrupting her. She feared that her message would be less persuasive because she couldn't offer time to an interviewer when she was free of other responsibilities.

However, despite the stereotypical representations of both the Natural-Moms and the public health official during the Fox News segment, the mothers appeared sympathetic and human in a way that the medical director did not. The signifiers of the public health director's professional expertise in fact made him seem unaware of the realities of people's lives. Thus, he came across as unpersuasive. At the next NaturalMoms meeting

after the news segment aired, the mothers agreed that the segment was sat-
isfactory, even successful. Wearing a red fleece hoodie, embroidered with
"Mrs. D____" on the front, perhaps something she wore in her job as a preschool teacher, Lucia exclaimed how much she loved that they'd referred to
her as "public enemy number one."

Mothers' Knowledge

Andrew Wakefield's 1998 article in the *Lancet* associating the MMR vaccine with autism persists as the origin story immunization advocates tell
about vaccine resistance.[17] In 2004, ten of the article's original twelve
authors retracted the findings. "We wish to make it clear . . . no causal link
was established between MMR vaccine and autism as the data were insufficient. However . . . such a link was raised and consequent events have
had major implications for public health. . . . Now is the appropriate time
that we should together formally retract. . . . these findings . . . according
to precedent"[18] In 2010, the *Lancet* formally retracted the Wakefield study
due to ethical violations in the research protocol.[19] Today, in the digital
version of the journal, every page is stamped with the word "Retracted" in
red. In addition, the UK medical register stripped Wakefield of his license
after the UK General Medical Council ruled that Wakefield had failed to
disclose financial conflicts of interest and had treated his research subjects
unethically.[20] Wakefield's study does appear to have led to a decrease in the
use of the MMR vaccine, especially in the UK, but its persistent impact on
vaccination rates is less clear.

However, the narrative that identifies Wakefield as the progenitor of
vaccine resistances is a myth. As historians of vaccines have shown, vaccine refusals have come and gone over the past several centuries.[21] Vaccine
skepticism has existed since the initial introduction of smallpox vaccination in the 1700s. In the 1970s and 1980s, concerns about the safety of
the diphtheria, tetanus, pertussis (DTP) vaccine affected vaccine rates
in the United Kingdom and in the United States.[22] Blume and Zanders
point out that pharmaceutical manufacturers had developed an acellular
pertussis vaccine as early as the 1920s, but they suggest that the high cost
of its production may have impeded its widespread use.[23] Public concerns
about the use of whole-cell pertussis in the DTP vaccine and its potential for serious adverse effects prompted lawsuits in the United States. In

response to their experiences with the DTP vaccine, two mothers established the National Vaccine Information Center, an advocacy organization that currently self-identifies as the "oldest and largest consumer led organization advocating for the institution of vaccine safety and informed consent protections in the public health system."[24] The National Vaccine Information Center has shaped legislation and public policy, including the National Childhood Vaccine Injury Act of 1986, which allows parents to seek compensation for claims of vaccine-related injury.[25] The high burden of vaccine-related litigation in the United States drove many pharmaceutical companies out of the U.S. market and contributed to policymakers' decision to use the diphtheria, tetanus, acellular pertussis (DTaP) vaccine as the U.S. pediatric standard in 1996.[26] DTaP requires five booster shots to be effective, but it has a shorter duration of immunity against pertussis, which some have blamed for the rise in pertussis infections over the last twenty years.[27]

Thus, Wakefield and McCarthy belong to a longer history of vaccine resistances. The scientific community considers there to be no connection between vaccination and autism.[28] Yet parents' concerns about vaccines are not just about autism. The mothers in NaturalMoms discussed nebulous fears about potential harms from vaccines and their distrust of the medical professionals who promoted a universal immunization schedule. In the context of a growing movement against required vaccines, parents distrusted pharmaceutical companies' profit motives and government policies that required vaccination. Merck's rush to legislate Gardasil fed the distrust of these parents.

Reminding me of Merck's "I Chose" advertisements for Gardasil, the mothers I interviewed invoked maternal intuition, insight, and responsibility for their children, regardless of whether they opposed or accepted vaccines. Julia, a member of NaturalMoms who appeared in the Fox News segment, spoke to me at length about the differences between the decision-making processes of parents and doctors, which she summed up as a question of individual needs versus the needs of a population. She asserted her right to question the safety of vaccines for her two sons. She attended all her sons' appointments with detailed questions and plans about which vaccines they would receive and which ones they would delay or skip. "[The doctor] has all this knowledge; but since his job is to protect his 3,000 patients as a whole, he is thinking in terms of the group. I am thinking in terms of the individual. I only have two people to worry about, so I can make decisions that I feel are tailored to these two kids. If I had 3,000 kids to worry about, then yeah, I would just give them all on the same schedule without worrying about whether Timmy had a cold today or whatever. But since I only have two, it makes sense to me that I be the one making the decisions, not him." Julia pointed out that the schedules for some vaccines, such as for hepatitis B, were guided by population-level analyses, not individualized needs: "To give a shot to a day-old baby because you don't trust that the promiscuous boy later on is going to come to the doctor when they need to . . . is not a good reason for me. That is why they do it, because the high-risk populations don't come and get shots." The fact that the hepatitis B vaccine is given in infancy to protect the baby in adulthood affirmed Julia's skepticism about the vaccine schedule. Lucia argued during her interview for the Fox News story that some kids have reactions to penicillin, so why wouldn't vaccines elicit different responses in different children? The mothers' objections resisted a foundational principle of medical research, which "operates on the notion that the immortal logic of science trumps individual mortality [or risks]."[29] Julia began our interview by telling me that although she had an advanced degree in biology, and her husband was a physicist and a professor, she was committed to the right of parents to question scientific findings. "I have never told [the physician] that I have a background in science. . . . I would rather just say because I am a parent, this is my right and have that open the door for other people who might not feel they have such a strong voice." Julia's declaration of authority parallels Jenny McCarthy's assertion of mother-as-expert. As McCarthy told Oprah, "my science is named Evan."

The Herd and the Individual

The mothers who participated in NaturalMoms did not speak about Gardasil specifically during their discussions of vaccines or on the local and national listservs. When I asked the mothers I interviewed directly about the vaccine, they averred that it was not different from other vaccines, but its novelty concerned many of the mothers I interviewed. Lindsey, a member of the Church of Jesus Christ of Latter-day Saints and who is not part of the NaturalMoms group, was the only mother who enthusiastically wanted to give it to her daughter. She and I met at a playground while two of her four children played. Her enthusiasm initially surprised me, since her Mormon faith was a central part of her family's identity, but she cared about Gardasil's promise to prevent cancer. Lindsey told me that her husband was an immunologist who had worked on cervical cancer in the late 1990s. Lindsey described her own understanding of HPV as "fuzzy," but she did know that the virus could cause cancer. Unlike the other mothers I met, she deferred to her husband about most medical and scientific knowledge. As she described it, her husband had not just read "a few" articles on vaccines, but rather had "boxes and boxes" of material about vaccines. He would assure her that "you can only do so much . . . you do the best you can." Lindsey chose to speak with me because she was a proponent of vaccines. "If you get exposed to the virus, you have something to help defend you, so you may not have to die. . . . I guess I have been fortunate that I have had very minor reactions to vaccines. I guess it is always in the back of your head—did I do the right thing?" Lindsey recognized that vaccines are "polarizing," as she put it. She did not have a strong opinion about the slow or non-vaccinating parents, but she thought mothers who didn't vaccinate were often ill informed.

Annette, a mother of ten-year-old male and female twins, compared her feelings about Gardasil to her distrust of the chicken pox vaccine: "I felt kind of like it was [like] the chicken pox vaccination because I remember [when] that came out in full glory. . . . I was reading a little bit about how the [Gardasil] studies haven't been completely conducted with the certain demographics, age appropriate and what are the side effects and does it have to be re-administered because its effectiveness wears off à la chicken pox?" Julia said explicitly that she preferred vaccines for which there were more longitudinal data, despite the conundrum that such data required people to get vaccines in order to generate the perspective on their safety: "I understand, in order to have longitudinal studies, people have to actually have the vaccine. But you know, very selfishly, I am not willing to do that. If I have a daughter, she would not be . . . part of the [longitudinal] study. I am not interested in that part." Most of the mothers focused on whether Gardasil ought to be required and none discussed the scientific data or the efficacy of the vaccine. Mary, a mother of four, resisted the HPV vaccine even though her preteen daughter was eligible. "That is the other thing, it [the HPV vaccine] is pretty new. I don't know how long . . . it has . . . been out. . . . They don't know the long-term side effects and that makes me anxious. That makes me not want to do it. Because like with the oral polio [vaccine], they had given it for a couple years, and then they found out it was causing problems and then they took it away.[30] So I don't want to be a guinea pig and I don't want my kids to be that way. So I would be really careful about giving it to her." Parents did not trust that the pharmaceutical companies and legislators prioritized their children's best interests.

Mary, a licensed social worker, told me that she knew how to read scientific documents and research reports. "Knowledge is power, so I would find out where the information [about the vaccine] is coming from. . . . If the study is done by the drug company making the vaccine, I'm not going to believe it as much." Mary talked about the birth control policy of the Catholic Church in a similar way. Describing to me her interpretation of the Vatican II decision that forbade birth control and the fact that the pope overrode the recommendation of a papal committee, she said that she preferred to "take what I like and leave the rest . . . in terms of doing what some *man* at some church tells me." In addition to questioning the source of information, mothers such as Mary also objected to expressions of authority that ignore the complexity of decision making. The pope's reasons for rejecting birth control did not take into consideration the many reasons that a faithful congregant, like Mary, might still believe that birth control was the right choice for her family. These mothers believed that those in authority were unaware of the realities of their lives, and they did not want to follow the guidance of experts who fail to understand the nuances of mothers' decisions.

Mothers did not find HPV's easy transmission to be an incentive to vaccinate their children, perhaps because all of the mothers I interviewed had children who were too young for the vaccine or who were newly eligible to receive it. This, of course, is a challenge with the HPV vaccine. To be effective, Gardasil needs to be given before sexual debut, but parents may not think about the future sexually active person their child will become. Thus, for these parents, its benefits may seem ambiguous. The mothers I interviewed interpreted it as another money-maker for pharmaceutical companies, part of what they judged to be an excess of childhood vaccines. Annette viewed the vaccine with suspicion: "I personally don't know anyone who has had cervical cancer, so I haven't heard about it that much except all of a sudden when this vaccination was brought out. So, the skeptic in me says, really? Is that your next thing?" Rebecca dismissed the new vaccine on the market as just like others: "I just kind of lumped it into all the other vaccines. I was like, oh, here they [pharmaceutical companies/scientists] go again, coming up with another vaccine. Even though I have had HPV, I still wouldn't want to give the vaccine to my daughter." I asked the mothers direct questions about their gynecological and sexual histories, but Rebecca was the only mother to admit that she had been diagnosed with a cervical abnormality in college. She described it as a traumatic event, yet her experiences with gynecological interventions did nothing to persuade her that Gardasil was appropriate for her daughter.[31]

None of the mothers recognized how ubiquitous HPV is. Rebecca and Julia told me that they would teach their children to make good decisions about their sexual partners. Neither woman stated that it would be impossible to detect whether a partner has a cancer-causing type of HPV. Julia framed the risk of HPV in language that evoked stigmas about other STIs, suggesting one could recognize an infected partner because of some distinctive attribute or evidence of disease. "I would rather teach [a daughter] . . . about safe sex and choosing your partners carefully—same thing I will teach my boys, choose your partners carefully. One thing my mom said to me, when you have sex with someone, you have sex with everyone they have had sex with in terms of transmission. She said that to me when I was a teenager. That sentence was so simple and so strong that it left an impression on me. . . . So I would rather teach them to make responsible decisions than to give them a shot and bank on that and then find that the immunity wears off, or you know, the virus mutated and now it doesn't protect against what we thought it would protect against." Julia's concerns about the HPV vaccine's lack of longitudinal data did not entirely explain her hesitancy to give her sons the vaccine when it became available for them. Rather, she described her parenting principles to include raising sons who are "responsible" and teaching them to be accountable for their sexual actions. These informed her lack of interest in giving her sons Gardasil.

In contrast to implications in the media that parents feared Gardasil would promote promiscuity, the mothers' arguments revealed more nuance. Julia and Rebecca both insisted that they would deliberately educate their children about sexual health and objected to Gardasil as a prophylactic solution to what they saw as essentially a moral responsibility issue. Lindsey, who as a practicing Mormon might have been more likely to distrust the vaccine's HPV protection, embraced it without hesitation. The differences in these mothers' attitudes demonstrated that they perceived Gardasil as a *vaccine* first and that it reflected their concerns and beliefs about vaccination more generally. They were not motivated by the idea of a prophylactic to protect the sexual health of their children. For Lindsey, the mother whose religious values seemed most likely to lead her to object to a vaccine for sexual activity, her comfort with vaccines took precedence. In contrast, the mothers who objected to vaccines could not see the value of Gardasil.

Like Julia, Rebecca focused on teaching her daughter to avoid having sex with an infected partner.

> My plan is to educate my daughter and talk to her openly about sexually transmitted diseases. . . . I think my mother attempted that. . . . She preached abstinence, and that just didn't happen. I don't know. I hope to be more open with my daughter about it so that she can make better choices. . . . I will probably show her what HPV looks like. It is funny, because the boyfriend that I had at the time, I did see warts on his penis. I saw them, but I didn't know what they were. . . . In retrospect, I go, aha! That is what they were. So I will show her what it looks like so that if for some reason she is intimate with a man that has it, she could recognize it and maybe choose not to go through with having sex or definitely make sure there is a condom. . . . I can't really say that I hope she chooses someone who is clean because I thought that the guy that I was with was clean.

Rebecca saw information as power. She planned to implement this form of empowerment as she educated her daughter about how to make decisions about sexual partners. Annette had a ten-year-old daughter who had already started menstruating, but Gardasil seemed to be a vaccine for some future person that Annette did not yet know. She told me, "Were she now a teenager and thinking to be sexually active, I don't know how I would think about [Gardasil]. It would so depend on her then, her maturity and what was going on with her. I would like to . . . instill in her again respect for her body. Like make the right choices but always respect herself first and foremost." As mothers like Annette tried to imagine the choices they might make for a sexually active teenager, they failed to understand the benefit in vaccinating before their children began to engage in sexual activity. The absence of education about what Gardasil could do to protect their children's sexual health left parents uncertain about the vaccine's utility. It is possible that mothers were unwilling to disclose their attitudes about their children's future sexual selves to me. Perhaps even mothers like Julia and Rebecca, who described themselves as cultivating a positive attitude about sex, were not entirely comfortable discussing their children's sexual development. But the mothers consistently articulated objections to Gardasil as an issue related to their distrust of vaccines. They expressed their concerns about Gardasil with the same language they used to describe their feelings about other vaccines.

Hesitance about Gardasil

Mothers' skepticism about Gardasil points to clear missed opportunities for health educators and physicians who introduced the vaccine to parents. There are limitations to Gardasil's utility, but there are good reasons to vaccinate, including the prevalence of HPV and how difficult it is to prevent. The mothers' lack of clarity about HPV and its relationship to cervical cancer illustrates how confusing the science and epidemiology of HPV are. Merck's Gardasil marketing failed to fully educate the public about these complexities. Would these mothers have embraced Gardasil more readily if it had been marketed explicitly as an STI preventive? The mothers wanted to teach their children about STIs and prepare them to make responsible choices, even if they couched these lessons in inaccurate notions of how to recognize an infection. But these mothers felt strongly about vaccines and did not want to subject their children's vulnerable bodies to the penetration of a needle that could, maybe, possibly, trigger something unpredictable. Just one adverse reaction made a number of mothers hesitant to proceed with future vaccines because no one could sufficiently answer their concerns or explain why the reaction happened. An immunologist casually commented to me that we know that things work, but we don't always understand exactly how or why. When experts claim authority but cannot satisfy parents' desire to know definitively why adverse events happen, they generate distrust. Doctors might find a fever or soreness unremarkable after vaccination, but it is stressful and worrisome to the caregiver, as Mary, Lucia, and others described. Mothers' stories of the ease with which doctors dismissed their concerns remind us that the priorities of doctors and mothers are not the same and are sometimes irreconcilable. Doctors focus on what is best for a population; mothers focus on their children for whom they invest a lot of love, time, and labor.

Since conducting this research, when I get a vaccine, I think about these mothers and their reasons for vaccine skepticism. When I sat down recently for a flu shot, I had a moment of anxiety: what if this time something bad happened? It is unnerving to choose to introduce a foreign substance into one's body. What will it do to my body? How might I change? Are its benefits truly worth the moment of uncertainty? Even though I am a proponent of vaccines, the persuasive skepticism of the NaturalMoms makes me hesitate before getting my own vaccines, and when my children need vaccines it is even more stressful. Making the choice to do something feels scarier than choosing to abstain. Abstinence suggests avoidance of risk, even if that assumption is false. Abstinence is a choice, too. A refusal of vaccines makes one vulnerable to harmful viruses or bacteria. But at the moment of vaccination, exposure to disease remains some vague time in the future and it seems like an uncontrollable, mostly unknowable event. The uncertainty of future potential infection contributes to parents' competing concerns.

Mothers who do not vaccinate declare that they will not deliberately introduce what they perceive as a potentially unsafe foreign substance into their children's bodies. They assume, often correctly because of the successes of widespread immunization in the United States, that the risk of contracting a preventable illness is low enough that there is no reason to accept the small risk of an adverse reaction. These two choices, to abstain from vaccines or to deliberately expose their children to a needle, are not commensurate. They are different fears and different type of decisions. When mothers perceive that clinicians do not respect other choices they have made about their children, an experience that mothers described as delegitimizing, then why wouldn't mothers see refusing vaccines as an opportunity to make clear their distrust of unreliable authority figures? Vaccines introduce a deliberative moment when mothers can assert their expertise by saying no. Few other moments of parenting present such discrete, clear decisions.

Still, it remains unclear why Gardasil has such low utilization in the United States. The MMR vaccine has generated far more public outcry than Gardasil did, partly driven by the 1998 spurious Andrew Wakefield study. Yet the MMR vaccination rates among eligible populations far exceed Gardasil's vaccination rate. One factor that has yet to be discussed in the literature about Gardasil's low acceptance is Merck's strategy to obscure Gardasil's HPV protection. My research suggests that this has impacted the widespread use of the vaccine. The clinicians I interviewed emphasized Gardasil's cancer protection as the primary reason to receive the vaccine. Across my fieldsites, clinical staff and public health professionals consistently described the vaccine as a cancer vaccine.

The low future risk of cervical cancer contributes to mothers' lack of incentive to vaccinate. One of the reasons the NaturalMoms I interviewed refused vaccines was because of the low odds of becoming ill with a vaccine-preventable condition. Cervical cancer is a rare (enough) condition for which there exists effective, albeit imperfect, treatments. No mother addressed how few U.S. women still die from cervical cancer, but the low numbers hardly create an urgent need for Gardasil. Even though clinicians cast Gardasil as a vaccine like any other, it does not fit neatly into classic tactics used to promote vaccination. Cervical cancer simply is not comparable to other vaccine preventable diseases. Ironically, parents may not know that the risk for cervical cancer mortality remains low in the United States, and HPV is in fact a persuasive reason for parents to accept the vaccine. Merck's deliberate marketing strategies failed to convince their target audience.

9

The "Tragically
Underused" Vaccine

Despite the cancer narrative Merck used to sell its vaccine in the first five years on the market, the HPV vaccine has not become a commonly used vaccine in the United States. In January 2016, the National Cancer Institute–designated Cancer Centers issued a consensus statement "urging" that the HPV vaccine be used to prevent cancer. The statement described the low rates of vaccination "as a serious public health threat. HPV vaccination represents a rare opportunity to prevent many cases of cancer that is tragically underused. As national leaders in cancer research and clinical care, we are compelled to jointly issue this call to action."[1] The language of the National Cancer Institute Cancer Centers' consensus statement echoed the language used in a 2014 report to the U.S. president encouraging an increased investment in HPV vaccination. As the report's authors described in their letter introducing the report, "Low vaccination rates reveal countless missed opportunities to prevent cancers and other serious diseases. HPV vaccines are underused not only in the U.S. but around the world. The Panel finds this a serious threat to progress against cancer. We are confident that vaccine uptake can be increased dramatically, starting now, if HPV vaccination is made a public health priority by many different organizations. We believe there is the will to do that."[2] In another example of HPV vaccine promotion, the CDC shared one physician's recommendations for encouraging vaccination, which the CDC titled "Top 10 List for HPV #VaxSuccess," to help other doctors reach the high rates of HPV immunization this doctor's practice had achieved.[3] While I was finishing this book, an article in the *Wall Street Journal* proclaimed that providers should adopt new strategies to promote the HPV vaccine.[4] Immunization promotion strategies have existed long before Gardasil, but these public health interventions suggest that clinicians and parents need new ways to think about the HPV vaccine.

These statements, taken individually or together, are strange. In his 2014 opinion editorial, Dr. Paul Offit, a leading vaccine researcher and advocate, titled his piece "Let's Not Talk About Sex," perpetuating and encouraging the invisibility of sex and sexual contact as the means of HPV transmission. The silence (let's not talk) and the speaking (what will you say) produce the affective states of urgency and concern. The moral imperative to vaccinate is not about knowledge or education, but rather a narrow emphasis on vaccination as the only real solution to the (hyped) threat of cervical cancer. Proposing a purportedly novel tactic, officials encouraged doctors *not* to talk about sex, as though clinicians were emphasizing sex whenever they introduced the HPV vaccine to parents. This strategy is not innovative. Health officials and clinicians have always cast the HPV vaccine as a narrative about cancer. What that narrative has never been about is HPV. The cancer narrative partly explains why the media, clinicians, and public health campaigns have rarely invoked sex, despite the fact that HPV infection is the most persuasive reason to vaccinate in the United States.

Merck has directly shaped and informed public comprehension of HPV, cervical cancer, and the promise of a cancer vaccine. This is a shame. Although I was not surprised by the pervasiveness of pharmaceutical company advertising or the pharma-sponsored components of the health education events I attended over the years, they were impossible to ignore. They were truly everywhere: the word "Gardasil" that was stamped on the pen that Mira, the director of a California city's Office of Women's Health, used; the pharma-funded lunches at the meetings of the southern California immunization coalition; the pharmaceutical company-subsidized lunch at the low-income clinic where Drs. Gonzalez, Santana, and Grayson worked; the pharmaceutical companies' sponsored events at the CDC's National Immunization Conference; the various free items included in the CCG's conference materials; the request for an honorarium from an older physician at the low-income clinic, revealing his assumption that such a fee was his due because pharma honoraria have historically been common. Each time I visited patient advocacy and women's health websites for this research, corporate sponsorship from pharmaceutical and medical diagnostic companies adorned the bottom of the pages.[5] The CCG's public service announcement in a women's fashion magazine was dominated by an intrusive message from Merck. Pharmaceutical corporations were so omnipresent that I have a hard time thinking of places where they *weren't*.

Many social scientists have demonstrated the ubiquity and influence of pharmaceutical corporations, yet new examples continue to proliferate.[6] Merck's strategies for disseminating information about Gardasil illustrate how much our conceptions of health, wellness, risk, and disease are designed by those who stand to make money when we absorb and act upon these ideas. What we know and how we know trace back to deliberate market creation by corporations. However, it is not simply the corporate production of information that shapes how we experience and understand our health, as individuals and as members of a larger public. The messages corporations disseminate become embedded in our politics, our cultural beliefs, and our public health practices. They become systemic. In the decade since Gardasil has become available, disparate actors have adopted Merck marketers' framing of HPV and have failed to challenge the corporately-shaped knowledge.

Merck marketed Gardasil as though new interventions and scientific discoveries will necessarily produce better health outcomes and a better quality of life. Among the problems with this assumption that technology is always an unqualified good, this optimism neglected persistent racial disparities in U.S. cervical cancer mortality rates. Further, betterness has prescriptive qualities, as we can see in Gardasil's advertisements over time.

Held in a State of Anticipation

The speculative discourse of anticipatory regimes imposes a dominant moral economy, brought to bear through a variety of methods that aspire toward this imagined "better" future.[7] Ten years after the marketing launch of quadrivalent Gardasil, Merck has intensified its portrayals of vulnerable future bodies with its "Know HPV" advertisements and their retrospective montages of young people who now have HPV-related cancer. Merck's earlier advertisements emphasized informing the public about the existence of HPV and preventive strategies to keep HPV at bay. In those advertisements, parents declared that they had chosen to protect their children. The doubling down in Merck's "new approach," which is hardly new, calls attention to failure, an emotionally charged warning. The tropes of commodified female empowerment to sell a pharmaceutical product have failed to sell the vaccine, and thus the marketers have shifted to an emphasis on parental responsibility now that Gardasil is approved for boys and girls.[8]

Instead of engaging with the concerns and needs of families that might consider Gardasil, Merck's story of bodies at risk persists and has been amplified from the incredulous "Cancer, caused by a virus?!" to young adults wondering why they had to get cancer. But these narratives ignore the continued inequities in medical management of HPV-related cancers: the oft-cited numbers of how many U.S. women die from cervical cancer obscured *whose* bodies continue to suffer most from cervical cancer mortality.[9] The anticipatory regimes Merck created with its advertisements for Gardasil have served to distract the public from unresolved inequities in access to and delivery of health care in the United States. New technologies may fail to address or simply ignore these inequalities. Few have asked what Gardasil will *not* change in gynecological care or why HPV screening is promoted for females and not for males.[10] However, it is the inequality revealed in the unacceptably high death rates from cervical cancer among black women and other women of color in the United States that should trouble us most. Gardasil's availability has done little to alter social, cultural, and economic inequities in gynecological health practices in the United States or abroad.

When the "Know HPV" advertisements first came out, I felt as though I were watching a parody advertisement I would have created to go along with this book. Yes, of course, I thought, this ad hits so many elements of the earlier ads, now condensed and imbued with heightened emotions. Perversely, the ad is not a parody. I also observed these newer advertisements from a different perspective from the one during my earlier research. In 2006, I was just barely too old for Gardasil. My friends and I had had intimate experiences with abnormal Pap smears and, for some of us, biopsies and the anxieties tied to semi-regular screenings. Now I am a parent who vaccinates more or less according to standard schedules and who will one day decide about Gardasil for my children.[11] The HPV ads have matured along with their audiences; they now target parents' nostalgia and use a blatantly emotional appeal to garner sales. Childhood vaccines invoke anticipatory logics—needles are presented, causing momentary pain for a (hopefully) lasting protection against a more serious harm that is not necessarily inevitable, but why risk it? Gardasil has been marketed with massive campaigns that focus on anxieties and future disease imaginaries. In many ways, Gardasil ought not to have merited much resistance; it should have been another childhood vaccine among many. Gardasil is not different. And yet it is.

Gardasil Today and Tomorrow

The policy debates in the years immediately after the FDA approved Gardasil have had a notable effect on current Gardasil immunization rates. A variety of officials urged clinicians and parents to view Gardasil as no different from other pediatric immunizations. Studies that analyze why parents and eligible young adults have yet to accept the HPV vaccine suggest the stigma CCG members sought to erase has not fully disappeared.[12] Clinicians report that they are uncomfortable promoting a vaccine for sexual behavior, and parents seem to believe that *their* children do not need the vaccine.[13] Thus, immunization proponents encourage clinicians to deemphasize Gardasil's role as a prophylactic against an STI and instead focus on it as a preventive tool. Since I conducted the core research for this book, Gardasil received FDA approval for boys. In December 2014, the FDA approved a newer more comprehensive vaccine, Gardasil 9, which protects against nine types of HPV, including seven HPV types that cause cancer. Do the critiques and analyses presented here still hold? Do people still imagine Gardasil as a gendered intervention?

The most recent data on Gardasil uptake in adolescents 13–17 show how much Gardasil coverage differs from the uptake of other vaccines. HPV vaccination rates lag behind the rate of previously controversial vaccines, such as the MMR, polio, or pertussis vaccines.[14] In a recent study based on 2013 data, more than 90 percent of the sample population had received the MMR vaccine, but only 57 percent of females had received at least one dose of the HPV vaccine. For individuals who had completed the three-dose series, the HPV vaccination rate was even lower.[15] More than 75 percent of the population had received the meningococcal vaccine, a less notorious and perhaps less well-known vaccine. The percentages of girls (37.6) and boys (13.9) who received all three doses of Gardasil stand out as distinctively low.[16] In 2016, the ACIP published guidelines that attempted to solve the failure of patients to complete all three doses of the vaccine. The ACIP has recommended that children aged 9–14 receive only two shots of Gardasil 9.[17] However, Gardasil has suffered doubly from its categorization as a vaccine and its association with an STI. Merck's marketing of it as a cancer preventive undermined public trust because the emphasis on cancer did not tell the whole story of the vaccine.

While protection from cancer is a persuasive reason to receive the vaccine, so are the related HPV morbidities. In 2009 at a Commonwealth Club panel, Dr. Joel Palefsky, a leading HPV researcher, emphasized Gardasil's ability to prevent HPV-related morbidity as the real value of the vaccine: "In this country, cancer rates are low . . . which isn't to say the vaccine isn't valuable. [We need] to recognize its primary value is here [in the United States], which is the prevention of the morbidity and the procedures and the stigmas in the treatment of genital warts and cancer precursors. . . . In the developing world it is a whole other story."[18] Studies have shown that greater HPV knowledge correlates with higher rates of Gardasil acceptance; in other words, education about HPV can influence willingness to vaccinate.[19] Merck made a mistake by not better educating the U.S. population about HPV's ubiquity. While we might not expect Merck to put public service over profits, the health officials and clinicians who are committed to the well-being of the public have a responsibility to educate people about the vaccine's benefits and to ensure that the public knows how common HPV is.

Women's confusion about HPV and its association with cervical cancer persists.[20] When clinicians insist that "this is a vaccine that kills cancer. No matter what you hear in the media, it kills cancer, a hundred percent of the time," as Dr. Grayson told me, or when clinicians suggest, as Dr. Gonzalez did, that faith in science is enough to motivate anyone to vaccinate, we have real problems with the dissemination of health care information. Merck has acknowledged that it crafted its current marketing strategy to address parents' low awareness of the relationship between HPV and cancer.[21] The company has yet to indicate that it seeks to improve comprehension beyond the fundamental connection between HPV and cancer. There remains much to educate the public about, including the fact that both men and women can develop HPV-related cancers.

The marketing of Gardasil and the subsequent debates about it point to how information gets manipulated by various interests. These manipulations have long-term consequences. If we are to persuade skeptics of the value of new medical interventions, we need new methods. One of the first steps is to challenge the messages that pharmaceutical companies produce. When we allow the slogans crafted by corporate marketers to define the discourse, when we fail to question the information (or lack thereof) in the ads of pharmaceutical companies, we become complicit in the spread of misinformation. It is possible to recognize the value of pharmaceutical products and remain critical of their marketing and distribution.

Faith and Disillusionment

Dr. Gonzalez, whom we met in Chapter 4, invoked the power of science and faith in medicine's revolutionary potential. Yet for me, this story is about the *loss* of faith. An HPV vaccine promised to be an important advancement in women's health. It promised to protect women, and eventually men, against a virus that we can do nothing to prevent, an invasive virus that may turn fatal. While the HPV vaccine does provide these benefits, the misinformation associated with the marketing of that vaccine highlights deeper problems with health care interventions that are commodities first and public goods second (or third). In response to the low uptake of HPV vaccines, clinicians and public health professionals continue to laud the vaccine, hoping to convert those who have chosen not to use it, but the "new" tactics vaccine proponents have suggested do not appear to alter past strategies. On the Seattle Children's Hospital's website, a weblog written by Dr. Swanson, a physician who calls herself "Seattle Mama Doc," begins with praise for the HPV vaccine and reassures parents: "Great news about reducing cancer risk. Nothing controversial here."[22] But is it controversy that has prevented the vaccine from gaining broader public use? Dr. Swanson's cheerful reassurance that the vaccine is "nothing controversial" reveals her defensive position. Although Gardasil generated controversy, advocates of the HPV vaccine consistently miss critical sources of parental distrust: Merck's attempts to impact policy in state legislatures;

the health community's emphasis on this vaccine as a revolutionary way to fight a cancer that few parents considered relevant for their preteen children; and perhaps even Merck's lack of honesty about the etiology of HPV and what HPV-related cancer risks are for most of the U.S. population. Neither Merck nor health officials offered straightforward guidance that HPV is everywhere; that most sexually active individuals will get the infection sometime in their lifetime; that we don't have good ways to prevent it; that it can lead to invasive interventions; that we don't test men; that it can cause a variety of cancers, not just cervical cancer; and that the vaccine will help protect our children from getting the infection in the first place. Instead, Gardasil's semi-duplicitous marketing strategy undermined the potential good that widespread vaccination against HPV might offer.

Invoking cancer is a scare tactic, not a health education strategy. The juxtaposition in the various iterations of Gardasil advertisements of the word "cancer" and the message "you can do something" put parents in a blameworthy position. The current advertisements for Gardasil 9 hardly mention the vaccine. Instead, in these ads children blame their parents for their failure to protect them from a potentially fatal illness. Parents, and mothers in particular, receive so many messages about their duty to be responsible and to manage their children's bodies diligently. This is where the position of vaccine resisters seems quite reasonable. The parents who choose a slower schedule or who choose not to vaccinate according to the pediatric schedule demonstrate an alternative interpretation of compliance: they believe they are being responsible. They choose not to leave decisions about their children's health to experts whose priorities are much broader than the particular needs of individual children. Vaccine resistances can be refusals informed by careful deliberation and heightened conscientiousness about the health needs of children. The logic of those decisions may be flawed, but the decisions are not made lightly. Julia questioned what she interpreted as other parents' blind acceptance of clinical requirements: "Other moms with babies the same age as my kids, they will say, 'Oh, I just went to the doctor and she got her four shots today. Oh, my gosh, it was so painful.' I will say, 'Which ones did she get?' 'Oh, I don't know, whichever ones were due today.'" One reason why Gardasil uptake rates are so low may be due to the moral imperative health officials call upon parents (mothers) to exercise: to make the right choices for their children. To refuse a vaccine that has been marketed with a disingenuous strategy can be interpreted as reasonable skepticism. Refusal then can be cast in the language of participation, perhaps not yielding the outcome officials wish, but a different interpretation than ignorance or disengagement.

The Gardasil story calls attention to how pharmaceutical companies commercialize health concerns and present inaccurate marketing messages about health. The low rates of Gardasil use in the U.S. reveal something more than just fears of nascent adolescent sexuality. In this case, Merck's marketing choices fostered distrust of the source. Merck is now in the position of trying to sell a product for which there is little demand. Gardasil is primarily a vaccine for HPV, not for cervical cancer. Would Gardasil have elicited similar resistance had it been marketed for what it is? Imagining a counterfactual set of circumstances is perhaps a hollow endeavor, and it is likely that marketing it as a vaccine for the most common STI would have also generated a host of objections. But what if Merck had waited to submit it for FDA review until their data for boys were adequate? What if Merck had waited to promote policy interventions for several years after FDA approval, when they would have had a better understanding of how parents and legislators perceived the vaccine? What if Merck's top priority had been to improve the health of the next generation of young men and women? These potential directions for what Gardasil *could* have been do not seem unreasonable standards by which to judge new products and procedures related to sexual health. What if a useful tool for battling one of the leading causes of mortality for women globally were not so prohibitively expensive? In these questions and in these imagined uses of the vaccine we can see the opportunities that were missed and whose interests were prioritized. In the United States, health care products are made by corporations who pursue their own interests. This doesn't mean that they do not lead to important advancements in health care. What matters is how these innovations come into the world and how they are promoted.

Acknowledgments

I could not have persevered with this project without the support and encouragement of many wonderful people.

I am grateful for the institutional and intellectual resources I received from the faculty at the Department of Anthropology at Johns Hopkins University. Jane Guyer provided incisive feedback throughout my time at the university. Veena Das's wisdom, perspective, and intellectual depths have had a deep impact on my work. Jonathan Ellen offered insight over the years and many times kept me on track, for which I will always be appreciative. Lori Leonard and Clara Han provided essential guidance and suggestions as this work evolved.

The support and intellectual camaraderie of my colleagues at Johns Hopkins have provided meaningful insights and advice through all stages of the project. Sameena Mulla's warm and astute critiques helped me clarify my thinking. Lauren Heidbrink merits more gratitude than I can articulate adequately here. She has been a constant across the years and the sagas, and I am so fortunate to have her support and generosity. Abigail Lance-DeVos's attention to philosophical and intellectual issues have enriched the text. Her generous friendship and care have sustained me. I feel lucky to have met such thoughtful and engaging women along the way.

Hadley Leach's labor and love pervade this text. This book would not have come to fruition without her perspectives, patience, and friendship.

Loring Pfeiffer provided one of the most detailed and reflective responses to the book in its early stage, and I thank her for being my idealized and actual reader. I am greatly indebted to William Muraskin for the wisdom and expertise he has shared with me over the years. Avi Brisman offered clever and provocative strategies in the early days of this project, and I appreciate his continued support of my work. Christine Holmberg has supported me through various stages in my career, and I am grateful for her invitation to the Vaccination, Society, and Politics Conference at the Charité Universitätsmedizin in Berlin in 2011, which helped me transform this project into the book it has become. I am lucky to have met a lifelong friend whose work has overlapped with mine in various ways but whose current employment requires that he remain anonymous. We bonded over our shared cynicism and skepticism in the early days of public health school, and I thank him for providing me with epidemiological perspectives on HPV, vaccines, and for reminding me not to get carried away with anthropologizing. I thank Emma Tsui, Laura Fanucchi, Fang Cai, Suzanne Jung Angell, Meridel Tobias, Cas McGee, Corey Datz-Greenberg, Kim Woodhouse, Sasha Hauswald, Forest and Brent Large, Jessica Watson, Shannon Smith-Bernadin, Susan Shennon, Jennifer Merin, Abigail Arons, Wendy Eberhart, Toby Sanderson, Caterina Rindi, Jesica Brennan, Nicoleta Timofti, Sarah Bennett (aka SB), and Rachel Sitkin Marks for the intellectual stimulation, fun, and emotional support they have provided over the years. Thanks also to Ramah McKay and Aviva Sinervo, who offered thoughtful feedback on earlier versions of this work.

At Rutgers University Press, Marlie Wasserman helped make this book a reality. I am incredibly fortunate to have had her as my champion. Kimberly Guinta's enthusiasm when she took over Marlie's role has made these later stages almost pleasurable. I thank the three anonymous reviewers whose encouragement and reflective criticisms have informed and improved the book immensely. Alissa Zarro's patience and dedicated efforts deserve public recognition. Kate Babbitt's editing has made this book even more itself. All errors, however, are mine alone.

This work was supported in its early stages with generous funding by the Wenner-Gren Foundation (2007), the National Science Foundation Science and Society Division (2007), and the Johns Hopkins University Women, Gender and Sexuality Summer Fellowship (2007).

This book could not exist without the generosity of my interlocutors, although I have not named all of them here. Their time, the perspectives they shared, and the help they gave me with fieldwork in venues that were often difficult to navigate will not be forgotten. One individual, to whom I refer as Lucy in this book, gave me invaluable access to a large county public health department. The time we worked together left me with a lasting impression of her commitment to sexual health and to remedying sexual inequalities. Although we are no longer in touch, I think of her and continue to admire her persistence and her wry insights.

My father, Richard Gottlieb, patiently read earlier versions of this work and supported me in myriad ways to bring this book to fruition. I hope to be half the parent and human being he is. My stepfather, Tim Webster, has helped make this book possible through all his labor, cross-country travels, love, and grandparenting. Childcare providers who work behind the scenes are too often made invisible, yet they are indispensable to parents who work. We have been lucky to encounter Arlette Earwood, Alida Ngollo, Delilah Paskowitz, Ruby Rogers, Justa Barrios, Naima Zarguit, Julia Colton, Courtney Duffy, and the loving teachers at Rockridge Little School and the French Maternal School.

This work has spanned lifetimes and life phases. The company of my children and their curiosity and enthusiasm about the world remind me of the importance of research and intellectual endeavors. Finally, but most essentially, Sean-Michael has absorbed the chaos, mostly, and nourished me throughout the many stages of this project. There is no one else with whom I'd rather do all the things.

Notes

Chapter 1—Introduction

1   As of January 2017, both advertisements could be viewed on a television commercial analytics website: https://www.ispot.tv/ad/Ap1V/merck-hpv-vaccination#.

2   Laurie McGinley, "Cancer Doctors Leading Campaign to Boost Use of HPV Vaccine," *Washington Post*, June 19, 2016; Lydia Ramsey, "A Shocking New Ad Is Shaming Parents for Not Giving Their Children This Unpopular Vaccine," *Business Insider*, July 15, 2016.

3   Vincanne Adams, Michelle Murphy, and Adele E. Clarke, "Anticipation: Technoscience, Life, Affect, Temporality," *Subjectivity* 28, no. 1 (2009): 251.

4   Ibid.

5   Robert Aronowitz, *Risky Medicine: Our Quest to Cure Fear and Uncertainty* (Chicago: University of Chicago Press, 2015), 96.

6   Adams, Murphy, and Clarke, "Anticipation," 249.

7   I use the term African American to reflect the language Lucy's public health department used to categorize a population at risk. Throughout the text, I use the terms the individuals I interviewed use to refer to themselves or to populations they manage.

8   In January 2017, Beavis, Gravitt, and Rositch published findings that corrected for past inclusions of women with hysterectomies in cervical cancer mortality data. They demonstrated that the mortality rate for cervical cancer among black women in the United States is more than double the rate for white women. Black women's mortality rates due to cervical cancer had been underestimated by more than 40 percent (Anna L. Beavis, Patti E. Gravitt, and Anne F. Rositch, "Hysterectomy-Corrected Cervical Cancer Mortality Rates Reveal a Larger Racial Disparity in the United States," *Cancer* 123, no. 6 (2017): 1044–1050).

9   Elisa J. Sobo, Arianna Huhn, Autumn Sannwald, and Lori Thurman, "Information Curation among Vaccine Cautious Parents: Web 2.0, Pinterest Thinking, and Pediatric Vaccination Choice," *Medical Anthropology* 35, no. 6 (2016): 529–546;

Anna Kirkland, "The Legitimacy of Vaccine Critics: What Is Left After the Autism Hypothesis?" *Journal of Health Politics, Policy and Law* 37, no. 1 (2012): 69–97; Melissa Leach and James Fairhead, *Vaccine Anxieties: Global Science, Child Health and Society* (Abingdon: Earthscan, 2007).

10   Shannon Stokley, Jenny Jeyarajah, David Yankey, Maria Cano, Julianne Gee, Jill Roark, R. C. Curtis, and Lauri Markowitz, "Human Papillomavirus Vaccination Coverage among Adolescents, 2007–2013, and Postlicensure Vaccine Safety Monitoring, 2006–2014—United States," *Morbidity and Mortality Weekly Report* 63, no. 29 (2014): 620–624.

11   McGinley, "Cancer Doctors Leading Campaign to Boost Use of HPV Vaccine"; Paul A. Offit, "Let's Not Talk about Sex," *New York Times*, August 19, 2014.

12   Adams, Murphy and Clarke, "Anticipation."

13   Irving Kenneth Zola, "Medicine as an Institution of Social Control," *Sociological Review* 20, no. 4 (1972): 502.

14   Adele E. Clarke, Janet K. Shim, Laura Mamo, Jennifer Ruth Fosket, and Jennifer R. Fishman, "Biomedicalization: Technoscientific Transformations of Health, Illness, and U.S. Biomedicine," *American Sociological Review* 68, no. 2 (2003): 162.

15   Stokley et al., "Human Papillomavirus Vaccination Coverage among Adolescents."

16   Laurie McGinley, "Do the New Merck HPV Ads Guilt-Trip Parents or Tell Hard Truths? Both," *Washington Post*, August 11, 2016.

17   Advisory Committee on Immunization Practices, "Quadrivalent Human Papillomavirus Vaccine," *Morbidity and Mortality Weekly Report* 56 (2007): 1–24.

18   Catriona Kennedy, Carol Gray Bunton, and Rhona Hogg, "'Just that Little Bit of Doubt': Scottish Parents', Teenage Girls' and Health Professionals' Views of the MMR, H1N1 and HPV Vaccines," *International Society of Behavioral Medicine* 21 (2014): 3–10.

19   Laura Mamo and Steven Epstein, "The Pharmaceuticalization of Sexual Risk: Vaccine Development and the New Politics of Cancer Prevention," *Social Science & Medicine* 101 (2014): 160.

20   See, for example, Janet G. Baseman and Laura A. Koutsky, "The Epidemiology of Human Papillomavirus Infections," *Journal of Clinical Virology* 32 (2005): 16–24.

21   Maura L. Gillison, Wayne M. Koch, Randolph B. Capone, Michael Spafford, William H. Westra, Li Wu, Marianna L. Zahurak, Richard W Daniel, Michael Viglione and David E. Symer, "Evidence for a Causal Association between Human Papillomavirus and a Subset of Head and Neck Cancers," *Journal of the National Cancer Institute* 92, no 9 (2000): 709–720.

22   Centers for Disease Control and Prevention, "STD Facts—Human Papillomavirus (HPV)," *Centers for Disease Control and Prevention*, http://www.cdc.gov/std/hpv/stdfact-hpv.htm, accessed February 4, 2014.

23   Maura L. Gillison, Tatevik Broutian, Robert K. L. Pickard, Zhen-yue Tong, Weihong Xiao, Lisa Kahle, Barry I. Graubard, and Anil K. Chaturvedi, "Prevalence of Oral HPV Infection in the United States, 2009–2010," *JAMA* 307, no. 7 (2012): 693–703; Gypsyamber D'Souza, Aimee R. Kreimer, Raphael Viscidi, Michael Pawlita, Carole Fakhry, Wayne M. Koch, William H. Westra, and Maura L. Gillison, "Case-Control Study of Human Papillomavirus and Oropharyngeal Cancer," *New England Journal of Medicine* 356, no. 19 (2007): 1944–1956.

24 Luiz Antonio Teixeiera and Ilana Löwy, "Imperfect Tools for a Difficult Job: Colposcopy, 'Colpocytology,' and Screening for Cervical Cancer in Brazil," *Social Studies of Science* 41, no. 4 (2011): 585–608.

25 Malcolm Griffiths, "Nuns, Virgins, and Spinsters: Rigoni-Stern and Cervical Cancer Revisited," *BJOG: An International Journal of Obstetrics & Gynaecology* 98, no. 8 (1991): 797–802.

26 "Influenza Is Caused by a Virus, not a Bacterium," *The Rockefeller University*, 2010, http://centennial.rucares.org/index.php?page=Influenza, accessed April 9, 2014.

27 Donald G. McNeil Jr., "How a Vaccine Search Ended in Triumph," *New York Times*, August 29, 2006.

28 Harald zur Hausen, "Human Genital Cancer: Synergism Between Two Virus Infections or Synergism Between a Virus Infection and Initiating Events?" *The Lancet*, December 18, 1982: 1370–1372.

29 Baseman and Koutsky, "The Epidemiology of Human Papillomavirus Infections."

30 One cause of cervical cancer is exposure to chemicals. There is evidence that women and fetuses exposed to diethylstilbestrol (DES) have a high incidence of cervical cancer. DES is no longer given to women.

31 Until Gargano et al. published 2013–2014 data on the prevalence of HPV infection in men, all male data were estimates based on small datasets of male HPV prevalence. See Julia W Gargano, Elizabeth R Unger, Gui Liu, Martin Steinau, Elissa Meites, Eileen Dunne and Lauri E Markowitz, "Prevalence of Genital Human Papillomavirus in Males, United States, 2013—2014," *Journal of Infectious Diseases* 215, no 7 (2017): 1070–1079.

32 F. Xavier Bosch and Silvia De Sanjosé, "Human Papillomavirus and Cervical Cancer Burden and Assessment of Causality," *JNCI Monographs* 2003, no. 31 (2003): 6.

33 Ibid.; Nubia Muñoz, F. Xavier Bosch, Silvia de Sanjosé, Rolando Herrero, Xavier Castellsagué, Keerti V. Shah, Peter J. F. Snijders, and Chris J. L. M. Meijer, "Epidemiologic Classification of Human Papillomavirus Types Associated with Cervical Cancer," *New England Journal of Medicine* 348, no. 6 (2003): 518–527; Udani Samarasekera and Richard Horton, "Women's Cancers: Shining a Light on a Neglected Health Inequity," *The Lancet* 389, no. 10071 (2016): 771–773.

34 International Agency for Research on Cancer, "Globocan 2012: Estimated Cancer Incidence, Mortality and Prevention Worldwide," *International Agency for Research on Cancer*, http://globocan.iarc.fr/Pages/fact_sheets_cancer.aspx, accessed November 3, 2016.

35 Bosch and De Sanjosé, "Human Papillomavirus and Cervical Cancer Burden and Assessment of Causality," 6.

36 L. W. Musselwhite, C. M. Oliveira, T. Kwaramba, N. de Paula Pantano, J. S. Smith, J. H. Fregnani, R. M. Reis, E. Mauad, F. L. Vazquez, and A. Longatto-Filho, "Racial/Ethnic Disparities in Cervical Cancer Screening and Outcomes," *Acta Cytologica* 60, no. 6 (2016): 518–526.

37 Eduardo L. Franco, Salaheddin M. Mahmud, Joseph Tot, Alex Ferenczy, and François Coutlée, "The Expected Impact of HPV Vaccination on the Accuracy of Cervical Cancer Screening: The Need for a Paradigm Change," *Archives of Medical Research* 40, no. 6 (2009): 482.

38 The data did not distinguish between women who had a full hysterectomy, preventing them from developing cervical cancer, and those who had a partial hysterectomy, leaving the cervix intact. The authors note that partial hysterectomies account

for less than 2 percent of U.S. hysterectomies, and therefore they do not believe the lack of stratification has a significant impact on their findings. See Anne F. Rositch, Rebecca G. Nowak, and Patti E. Gravitt, "Increased Age and Race-Specific Incidence of Cervical Cancer after Correction for Hysterectomy Prevalence in the United States from 2000 to 2009," *Cancer* 120, no. 13 (2014): 2032–2038.

39   Beavis et al., "Hysterectomy-Corrected Cervical Cancer Mortality Rates Reveal a Larger Racial Disparity in the United States."

40   Ibid.

41   Patricia Jeudin, Elizabeth Liveright, Marcela G. del Carmen, and Rebecca B. Perkins, "Race, Ethnicity and Income as Factors for HPV Vaccine Acceptance and Use," *Human Vaccines & Immunotherapeutics* 9, no. 7 (2013): 1413.

42   National Cancer Institute, "Cancer Disparities," *National Cancer Institute*, https://www.cancer.gov/about-cancer/understanding/disparities, accessed January 17, 2017; Rebecca L. Siegel, Kimberly D. Miller, and Ahmedin Jemal, "Cancer Statistics, 2016," *CA: A Cancer Journal for Clinicians* 66, no. 1 (2016): 7–30.

43   Ibid.

44   Aronowitz points out that this may reflect an increase in hysterectomies among U.S. women after World War II, but he supports the value of cervical screening and sees it as linked to the decline in cervical cancer. Aronowitz, *Risky Medicine*, 243n13.

45   Gillison et al., "Prevalence of Oral HPV Infection in the United States, 2009–2010"; Maura L. Gillison, Wayne M. Koch, Randolph B. Capone, Michael Spafford, William H. Westra, Li Wu, Marianna L. Zahurak, Richard W. Daniel, Michael Viglione, and David E. Symer, "Evidence for a Causal Association between Human Papillomavirus and a Subset of Head and Neck Cancers," *Journal of the National Cancer Institute* 92, no. 9 (2000): 709–720.

46   Ahmedin Jemal, Freddie Bray, Melissa M. Center, Jacques Ferlay, Elizabeth Ward, and David Forman, "Global Cancer Statistics," *CA: A Cancer Journal for Clinicians* 61, no. 2 (2011): 69–90; Ophira Ginsburg, Freddie Bray, Michel P. Coleman, Verna Vanderpuye, Alexandru Eniu, S Rani Kotha, Malabika Sarker, et al., "The Global Burden of Women's Cancers: A Grand Challenge in Global Health," *The Lancet* 389, no. 10071 (2016): 847–860.

47   Muñoz et al., "Epidemiologic Classification of Human Papillomavirus Types Associated with Cervical Cancer." The quadrivalent vaccine protects against HPV 6, HPV 11, HPV 16 and HPV 18. The FDA approved a new vaccine in December 2014, eight years after the approval for the quadrivalent vaccine that was the focus of this study. This newer vaccine, Gardasil 9, includes protection against more types of HPV. Despite the update to the vaccine, the arguments made in this book still hold.

48   Fouzieyha Towghi, "The Biopolitics of Reproductive Technologies beyond the Clinic: Localizing HPV Vaccines in India," *Medical Anthropology* 32, no. 4 (2013): 325–342. Although pharmaceutical companies often identify the markets for their products based on epidemiological data, they also develop products based on other criteria, such as imagined market share. At one meeting I attended in 2010 while working as a pharmaceutical consultant, a biotech client discussed how to create the demand for the product they had developed, even though there was no formal clinical need for their drug. The client asked my boss how she would position their new drug given the absence of a diagnostic category for their product.

49 The 2010 Affordable Care Act has changed this landscape, as cervical cancer screening and the HPV vaccine are both part of preventive health care services. However, women still need to seek out care. Thus, the barriers are not just about affordability but also reflect cultural and social phenomena. Kevin A. Henry, Antoinette M Stroup, Echo L. Warner, and Deanna Kepka, "Geographic Factors and Human Papillomavirus (HPV) Vaccination Initiation among Adolescent Girls in the United States," *Cancer Epidemiology Biomarkers & Prevention* 25, no. 2 (2016): 309–317. Political changes due to the 2016 U.S. elections suggest that the advances made in women's health care during the Obama presidency may also be rolled back.

50 Centers for Disease Control and Prevention, "2013 Cancer Types Grouped by Race and Ethnicity," *Centers for Disease Control and Prevention*, https://nccd.cdc.gov/uscs/cancersbyraceandethnicity.aspx.

51 Harold P. Freeman and Barbara K. Wingrove, *Excess Cervical Cancer Mortality: A Marker for Low Access to Health Care in Poor Communities: An Analysis* (Rockville, MD: National Cancer Institute, Center to Reduce Cancer Health Disparities, 2005); National Cancer Institute, "Cancer Health Disparities—National Cancer Institute," *National Cancer Institute*, March 11, 2008, http://www.cancer.gov/cancertopics/factsheet/disparities/cancer-health-disparities, accessed February 6, 2014.

52 Matthew G. Mazzefa to GSKDirect Customers, August 18, 2016, available at https://www.gskdirect.com/medias/GSKDirect-Cervarix-Tip-Lok-Syringe-Discontinuation-8.18.2016.pdf?context=bWFzdGVyfHJvb3R8OTgiNDB8YX BwbGljYXRpb24vcGRmfGhmMi90YTUvODgoMTAyNTM4ODU3NC5w ZGZ8NmE4NzUzYWUwMzYwMTE0Mjg2NmRhMmMwODQwOTY1Y TA1ZDQ3YjliMGZlODY2ZmYwOGE5ZmU3YmEyODQxOTFjOA, accessed November 2, 2016.

53 This work is not directly analyzed here, but it informs the analysis of public health officials' conversations about and aspirations for the HPV vaccine.

54 The only real names that appear in this book are Merck representatives, the medical director of the Los Angeles Unified School District, and a few public figures, such as Dr. Paul Offit and Jenny McCarthy. To protect the confidentiality of my fieldwork participants, I have changed the names of anyone I interviewed or observed.

55 He wrote, "We may want to make sure she actually is a graduate student at JHU. . . . Let me know." Carlos A. Sattler to Richard M. Haupt, e-mail, April 19, 2006.

56 J. Waller, K. McCaffery, S. Forrest, A. Szarewski, L. Cadman, and J. Wardle, "Awareness of Human Papillomavirus among Women Attending a Well Woman Clinic," *Sexually Transmitted Infections* 79, no. 4 (2003): 320–322; Ellen M. Daley, Karen Kay M. Perrin, Cheryl Vamos, Candace Webb, Trish Mueller, Jennifer L. Packing-Ebuen, Holly L. Rayko, Mary McFarlane, and Robert J. McDermott, "HPV Knowledge among HPV+ Women," *American Journal of Health Behavior* 32, no. 5 (2008): 477–487; Nidhi Jain, Gary L. Euler, Abigail Shefer, Pengjun Lu, David Yankey, and Lauri Markowitz, "Human Papillomavirus (HPV) Awareness and Vaccination Initiation among Women in the United States, National Immunization Survey—Adult 2007," *Preventive Medicine* 48, no. 5 (2009): 426–431; Stefanie J. Klug, Meike Hukelmann, and Maria Blettner, "Knowledge about Infection with Human Papillomavirus: A Systematic Review," *Preventive Medicine* 46, no. 2 (2008): 87–98; John S. Luque, Heide Castañeda, Dinorah Martinez Tyson, Natalia Vargas, Sara Proctor, and Cathy D. Meade, "HPV Awareness among Latina Immigrants and

Anglo-American Women in the Southern United States: Cultural Models of Cervical Cancer Risk Factors and Beliefs," *NAPA Bulletin* 34, no. 1 (2010): 84–104; Laura A. V. Marlow, Gregory D. Zimet, Kirsten J. McCaffery, Remo Ostini, and Jo Waller, "Knowledge of Human Papillomavirus (HPV) and HPV Vaccination: An International Comparison," *Vaccine* 31, no. 5 (2013): 763–769.

Chapter 2—Imminent Vulnerability and Commodified Empowerment

1 Laura Mamo, Amber Nelson, and Aleia Clark, "Producing and Protecting Risky Girlhoods," in *Three Shots at Prevention*, edited by Keith Wailoo, Julie Livingston, Steven E. Epstein, and Robert Aronowitz (Baltimore: Johns Hopkins University Press, 2010): 121–145.

2 Merck did not respond to the request to reprint these postcards for the book.

3 I found ten versions of the postcards during my research. A selection of these cards can still be seen on an archived version of the website, although not all the images I found are represented on the original Merck website. See *Merck Pharmaceuticals Tell Someone*, website archive, https://web.archive.org/web/20060427091530/http://tell-someone.hpv.com:80/postcard.html, accessed June 13, 2017.

4 When I requested permission to use the image in this book, the website's founder consented but asked me to send in a secret of my own.

5 Deborah Lupton, "Risk and Emotion: Towards an Alternative Theoretical Perspective," *Health, Risk & Society* 15, no. 8 (2013): 634–647.

6 Ibid.

7 Elizabeth Monk-Turner, Kristy Wren, Leanne McGill, Chris Matthiae, Stephan Brown, and Derrick Brooks, "Who Is Gazing at Whom? A Look at How Sex Is Used in Magazine Advertisements," *Journal of Gender Studies* 17, no. 3 (2008): 201–209.

8 The 2016 Centers for Disease Control's admonition that any woman who is sexually active but not using contraceptives ought to avoid alcohol provides a recent example of this attitude toward the reproductive potential of female bodies. See Centers for Disease Control, "More Than 3 Million US Women at Risk for Alcohol-exposed Pregnancy," February 2, 2016. http://www.cdc.gov/media/releases/2016/p0202-alcohol-exposed-pregnancy.html, accessed September 29, 2016; and Daniel Victor, "C.D.C. Defends Advice to Women on Drinking and Pregnancy," *New York Times*, February 5, 2016.

9 Carolyn B. Sufrin and Joseph S. Ross, "Pharmaceutical Industry Marketing: Understanding Its Impact on Women's Health," *Obstetrical & Gynecological Survey* 63, no. 9 (2008): 586.

10 Michael Applebaum, "Beverly J. Lybrand, Merck Vaccines," *Adweek*, October 8, 2007.

11 "Tell Someone" television advertisement, Merck Pharmaceuticals website, http://www.hpv.com:80/hpv-tv-commercial.html, accessed May 2006.

12 Ibid.

13 Merck revealed its assumptions about the activities girls might do in both the Tell Someone postcards and its television advertisements. In the "One Less" television advertisement, it is unclear why a girl who speaks Spanish would necessarily be dancing a Spanish dance. A girl who speaks Spanish in the United States might be doing all the things her non-Latina or non-Spanish

counterparts might be doing, like boxing, riding horses, or hanging out with her friends.

14 Joseph Dumit, *Drugs for Life: How Pharmaceutical Companies Define Our Health* (Durham, NC: Duke University Press, 2012); Margaret Lock, "The Tempering of Medical Anthropology: Troubling Natural Categories," *Medical Anthropology Quarterly* 15, no. 4 (2001): 478–492.

15 Simon J. Williams, Paul Martin, and Jonathan Gabe, "The Pharmaceuticalisation of Society? A Framework for Analysis," *Sociology of Health & Illness* 33, no. 5 (2011): 710–725.

16 Maren Klawiter, "Risk, Prevention and the Breast Cancer Continuum: The NCI, the FDA, Health Activism and the Pharmaceutical Industry," *History and Technology* 18, no. 4 (2002): 313.

17 Michael J. Oldani, "Thick Prescriptions: Toward an Interpretation of Pharmaceutical Sales Practices," *Medical Anthropology Quarterly* 18, no. 3 (2004): 325–356.

18 S. Lochlann Jain, "Cancer Butch," *Cultural Anthropology* 22, no. 4 (2007): 501–538.

19 Casper, Monica J., and Laura M. Carpenter, "Sex, Drugs, and Politics: The HPV Vaccine for Cervical Cancer," *Sociology of Health & Illness* 30, no. 6 (2008): 886–899.

20 Malcolm Gladwell, "John Rock's Error," *New Yorker*, March 13, 2000.

21 Seasonale website, http://www.seasonale.com, accessed December 28, 2008.

22 Janelle S. Taylor, "Surfacing the Body Interior," *Annual Review of Anthropology* 34 (2005): 749.

23 Emily Martin, "The Egg and the Sperm: How Science Has Constructed a Romance Based on Stereotypical Male-Female Roles," *Signs* 16, no. 3 (1991): 485–501.

24 Stuart Hogarth, Michael M. Hopkins, and Victor Rodriguez, "A Molecular Monopoly? HPV Testing, the Pap Smear and the Molecularisation of Cervical Cancer Screening in the USA," *Sociology of Health & Illness* 34, no. 2 (2012): 234–250.

25 Rob Stein, "Specialists Split over HPV Test's Role in Cancer Screening," *Shots: Health News from NPR*, January 8, 2015, http://www.npr.org/blogs/health/2015/01/08/375619687/specialists-split-over-hpv-tests-role-in-cancer-screening, accessed January 8, 2015; "FDA Approves First Human Papillomavirus Test for Primary Cervical Cancer Screening," *U.S. Food and Drug Administration*, April 24, 2014, http://www.fda.gov/NewsEvents/Newsroom/PressAnnouncements/ucm394773.htm, accessed January 19, 2015; Maria T. Sandri, Paola Lentati, Elvira Benini, Patrizia Dell'Orto, Laura Zorzino, Francesca M Carozzi, Patrick Maisonneuve, Rita Passerini, Michela Salvatici, and Chiara Casadio, "Comparison of the Digene HC2 Assay and the Roche AMPLICOR Human Papillomavirus (HPV) Test for Detection of High-risk HPV Genotypes in Cervical Samples," *Journal of Clinical Microbiology* 44, no. 6 (2006): 2141–2146.

26 Julie Beck, "The Different Stakes of Male and Female Birth Control," *The Atlantic*, November 1, 2016; Hermann M. Behre, Michael Zitzmann, Richard A. Anderson, David J. Handelsman, Silvia W. Lestari, Robert I. McLachlan, M. Cristina Meriggiola, Man Mohan Misro, Gabriela Noe, and Frederick C. W. Wu, "Efficacy and Safety of an Injectable Combination Hormonal Contraceptive for Men," *Journal of Clinical Endocrinology & Metabolism* 101, no. 12 (2016): 4779–4788; Nelly Oudshoorn, *The Male Pill: A Biography of a Technology in the Making* (Durham, NC: Duke University Press, 2003).

27 Emily Martin, *The Woman in the Body: A Cultural Analysis of Reproduction* (Boston: Beacon Press. 2001), xxvii.

28 Jessika van Kammen, "Representing Users' Bodies: The Gendered Development of Anti-Fertility Vaccines," *Science, Technology & Human Values* 24, no. 3 (1999): 307–337.

29 Melissa Hendricks, "HPV Vaccine: Who Chooses?" *Los Angeles Times*, February 5, 2007; Bill Maher, "Christians Crusade Against Cancer Vaccine," *Salon.com*, March 2, 2007, http://www.salon.com/2007/03/02/hpv_7/, accessed March 4, 2007; Katha Pollitt, "Virginity or Death!" *The Nation*, May 30, 2005.

30 See Chapter 6 for the discussion of Rick Perry's executive order to require the HPV vaccine and his goal of protecting women and girls who conformed to his concept of virtue.

31 Sheila Jasanoff, "Science and Citizenship: A New Synergy," *Science and Public Policy* 31, no. 2 (2004): 90–94.

32 The story of the organization's founding is explored in greater depth in Chapter 7.

33 National Cancer Institute, "Cancer Stat Facts: Cancer of the Cervix Uteri," *National Cancer Institute: Surveillance, Epidemiology, and End Results Program*, http://seer.cancer.gov/statfacts/html/cervix.html, accessed January 12, 2017.

34 Merck's perfectly pitched marketing for CCG members exemplifies a well-researched market strategy, one that advertising magazines praised the company for in the first year of the Gardasil launch. See "Gardasil Campaign Taps Public Fear of Cancer," *Pharmaceutical Executive*, November 2006; and Applebaum, "Beverly Lybrand, Merck Vaccines."

35 I do not cite the magazine here, as I wish to preserve the anonymity of CCG.

36 Eric Sagonowsky, "GSK Exits U.S. Market with Its HPV Vaccine Cervarix." *Fierce Pharma*, October 21, 2016, http://www.fiercepharma.com/pharma/gsk-exits-u-s -market-its-hpv-vaccine-cervarix, accessed November 1, 2016.

37 Laurie McGinley, "Do the New Merck HPV Ads Guilt-Trip Parents or Tell Hard Truths? Both," *Washington Post*, August 11, 2016.

Chapter 3—The Pap Smear, Racist Histories, and "Cervix" Cancer

1 The buttons actually used a different word for vagina, but in order to protect the identity of the organization I am referring to as CCG, and as the original slang word is rarely used to connote vagina, I have changed it to a more commonly used word for clarity and confidentiality.

2 Michael Applebaum, "Beverly J. Lybrand, Merck Vaccines," *Adweek*, October 8, 2007.

3 "About the AIDS Memorial Quilt, History, Save America's Treasures, Fact Sheet—The Names Project," http://www.aidsquilt.org/about/the-aids-memorial -quilt, accessed February 3, 2015.

4 Diane Cooper, Margaret Hoffman, Henri Carrara, Lynn Rosenberg, Judy Kelly, Ilse Stander, Lynnette Denny, Anna-Lise Williamson, and Samuel Shapiro, "Determinants of Sexual Activity and Its Relation to Cervical Cancer Risk among South African Women," *BMC Public Health* 7, no. 1 (2007): 341. Although my questioning the quilt square maker's use of "early sex" may seem like semantic quibble, it is precisely the complexity of epidemiological risk assessment that matters so much in educating the public about HPV and cancer risks. Stating that early sex *causes*

cervical cancer inaccurately blames the behavior for the progression to cancer. Progression to cancer is due a variety of factors, not the sex itself. The risk for cervical cancer is greater due to earlier sexual debut, but blaming an individual's age at sexual initiation implies the girl's responsibility for her future cancer. Odds ratios, risk, and causalities are not absolute values or straightforward analyses and require a commitment to data parsing that current education about HPV and cervical cancer does not provide.

5   Alexandra Howson, "Surveillance, Knowledge and Risk: The Embodied Experience of Cervical Screening," *Health* 2, no. 2 (1998): 199.

6   Michelle Murphy, *Seizing the Means of Reproduction: Entanglements of Feminism, Health, and Technoscience* (Durham, NC: Duke University Press, 2012), 101.

7   Michelle Murphy, *Seizing the Means of Reproduction: Entanglements of Feminism, Health, and Technoscience*, 101, 81.

8   Anna Louise Beavis and Kimberly L. Levinson, "Preventing Cervical Cancer in the United States: Barriers and Resolutions for HPV Vaccination," *Frontiers in Oncology* 6 (2016): 19; Monica J. Casper and Adele E. Clarke, "Making the Pap Smear into the 'Right Tool' for the Job: Cervical Cancer Screening in the USA, Circa 1940–95," *Social Studies of Science* 28, no. 2 (1998): 255–290; Ralph M. Richart and Thomas C. Wright, "Controversies in the Management of Low-Grade Cervical Intraepithelial Neoplasia," *Cancer* 71, no. 4 (supplement) (1993): 1413–1421.

9   Margarete Sandelowski, "'This Most Dangerous Instrument': Propriety, Power, and the Vaginal Speculum," *Journal of Obstetric, Gynecologic & Neonatal Nursing* 29, no. 1 (2000): 73–82.

10 Thomas Walter Laqueur, *Making Sex: Body and Gender from the Greeks to Freud* (Cambridge, MA: Harvard University Press, 1990).

11 Emily Martin, *The Woman in the Body: A Cultural Analysis of Reproduction* (Boston: Beacon Press, 2001), 34–35.

12 Terri Kapsalis, *Public Privates: Performing Gynecology from Both Ends of the Speculum* (Durham, NC: Duke University Press, 1997), 39.

13 Ibid.

14 Laura Briggs, "The Race of Hysteria: 'Overcivilization' and the 'Savage' Woman in Late Nineteenth-Century Obstetrics and Gynecology," *American Quarterly* 52, no. 2 (2000): 246–273.

15 Ibid., 247.

16 Kapsalis, *Public Privates*; Briggs, "The Race of Hysteria."

17 Harriet A. Washington, *Medical Apartheid: The Dark History of Medical Experimentation on Black Americans From Colonial Times to the Present* (New York: Doubleday Books, 2006).

18 Sandelowski, "'This Most Dangerous Instrument,'" 73.

19 Casper and Clarke, "Making the Pap Smear into the 'Right Tool' for the Job," 255; Adele E. Clarke and Joan H. Fujimura, *The Right Tools for the Job: At Work in Twentieth-Century Life Sciences* (Princeton, NJ: Princeton University Press, 1992).

20 Adele E. Clarke and Monica J. Casper, "From Simple Technology to Complex Arena: Classification of Pap Smears, 1917–90," *Medical Anthropology Quarterly* 10, no. 4 (1996): 601–623; Casper and Clarke, "Making the Pap Smear into the 'Right Tool' for the Job"; Margaret J. Foulks, "The Papanicolaou Smear: Its Impact on the Promotion of Women's Health," *Journal of Obstetric, Gynecologic, & Neonatal Nursing* 27, no. 4 (1998): 367–373; Stylianos P. Michalas, "The Pap Test: George N.

Papanicolaou (1883–1962): A Screening Test for the Prevention of Cancer of Uterine Cervix," *European Journal of Obstetrics & Gynecology and Reproductive Biology* 90, no. 2 (2000): 135–138.

21 Casper and Clarke, "Making the Pap Smear into the 'Right Tool' for the Job"; Foulks, "The Papanicolaou Smear."

22 Casper and Clarke, "Making the Pap Smear into the 'Right Tool' for the Job."

23 Clarke and Casper, "From Simple Technology to Complex Arena."

24 Murphy, *Seizing the Means of Reproduction*, 107.

25 Anna L. Beavis, Patti E. Gravitt, and Anne F. Rositch, "Hysterectomy-Corrected Cervical Cancer Mortality Rates Reveal a Larger Racial Disparity in the United States," *Cancer* 123, no. 6 (2017): 1044–1050.

26 Foulks, "The Papanicolaou Smear"; Rose M. Mays, G. D. Zimet, Y. Winston, R. Kee, J. Dickes, and L. Su, "Human Papillomavirus, Genital Warts, Pap Smears, and Cervical Cancer: Knowledge and Beliefs of Adolescent and Adult Women," *Health Care for Women International* 21, no. 5 (2000): 361–374; Michalas, "The Pap Test."

27 Clarke and Casper, "From Simple Technology to Complex Arena"; Casper and Clarke, "Making the Pap Smear into the 'Right Tool' for the Job"; Foulks, "The Papanicolaou Smear."

28 Clarke and Casper, "From Simple Technology to Complex Arena."

29 Alexandra Howson, "Locating Uncertainties in Cervical Screening," *Health, Risk & Society* 3, no. 2 (2001): 167–179.

30 Monica J. Casper and Adele E. Clarke, "Making the Pap Smear into the 'Right Tool' for the Job: Cervical Cancer Screening in the USA, Circa 1940–95," *Social Studies of Science* 28, no. 2 (1998): 255–290.

31 Adele E. Clarke and Monica J. Casper, "From Simple Technology to Complex Arena: Classification of Pap Smears, 1917–90," *Medical Anthropology Quarterly* 10, no. 4 (1996): 601–623.

32 Ibid.

33 Baseman and Koutsky, "The Epidemiology of Human Papillomavirus Infections."

34 Ibid.; Richard C. Boronow, "Death of the Papanicolaou Smear? A Tale of Three Reasons," *American Journal of Obstetrics and Gynecology* 179, no. 2 (1998): 391–396; Casper and Clarke, "Making the Pap Smear into the 'Right Tool' for the Job."

35 Casper and Clarke, "Making the Pap Smear into the 'Right Tool' for the Job," 262.

36 George F. Sawaya and Karen Smith-McCune, "Cervical Cancer Screening," *Obstetrics & Gynecology* 127, no. 3 (2016): 465–466.

37 Alexandra Howson, "'Watching You—Watching Me': Visualising Techniques and the Cervix," *Women's Studies International Forum* 24, no. 1 (2001): 97–109.

38 Nikolas Rose and Carlos Novas, "Biological Citizenship," in *Global Assemblages: Technology, Politics, and Ethics as Anthropological Problems*, edited by Aihwa Ong and Stephen J. Collier (Oxford: Blackwell Publishing, 2005), 439–463; Carlos Novas and Nikolas Rose, "Genetic Risk and the Birth of the Somatic Individual," *Economy and Society* 29, no. 4 (2000): 485–513.

39 Rebecca Dimond, Andrew Bartlett, and Jamie Lewis, "What Binds Biosociality? The Collective Effervescence of the Parent-Led Conference," *Social Science & Medicine* (February 2015): 2.

40 Pascale Lehoux and Stuart Blume, "Technology Assessment and the Sociopolitics of Health Technologies," *Journal of Health Politics, Policy and Law* 25, no. 6 (2000):

1088. See also Michel Callon, P. Lascoumes, and Y. Barthe, *Acting in an Uncertain World: An Essay on Technological Democracy* (Cambridge, MA: MIT Press, 2009); Steven Epstein, "The Construction of Lay Expertise: AIDS Activism and the Forging of Credibility in the Reform of Clinical Trials," *Science, Technology & Human Values* 20, no. 4 (1995): 408–437.

41 Susanne Dalsgaard Reventlow, Lotte Hvas, and Kirsti Malterud, "Making the Invisible Body Visible. Bone Scans, Osteoporosis and Women's Bodily Experiences," *Social Science & Medicine* 62, no. 11 (2006): 2720–2731; Anne M. Kavanagh and Dorothy H. Broom, "Embodied Risk: My Body, Myself?" *Social Science & Medicine* 46, no. 3 (1998): 437–444.

42 Kapsalis, *Public Privates*.

43 Most of the women at the conference who spoke with me were in their 20s or early 30s. I was in my late 20s at the time. They may have been willing to talk to me because our ages were similar, or it may be the case that younger women are more comfortable discussing their diagnoses. I disclosed my role as a researcher as soon as I met conference attendees.

44 On the CCG's website, the color associated with cervical cancer is now teal. An organization founded in 2011 called Color of Teal (not a pseudonym) is an HPV awareness and gynecological cancer advocacy organization and offers financial assistance for low-income women receiving treatment for gynecological cancers. Incongruously, however, its 2015 sponsors included Summer's Eve, a douche product known to be harmful to women. Color of Teal features women of color as speakers and participants on its website. As it was founded after I concluded the majority of my primary research, Color of Teal is not included in this discussion. Although Color of Teal does not identify itself as specifically an organization for women of color, its diversity is distinctive from many of the other cervical cancer organizations that do not have as visibly diverse women as spokespeople. Denise, a speaker at the CCG conference, was an exception; but, her organization does not focus on the specific cervical cancer concerns of women of color, even though it was founded by a young black woman.

45 Laurie Gilmore Selleck, "Pretty in Pink: The Susan G. Komen Network and the Branding of the Breast Cancer Cause," *Nordic Journal of English Studies* 9, no. 3 (2010):123.

46 See Carla Willig, "Cancer Diagnosis as Discursive Capture: Phenomenological Repercussions of Being Positioned within Dominant Constructions of Cancer," *Social Science & Medicine* 73, no. 6 (2011): 897–903; Siddhartha Mukherjee, *The Emperor of All Maladies: A Biography of Cancer* (New York: Simon and Schuster, 2010); and Susan Sontag, Illness as Metaphor *and* AIDS and Its Metaphors (New York: Macmillan, 2001).

47 I discuss the concern about funding and reimbursement for cervical cancer screening that informed the founding of CCG in Chapter 7.

48 CCG website, accessed October 21, 2008.

49 CDC data published in 2016 noted that among the 38,793 HPV-related cancers that are diagnosed each year, 28,500 are attributable to the nine types of HPV included in the newer version of Gardasil. This means that more than 25 percent of HPV-related cancers will not be prevented by Gardasil 9. Laura J. Viens, Jane Henley, Meg Watson, Lauri E. Markowitz, Cheryll C. Thomas, Trevor D. Thompson, Hilda Razzaghi, and Mona Saraiya, "Human Papillomavirus–Associated

Cancers—United States, 2008–2012," *Morbidity and Mortality Weekly Report* 65 (2016): 661–666.

50 Alexandra Howson, "Locating Uncertainties in Cervical Screening," *Health, Risk & Society* 3, no. 2 (2001): 167–179.

51 Viens et al, "Human Papillomavirus—Associated Cancers;" Laurie D. Elam-Evans, David Yankey, Jenny Jeyarajah, James A. Singleton, R. C. Curtis, Jessica MacNeil, and Susan Hariri, "National, Regional, State, and Selected Local Area Vaccination Coverage among Adolescents Aged 13–17 Years: United States, 2013," *Morbidity and Mortality Weekly Report* 63, no. 29 (2014): 625–633; Laurie McGinley, "Cancer Doctors Leading Campaign to Boost Use of HPV Vaccine," *Washington Post*, June 19, 2016.

52 L. W. Musselwhite, C. M. Oliveira, T. Kwaramba, N. de Paula Pantano, J. S. Smith, J. H. Fregnani, R. M. Reis, E. Mauad, F. L. Vazquez, and A. Longatto-Filho, "Racial/Ethnic Disparities in Cervical Cancer Screening and Outcomes," *Acta Cytologica* 60, no. 6 (2016): 518–526; Beavis et al., "Hysterectomy-Corrected Cervical Cancer Mortality Rates Reveal a Larger Racial Disparity in the United States"; Anne F. Rositch, Rebecca G. Nowak, and Patti E. Gravitt, "Increased Age and Race-Specific Incidence of Cervical Cancer after Correction for Hysterectomy Prevalence in the United States from 2000 to 2009," *Cancer* 120, no. 13 (2014): 2032–2038.

53 Marc Berg and Paul Harterink, "Embodying the Patient: Records and Bodies in Early 20th-century US Medical Practice," *Body & Society* 10, no. 2–3 (2004): 15.

54 Murphy, *Seizing the Means of Reproduction*, 72.

Chapter 4—Educate the Educators

1 Jerome Groopman, "Contagion: Papilloma Virus," *New Yorker*, September 13, 1999.

2 Monica J. Casper and Adele E. Clarke, "Making the Pap Smear into the 'Right Tool' for the Job: Cervical Cancer Screening in the USA, Circa 1940–95," *Social Studies of Science* 28, no. 2 (1998): 255–290.

3 Accent Health, http://www.accenthealth.com/, accessed September 10, 2007.

4 Jasmin A. Tiro, Helen I. Meissner, Sarah Kobrin, and Veronica Chollette, "What Do Women in the US Know about Human Papillomavirus and Cervical Cancer?" *Cancer Epidemiology Biomarkers & Prevention* 16, no. 2 (2007): 288–294; Sandi L. Pruitt, Patricia A. Parker, Susan K. Peterson, Tao Le, Michele Follen, and Karen Basen-Engquist, "Knowledge of Cervical Dysplasia and Human Papillomavirus among Women Seen in a Colposcopy Clinic," *Gynecologic Oncology* 99, no. 3 (2005): S236–S244; Rebecca Anhang, Annekathryn Goodman, and Sue J. Goldie, "HPV Communication: Review of Existing Research and Recommendations for Patient Education," *CA: A Cancer Journal for Clinicians* 54, no. 5 (2004): 248–259; Marian Pitts and Tracy Clarke, "Human Papillomavirus Infections and Risks of Cervical Cancer: What Do Women Know?" *Health Education Research* 17, no. 6 (2002): 706–714; Heather Baer, Susan Allen, and Lundy Braun, "Knowledge of Human Papillomavirus Infection among Young Adult Men and Women: Implications for Health Education and Research," *Journal of Community Health* 25, no. 1 (2000): 67–78.

5 Ray Moynihan, Iona Heath, and David Henry, "Selling Sickness: The Pharmaceutical Industry and Disease Mongering Commentary: Medicalisation of Risk Factors," *BMJ* 324, no. 7342 (2002): 886–891; Howard Wolinsky, "Disease Mongering

and Drug Marketing," *EMBO Reports* 6, no. 7 (2005): 612–614; Leonore Tiefer, "Female Sexual Dysfunction: A Case Study of Disease Mongering and Activist Resistance," *PLoS Medicine* 3, no. 4 (2006): e178.

6 In 2010–2011, when I was working as a consultant in biotechnology, I sat in on a meeting with a large biotech company that discussed this very idea of wanting to create a new medical condition to justify a use for their product.

7 Vincanne Adams, Michelle Murphy, and Adele E. Clarke, "Anticipation: Techno-science, Life, Affect, Temporality," *Subjectivity* 28, no. 1 (2009): 252.

8 Ibid., 253.

9 Michael Applebaum, "Beverly J. Lybrand, Merck Vaccines," *Adweek*, October 8, 2007.

10 Kalman Applbaum, "Consumers Are Patients! Shared Decision-Making and Treatment Non-Compliance as Business Opportunity," *Transcultural Psychiatry* 46, no. 1 (2009): 115.

11 Merck, "Educate the Educators," n.d.

12 Michael J. Oldani, "Thick Prescriptions: Toward an Interpretation of Pharmaceutical Sales Practices," *Medical Anthropology Quarterly* 18, no. 3 (2004): 325–356.

13 Daniel Carlat, "Dr. Drug Rep," *New York Times*, November 25, 2007.

14 This is a pseudonym.

15 Eduardo L. Franco, Nicolas F. Schlecht, and Debbie Saslow, "The Epidemiology of Cervical Cancer," *Cancer Journal* 9, no. 5 (2003): 351.

16 Rachel L. Winer, James P. Hughes, Qinghua Feng, Sandra O'Reilly, Nancy B. Kiviat, King K. Holmes, and Laura A. Koutsky, "Condom Use and the Risk of Genital Human Papillomavirus Infection in Young Women," *New England Journal of Medicine* 354, no. 25 (2006): 2645–2654.

17 National Vaccine Advisory Committee, "Overcoming Barriers to Low HPV Vaccine Uptake in the United States: Recommendations from the National Vaccine Advisory Committee," *Public Health Reports* 131, no. 1 (2016): 17.

18 I use this term here to refer to the prevalence of HPV.

19 See Carlat, "Dr. Drug Rep."

20 The number of physicians interviewed one on one for this project was low, although I observed doctors speaking on panels at the quarterly immunization coalition meeting and at the CDC annual immunization meeting. I also draw on transcripts of interviews conducted by research assistants with physicians and clinical staff at two low-income clinics for a separate research project funded by the CDC.

21 Not a pseudonym, as the Commonwealth Club makes its sessions available via streaming video online.

22 "Douglas S. Diekema, Responding to Parental Refusals of Immunization of Children," *Pediatrics* 115, no. 5 (2005): 1429, italics added.

23 Parents mentioned the varicella (chicken pox) vaccine as an example of a vaccine with limited utility. Although people are now vaccinated during childhood, the immunity to the virus appears to wane around the same time that varicella can become quite severe. Adult infection, known as shingles, can be extremely debilitating. A vaccine for shingles has also been developed, but many parents wonder why yet another vaccine is necessary. They questioned whether a follow-up injection against shingles is just a business opportunity. They interpreted the varicella vaccine as a way to necessitate yet another vaccine in order to preserve immunity into adulthood. The NaturalMoms mothers, both in person and on the listservs, said they

preferred chicken pox parties, where children might be exposed to the infection "naturally." They hoped to lessen the severity of the illness or to plan for it. Chicken pox parties occurred well before the development of the varicella vaccine, but they are now commonly associated with the vaccine resistant community as a way to develop natural immunity without vaccinating. Of course, not everyone who gets chicken pox will have immunity later in life. As I discovered during pregnancy, even though I had had the disease, I did not have immunity and needed to get a vaccine after my first child was born.

24 Ohid Yaqub, Sophie Castle-Clarke, Nick Sevdalis, and Joanna Chataway, "Attitudes to Vaccination: A Critical Review," *Social Science & Medicine* 112 (2014): 7.

25 Elisa J. Sobo, Arianna Huhn, Autumn Sannwald, and Lori Thurman, "Information Curation among Vaccine Cautious Parents: Web 2.0, Pinterest Thinking, and Pediatric Vaccination Choice," *Medical Anthropology* 35, no. 6 (2016): 529–546; Anna Kirkland, "The Legitimacy of Vaccine Critics: What Is Left After the Autism Hypothesis?" *Journal of Health Politics, Policy and Law* 37, no. 1 (2012): 69–97.

26 Centers for Disease Control, "Incidence, Prevalence, and Cost of Sexually Transmitted Diseases in the United States," *Centers for Disease Control and Prevention*, https://www.cdc.gov/std/stats/sti-estimates-fact-sheet-feb-2013.pdf, accessed June 17, 2017.

27 Stuart Hogarth, Michael M. Hopkins, and Victor Rodriguez, "A Molecular Monopoly? HPV Testing, the Pap Smear and the Molecularisation of Cervical Cancer Screening in the USA," *Sociology of Health & Illness* 34, no. 2 (2012): 234–250.

28 Digene Corporation, "Digene Consumer Ad Wins Industry Award for Best Product Launch," *PR Newswire*, November 17, 2005, http://www.prnewswire.com/news-releases/digene-consumer-ad-wins-industry-award-for-best-product-launch-55703912.html, accessed April 7, 2017.

29 *Make the Connection*, http://web.archive.org/web/20060602075952/http://www.maketheconnection.org:80/, accessed June 17, 2017.

30 Applebaum, "Beverly J. Lybrand, Merck Vaccines."

Chapter 5—Merck and the FDA

1 Katha Pollitt, "Virginity or Death!" *The Nation*, May 30, 2005.

2 Michael Specter, "Reporter at Large—Political Science," *New Yorker*, March 13, 2006.

3 Lisa L. Wynn and James Trussell, "The Social Life of Emergency Contraception in the United States: Disciplining Pharmaceutical Use, Disciplining Sexuality, and Constructing Zygotic Bodies," *Medical Anthropology Quarterly* 20, no. 3 (2006): 297–320.

4 Although I attended the meeting and recorded some of its proceedings, I quote the FDA transcript here to provide publicly available evidence.

5 Joanne Silberner, "FDA to Review Vaccine for Cancer-Causing Virus," *NPR*, May 18, 2006, http://www.npr.org/templates/story/story.php?storyId=5413896, accessed May 18, 2006.

6 Julie Steenhuysen, "Merck Cancer Vaccine Faces Christian Right Scrutiny," *Reuters*, May 22, 2006.

7   Ibid.

8   Minutes of meeting of Vaccines and Related Biological Products Advisory Committee, Food and Drug Administration, Center for Biologics Evaluation and Research, May 18, 2006, 11, https://www.fda.gov/OHRMS/DOCKETS/ac/06/transcripts/2006-4222t1.pdf, accessed October 12, 2008.

9   Ibid, 13.

10 Ibid.

11 Ibid.

12 Ibid., 20.

13 Ibid., 28.

14 Ibid., 23.

15 Ibid., 26–27; Beth Herskovits, "Brand of the Year," *Pharmaceutical Executive*, February 1, 2007.

16 Ibid., 26–27.

17 U.S. Food and Drug Administration, "Fast Track," *U.S. Food and Drug Administration*, http://www.fda.gov/forconsumers/byaudience/forpatientadvocates/speeding accesstoimportantnewtherapies/ucm128291.html, accessed February 10, 2014.

18 Alex Berenson, "Merck Agrees to Pay $4.85 Billion in Vioxx Claims," *New York Times*, November 9, 2007.

19 Stephanie Saul, "Merck Wrote Drug Studies for Doctors," *New York Times*, April 16, 2008.

20 Duff Wilson, "Merck to Pay $950 Million over Vioxx," *New York Times*, November 22, 2011.

21 Vaccines and Related Biological Products Advisory Committee minutes, May 18, 2006, 11–12.

22 Ibid., 12.

23 Ibid., 18–19.

24 Ibid., 34.

25 Ibid., 29.

26 Vincanne Adams, Michelle Murphy, and Adele E. Clarke, "Anticipation: Technoscience, Life, Affect, Temporality," *Subjectivity* 28, no. 1 (2009): 253.

27 Ibid., 254.

28 Vaccines and Related Biological Products Advisory Committee minutes, May 18, 2006, 72–73.

29 Ibid., 72–73.

30 Ibid., 72–73.

31 Ibid., 175.

32 Ibid., 177.

33 Ibid., 113.

34 Julie Beck, "The Different Stakes of Male and Female Birth Control," *The Atlantic*, November 1, 2016; Hermann M. Behre, Michael Zitzmann, Richard A. Anderson, David J. Handelsman, Silvia W. Lestari, Robert I. McLachlan, M. Cristina Meriggiola, Man Mohan Misro, Gabriela Noe, and Frederick C. W. Wu, "Efficacy and Safety of an Injectable Combination Hormonal Contraceptive for Men," *Journal of Clinical Endocrinology & Metabolism* 101, no. 12 (2016): 4779–4788; Nelly Oudshoorn, "On Masculinities, Technologies, and Pain: The Testing of Male Contraceptives in the Clinic and the Media," *Science, Technology & Human Values* 24, no. 2 (1999): 265–289.

35 Nelly Oudshoorn, *The Male Pill: A Biography of a Technology in the Making* (Durham, NC: Duke University Press, 2003).

36 Emily Martin, *The Woman in the Body: A Cultural Analysis of Reproduction* (Boston: Beacon Press, 2001).

37 Vaccines have not been mandatory in the United States since World War I; see J. L. Schwartz, A. L. Caplan, R. R. Faden, and J. Sugarman, "Lessons from the Failure of Human Papillomavirus Vaccine State Requirements," *Clinical Pharmacology & Therapeutics* 82, no. 6 (2007): 760–763. There is a policy difference between mandatory and required. The former means that no exceptions are permitted and the latter means that there may be exceptions to the policy.

38 Nancy Gibbs, "Defusing the War over the 'Promiscuity' Vaccine," *Time*, June 21, 2006.

39 James Colgrove, "The Ethics and Politics of Compulsory HPV Vaccination," *New England Journal of Medicine* 355, no. 23 (2006): 2389–2391.

Chapter 6—Vaccines and Politics

1 Quote in Joseph Dumit, *Drugs for Life: How Pharmaceutical Companies Define Our Health* (Durham, NC: Duke University Press, 2012), 13. See also Kalman Applbaum, "Pharmaceutical Marketing and the Invention of the Medical Consumer," *PLoS Medicine* 3, no. 4 (2006): e189; Adriana Petryna, Andrew Lakoff, and Arthur Kleinman, *Global Pharmaceuticals: Ethics, Markets, Practices* (Durham, NC: Duke University Press, 2006); Ray Moynihan, Iona Heath, and David Henry, "Selling Sickness: The Pharmaceutical Industry and Disease Mongering. Commentary: Medicalisation of Risk Factors," *BMJ* 324, no. 7342 (2002): 886–891; Susan Reynolds Whyte, Sjaak van der Geest, and Anita Hardon, *Social Lives of Medicines* (Cambridge: Cambridge University Press, 2002); Nancy Vuckovic and Mark Nichter, "Changing Patterns of Pharmaceutical Practice in the United States," *Social Science & Medicine* 44, no. 9 (1997): 1285–1302.

2 Nick J. Fox and Katie J. Ward, "Pharma in the Bedroom . . . and the Kitchen: The Pharmaceuticalisation of Daily Life," *Sociology of Health & Illness* 30, no. 6 (2008): 856–868.

3 Pieter Streefland, A. M. R. Chowdhury, and Pilar Ramos-Jimenez, "Patterns of Vaccination Acceptance," *Social Science & Medicine* 49, no. 12 (1999): 1705–1716.

4 Melissa Leach and James Fairhead, *Vaccine Anxieties: Global Science, Child Health and Society* (Abingdon: Earthscan, 2007); Daniel A. Salmon, Stephen P. Teret, C. Raina MacIntyre, David Salisbury, Margaret A. Burgess, and Neal A. Halsey, "Compulsory Vaccination and Conscientious or Philosophical Exemptions: Past, Present, and Future," *The Lancet* 367, no. 9508 (2006): 436–442; S. S. Blume and D. Rose, "Citizens as Users of Technology: An Exploratory Study of Vaccines and Vaccination," in *How Users Matter: The Co-Construction of Users and Technology* (Cambridge, MA: MIT Press, 2005), 103–132.

5 Leach and Fairhead, *Vaccine Anxieties*.

6 William A. Muraskin, *Polio Eradication and Its Discontents: An Historian's Journey through an International Public Health (Un)Civil War* (Himayatnagar, Hyderabad: Orient Blackswan, 2012).

7 Ann Robertson, "Biotechnology, Political Rationality and Discourses on Health Risk," *Health* 5, no. 3 (2001): 294–295.

8   Streefland et al., "Patterns of Vaccination Acceptance."

9   Mark Fischetti, "Too Many Children Go Unvaccinated," *Scientific American*, May 14, 2013.

10 Carla L. Black, David Yankey, and Maureen Kolasa, "National, State, and Local Area Vaccination Coverage among Children Aged 19–35 Months—United States, 2012," *Morbidity and Mortality Weekly Report* 62, no. 36 (2013): 733–737.

11 Ibid., 733.

12 Amrita Mishra and Janice E Graham, "Risk, Choice and the 'Girl Vaccine': Unpacking Human Papillomavirus (HPV) Immunisation," *Health, Risk & Society* 14, no. 1 (2012): 57–69.

13 The Lyme disease vaccine is an example of direct-to-consumer advertising for a vaccine, but vaccine advertisements are uncommon. Robert Aronowitz, *Risky Medicine: Our Quest to Cure Fear and Uncertainty* (Chicago: University of Chicago Press, 2015), 128.

14 Michelle M. Mello, Sara Abiola, and James Colgrove, "Pharmaceutical Companies' Role in State Vaccination Policymaking: The Case of Human Papillomavirus Vaccination," *American Journal of Public Health* 102, no. 5 (2012): 893–898.

15 "HPV Vaccine and State Legislatures," *National Conference of State Legislatures*, April 4, 2017, http://www.ncsl.org/research/health/hpv-vaccine-state-legislation -and-statutes.aspx, accessed April 7, 2017.

16 Lynn Doan, "Schools to Offer STD Vaccine," *Los Angeles Times*, July 24, 2006.

17 Ibid.

18 Not a pseudonym.

19 Streefland et al., "Patterns of Vaccination Acceptance."

20 Irina Todorova, "Introduction to the Special Section: Cross-Cultural Beliefs, Attitudes, and Dilemmas about Vaccination," *International Journal of Behavioral Medicine* 21, no. 1 (2014): 1; Leach and Fairhead, *Vaccine Anxieties*.

21 Vincanne Adams, Michelle Murphy, and Adele E. Clarke, "Anticipation: Technoscience, Life, Affect, Temporality," *Subjectivity* 28, no. 1 (2009): 246–265.

22 ACIP, a federal body, describes itself as "a group of medical and public health experts that develop[s] recommendations on the use of vaccines in the civilian population of the United States." "ACIP," *Centers for Disease Control and Prevention*, accessed May 31, 2017, https://www.cdc.gov/vaccines/acip/. Members of the board are selected by the secretary of the U.S. Department of Health and Human Services.

23 Gardiner Harris, "U.S. Approves Cervical Cancer Vaccine," *New York Times*, June 8, 2006.

24 Thalia Longoria, "Human Papillomavirus Vaccination Requirement for Immigrants Raises Concerns," *Dallas Morning News*, September 27, 2008. The U.S. Citizenship and Immigration Services is now known as Immigration and Customs Enforcement (ICE).

25 In 2016, the price of Gardasil 9, which protects against five more types of HPV than the original Gardasil, was $580 for all three doses. CDC Vaccine Price List, http://www.cdc.gov/vaccines/programs/vfc/awardees/vaccine-management/price-list/, accessed September 19, 2016.

26 Ann Haddix, "Criteria for Vaccination Requirements for U.S. Immigration Purposes," *Federal Register* 74, no. 218 (2009).

27 Susan Sontag, Illness as Metaphor *and* AIDS and Its Metaphors (New York: Macmillan, 2001); Barbara Ehrenreich, "Slap on a Pink Ribbon and Call It a Day,"

Salon.com, December 2, 2009, http://www.salon.com/2009/12/02/womens
_health_2/, accessed June 29, 2011; Samantha King, "Pink Ribbons Inc: Breast
Cancer Activism and the Politics of Philanthropy," *International Journal of Qualitative Studies in Education* 17, no. 4 (2004): 473–492; Maren Klawiter, "Racing for
the Cure, Walking Women, and Toxic Touring: Mapping Cultures of Action within
the Bay Area Terrain of Breast Cancer," *Social Problems* 46, no. 1 (1999): 104–126;
Katha Pollitt, "Virginity or Death!" *The Nation*, May 30, 2005; Michael Specter,
"Reporter at Large—Political Science," *New Yorker*, March 13, 2006.

28 James G. Hodge Jr. and Lawrence O. Gostin, *School Vaccination Requirements:
Legal and Social Perspectives* (Denver: National Conference of State Legislatures,
2002), 2.

29 James Keith Colgrove, *State of Immunity: The Politics of Vaccination in Twentieth-
Century America* (Berkeley: University of California Press, 2006), 72.

30 Ibid.; Salmon et al., "Compulsory Vaccination and Conscientious or Philosophical
Exemptions."

31 Michel Foucault, "The Means of Correct Training," in *The Foucault Reader*, edited
by Paul Rabinow (New York: Pantheon, 1984), 192.

32 Jacques Donzelot, *The Policing of Families* (New York: Pantheon, 1979), 267.

33 Anna Kirkland, "The Legitimacy of Vaccine Critics: What Is Left After the Autism
Hypothesis?" *Journal of Health Politics, Policy and Law* 37, no. 1 (2012): 69–97.

34 Women in Government Press Release, "Michigan State Senator Hammerstrom
Introduces Nation's First Legislation Requiring Cervical Cancer Vaccination for
School Entry," *Pharmalive.com*, September 12, 2006, http://www.pharmalive.com/
News/Print.cfm?articleid=372248, accessed September 19, 2006.

35 Nancy Gibbs, "Defusing the War over the 'Promiscuity' Vaccine," *Time*, June 21,
2006.

36 Rick Perry, "Statement of Gov. Rick Perry on HPV Vaccine Executive Order," *La
Prensa* 13, no. 22 (2007): 18.

37 "Public Hearing on HPV Vaccine Went until Midnight," *KXAN.com*, February 20,
2007, accessed February 21, 2007.

38 Thanh Tan, "31 Days, 31 Ways: Family Planning Funding Slashed," *Texas Tribune*,
August 15, 2011, https://www.texastribune.org/2011/08/15/day-15/, accessed
April 25, 2015; Tara Culp-Ressler, "Texas May Slash Cancer Screenings for Low-
Income Women," *Think Progress*, January 29, 2015, https://thinkprogress.org/
texas-may-slash-cancer-screenings-for-low-income-women-7289cd186c48?gi=
9cc1325f91a0, accessed April 23, 2015.

39 Ralph Blumenthal, "Texas Is First to Require Cancer Shots for Schoolgirls," *New
York Times*, February 3, 2007.

40 Ibid.

41 Andrew Pollack and Stephanie Saul, "Merck to Halt Lobbying for Vaccine for
Girls," *New York Times*, February 21, 2007.

42 Ibid.

43 "A Bill to Prohibit Federal Funding or Other Assistance for Mandatory Human
Papillomavirus (HPV) Vaccination Programs," HR 1153, 111th Congress, Febru-
ary 16, 2007, https://www.govtrack.us/congress/bills/111/hr3188/text, accessed
July 20, 2007.

44 Ibid. Of course, HPV is spread through other ways besides intercourse, including
nonpenetrative genital contact.

45 Dan Eggen, "Rick Perry Reverses Himself, Calls HPV Vaccine Mandate a 'Mistake,'" *Washington Post*, September 13, 2011.

46 "A Roadmap for Success: The State of Cervical Cancer Prevention in America 2010," *Women in Government*, www.womeningovernment.org, accessed November 10, 2011. This document is no longer available on their site.

47 "Oncology," *Women in Government*, n.d., https://web.archive.org/web/20110421020920/http://www.womeningovernment.org:80, accessed August 15, 2017.

48 Judith Siers-Poisson, "Women in Government, Merck's Trojan Horse: Part Three in a Series on the Politics and PR of Cervical Cancer," *Center for Media and Democracy PR Watch.org*, https://web.archive.org/web/20081201131753/http://www.prwatch.org/node/6232/, accessed November 9, 2008. For a discussion of Women in Government's strategic relationship with Merck, see also Mello, Abiola, and Colgrove, "Pharmaceutical Companies' Role in State Vaccination Policymaking."

49 Siers-Poisson, "Women in Government, Merck's Trojan Horse: Part Three in a Series on the Politics and PR of Cervical Cancer."

50 Jesse McKinley, "Lawmaker Ends Effort to Make Spanking a Crime," *New York Times*, February 23, 2007.

51 Mike Zapler, "Local Assemblywoman Drops Cervical Cancer Bill," *Palo Alto Daily News*, February 2, 2007.

52 AB 16 (Hernandez), amended on May 2, 2007, ftp://www.leginfo.ca.gov/pub/07-08/bill/asm/ab_0001-0050/ab_16_cfa_20070602_170621_asm_floor.html, accessed August 16, 2017.

53 SB 277, June 30, 2015, https://leginfo.legislature.ca.gov/faces/billNavClient.xhtml?bill_id=201520160SB277; Phil Willon and Melanie Mason, "California Gov. Jerry Brown Signs New Vaccination Law, One of Nation's Toughest," *Los Angeles Times*, June 30, 2015, http://www.latimes.com/local/political/la-me-ln-governor-signs-tough-new-vaccination-law-20150630-story.html, accessed August 15, 2017.

54 "Women in Government Challenge to Eliminate Cervical Cancer Campaign Activity," *Women in Government*, http://womeningovernment.org/prevention, accessed November 10, 2008.

55 "HPV Vaccine and State Legislatures."

56 Rhode Island's requirement went into effect in August 2015. Richard Salit, "HPV Vaccination Rate for R.I. Seventh Graders 'Extremely Encouraging,'" *Providence Journal*, November 19, 2015. Nearly three-quarters of students had received the vaccine at the beginning of the 2015–2016 school year.

57 President's Cancer Panel, *Accelerating HPV Vaccine Uptake: Urgency for Action to Prevent Cancer* (Bethesda, MD: U.S. Department of Health and Human Services, 2014), v, https://deainfo.nci.nih.gov/advisory/pcp/annualReports/HPV/PDF/PCP_Annual_Report_2012-2013.pdf, accessed September 13, 2016.

58 Colgrove, *State of Immunity*, 239.

59 Ed Silverman, "Pharmalot, Pharmalittle: Was the FDA Commissioner Paid by Drug Makers Last Year?" *STAT*, July 5, 2016, https://www.statnews.com/pharmalot/2016/07/05/robert-califf-fda-generics-teva/, accessed February 1, 2017.

Chapter 7—Complicity and Corporations

1 Michael Applebaum, "Beverly J. Lybrand, Merck Vaccines," *Adweek*, October 8, 2007.

2 Pamela Hartzband and Jerome Groopman, "The New Language of Medicine," *New England Journal of Medicine* 365 (2011): 1372–1373.

3 Ibid.

4 The patient testimonials to the FDA for Avastin exemplify this practice. See Andrew Pollack, "F.D.A. Revokes Approval of Avastin for Use as Breast Cancer Drug," *New York Times*, November 18, 2011.

5 Ed Silverman, "Drug Firms Still Abuse Citizen Petitions, FDA Tells Congress," *STAT*, August 22, 2016, https://www.statnews.com/pharmalot/2016/08/22/fda -generics-citizen-petition/, accessed September 6, 2016.

6 "Gardasil Campaign Taps Public Fear of Cancer," *Pharmaceutical Executive*, November 26, 2006.

7 In the period 2006–2012, the median age of women diagnosed with cervical cancer was 49. "Cervical Cancer Facts and Stats," *The Training Center*, March 6, 2017, https://qap.sdsu.edu/screening/cervicalcancer/facts.html, accessed June 1, 2017.

8 The line that Harriet referred to does not appear to be in the poem, but the sentiment she evoked in her rendition is an accurate description of the poem's content.

9 My time working in public health research included projects that left me feeling as though we were mining information and extracting data from people who needed more than a short-term intervention in the service of a future greater good, although not all public health interventions function this way.

10 Harold P. Freeman, "Why Black Women Die of Cancer," *New York Times*, March 13, 2014.

11 Shalanda A. Bynum, Heather M. Brandt, Patricia A. Sharpe, Michelle S. Williams, and Jelani C. Kerr, "Working to Close the Gap: Identifying Predictors of HPV Vaccine Uptake among Young African American Women," *Journal of Health Care for the Poor and Underserved* 22, no. 2 (2011): 549–561; Freeman, "Why Black Women Die of Cancer."

12 Darcell P. Scharff, Katherine J. Mathews, Pamela Jackson, Jonathan Hoffsuemmer, Emeobong Martin, and Dorothy Edwards, "More Than Tuskegee: Understanding Mistrust about Research Participation," *Journal of Health Care for the Poor and Underserved* 21, no. 3 (2010): 879–897; Rebecca Skloot, *The Immortal Life of Henrietta Lacks* (New York: Broadway Books, 2010).

13 Emily Martin, *The Woman in the Body: A Cultural Analysis of Reproduction* (Boston: Beacon Press, 2001); Terri Kapsalis, *Public Privates: Performing Gynecology from Both Ends of the Speculum* (Durham, NC: Duke University Press, 1997).

14 Veronika Lipphardt and Jörg Niewöhner, "Producing Difference in an Age of Biosociality: Biohistorical Narratives, Standardisation and Resistance as Translations," *Science, Technology & Innovation Studies* 3, no. 1 (2007): 45–65; Mindy Thompson Fullilove, "Comment: Abandoning 'Race' as a Variable in Public Health Research: An Idea Whose Time Has Come," *American Journal of Public Health* 88, no. 9 (1998): 1297–1298.

15 Jonathan Kahn, "Race, Pharmacogenomics, and Marketing: Putting BiDil in Context," *American Journal of Bioethics* 6, no. 5 (2006): W1–W5.

16 Linda M. Hunt, Nicole D. Truesdell, and Meta J. Kreiner, "Genes, Race, and Culture in Clinical Care," *Medical Anthropology Quarterly* 27, no. 2 (2013): 253–271; Lundy Braun, Anne Fausto-Sterling, Duana Fullwiley, Evelynn M. Hammonds, Alondra Nelson, William Quivers, Susan M. Reverby, and Alexandra E. Shields, "Racial Categories in Medical Practice: How Useful Are They?" *PLoS Med* 4, no. 9 (2007): 1423–1428.

17 Laura J. Viens, Jane Henley, Meg Watson, Lauri E. Markowitz, Cheryll C. Thomas, Trevor D. Thompson, Hilda Razzaghi, and Mona Saraiya, "Human Papillomavirus—Associated Cancers—United States, 2008–2012," *Morbidity and Mortality Weekly Report* 65 (2016): 661–666.

18 Charles L. Briggs, "Communicability, Racial Discourse, and Disease," *Annual Review of Anthropology* 34 (2005): 277.

19 Skloot, *The Immortal Life of Henrietta Lacks*.

20 Laurie Gilmore Selleck, "Pretty in Pink: The Susan G. Komen Network and the Branding of the Breast Cancer Cause," *Nordic Journal of English Studies* 9, no. 3 (2010): 119–138; Barbara Ehrenreich, "Slap on a Pink Ribbon and Call It a Day," *Salon.com*, December 2, 2009, http://www.salon.com/2009/12/02/womens_health_2/, accessed June 29, 2011; Samantha King, "Pink Ribbons Inc.: Breast Cancer Activism and the Politics of Philanthropy," *International Journal of Qualitative Studies in Education* 17, no. 4 (2004): 473–492; Emily S. Kolker, "Framing as a Cultural Resource in Health Social Movements: Funding Activism and the Breast Cancer Movement in the US 1990–1993," *Sociology of Health & Illness* 26, no. 6 (2004): 820–844.

21 Susan Reynolds Whyte, "Health Identities and Subjectivities," *Medical Anthropology Quarterly* 23, no. 1 (2009): 9.

22 Rebecca Dimond, Andrew Bartlett, and Jamie Lewis, "What Binds Biosociality? The Collective Effervescence of the Parent-Led Conference," *Social Science & Medicine* 126 (2014): 2. See also Carlos Novas and Nikolas Rose, "Genetic Risk and the Birth of the Somatic Individual," *Economy and Society* 29, no. 4 (2000): 485–513.

23 Whyte, "Health Identities and Subjectivities," 13.

24 Contemporary theories explore the interplay between actors and institutions, including the meaning actors attribute to institutional philosophies and their agency in shaping institutional values and practices. See, for example, Mayer N. Zald and Patricia Denton, "From Evangelism to General Service: The Transformation of the YMCA," *Administrative Science Quarterly* 9, no. 2 (1963): 214–234; Pamela S. Tolbert and Lynne G. Zucker, "The Institutionalization of Institutional Theory," *Studying Organization: Theory & Method* (1999): 169–184; and Tammar B. Zilber, "Institutionalization as an Interplay between Actions, Meanings, and Actors: The Case of a Rape Crisis Center in Israel," *Academy of Management Journal* 45, no. 1 (2002): 234–254. The recognition that institutions are not abstract monoliths, or "thinglike" (251), but exist in the world, created, led by, and affected by politics, processes, and cultural influences has been an important contribution of this discourse, informed partly by anthropologists such as Clifford Geertz. See Tolbert and Zucker, "The Institutionalization of Institutional Theory," 195.

25 The Internet Archive (www.archive.org) allows one to enter a website address and track the site's changes over time.

26 Capitalization in original.

27 CCG's website from cached version March 2000.

28 Michelle Murphy, *Seizing the Means of Reproduction: Entanglements of Feminism, Health, and Technoscience* (Durham, NC: Duke University Press, 2012), 147.

29 S. Lochlann Jain, "Cancer Butch," *Cultural Anthropology* 22, no. 4 (2007): 520.

30 Ibid., 528.

31 The cancer drug Avastin is an example of pharmaceutical companies deploying patients as their ideal advertisers for their product. During the FDA review of Avastin's breast cancer indication, Genentech, the drug's manufacturer, included a group of patients who testified about the benefits they'd seen from the drug. Despite Genentech's strategy, the FDA revoked its breast cancer indication. Pollack, "F.D.A. Revokes Approval of Avastin."

32 Michelle M. Mello, Sara Abiola, and James Colgrove, "Pharmaceutical Companies' Role in State Vaccination Policymaking: The Case of Human Papillomavirus Vaccination," *American Journal of Public Health* 102, no. 5 (2012): 893–898.

33 Laura Mamo and Steven Epstein, "The Pharmaceuticalization of Sexual Risk: Vaccine Development and the New Politics of Cancer Prevention," *Social Science & Medicine* 101 (2014): 156.

34 Aaron Smith, "Street Divided over Numbers from Big Pharma," *CNN Money*, April 20, 2007, http://money.cnn.com/2007/04/19/news/companies/drug_wrap/, accessed October 19, 2007.

35 Carolyn B. Sufrin and Joseph S. Ross, "Pharmaceutical Industry Marketing: Understanding Its Impact on Women's Health," *Obstetrical & Gynecological Survey* 63, no. 9 (2008): 585–596.

36 Matthew Arnold, "MM&M All-Stars Company of the Year: Merck," *Medical Marketing & Media*, January 1, 2008.

37 Viens et al., "Human Papillomavirus—Associated Cancers—United States, 2008–2012."

38 Anna L. Beavis, Patti E. Gravitt, and Anne F. Rositch, "Hysterectomy-Corrected Cervical Cancer Mortality Rates Reveal a Larger Racial Disparity in the United States," *Cancer* 123, no. 6 (2017): 1044–1050; Anne F. Rositch, Rebecca G. Nowak, and Patti E. Gravitt, "Increased Age and Race-Specific Incidence of Cervical Cancer after Correction for Hysterectomy Prevalence in the United States from 2000 to 2009," *Cancer* 120, no. 13 (2014): 2032–2038; Gopal K. Singh, "Rural-Urban Trends and Patterns in Cervical Cancer Mortality, Incidence, Stage, and Survival in the United States, 1950–2008," *Journal of Community Health* 37, no. 1 (2012): 217–223.

39 I reflect on the Gwendolyn Brooks poem because of the short duration of my time with BWHG. I wonder if Harriet perceived my short stint as emblematic of Brooks's criticism of self-righteous public health interventionists. My reasons for cutting the volunteering short had to do with other extenuating circumstances, and I regret not spending more time with Harriet's group.

40 Mello et al., "Pharmaceutical Companies' Role in State Vaccination Policymaking."

41 Mamo and Epstein, "The Pharmaceuticalization of Sexual Risk," 156.

Chapter 8—Mothers and Gardasil

1 The Merck executive in charge of these advertisements, Bev Lybrand, has explicitly acknowledged this strategy. See Matthew Arnold, "MM&M All-Stars Company of the Year: Merck," *Medical Marketing & Media*, January 1, 2008: 47.

2 *Gardasil.com*, http://www.gardasil.com/gardasil-information/vaccine-for-cervical-cancer/index.html, accessed December 29, 2009.

3 Another group for mothers gathered at a coffee shop not far from the meeting location where NaturalMoms met. On the night that I attended this other mothers' group, which was also part of a national organization, they held a WOW meeting, which stood for "Work on Whatever." As the group of twelve mothers arrived, they started bringing out various activities, papers, and craft projects, which they focused on while simultaneously socializing with each other. One mother admired another's foresight in bringing her coupons to clip. The group leader, Dara, explained that WOW day allowed mothers to do other tasks. As she ate her dinner, she clarified: "Multitask." In addition to the WOW theme, it was also "Chat in the Hat Day," which meant they would discuss questions by passing a hat that contained questions. It was unclear whether these questions had been recommended by the organization or if the group had written them as an activity in the past. I did not conduct fieldwork with this group after my first visit, as they were less receptive than the NaturalMoms group to having a researcher in their midst. The NaturalMoms' chapter leader invited me to attend the first meeting and asked me to pay dues to continue attending the group's meetings. Attendees were informed that I was a researcher at the beginning of each of the nine monthly meetings I observed.

4 Katharine McCabe, "Mothercraft: Birth Work and the Making of Neoliberal Mothers," *Social Science & Medicine* 162 (2016): 177–184.

5 Aimée Morrison, "Autobiography in Real Time: A Genre Analysis of Personal Mommy Blogging," *Cyberpsychology: Journal of Psychosocial Research on Cyberspace* 42, no. 2: article 5; Lisa Belkin, "Queen of the Mommy Bloggers," *New York Times*, February 23, 2011.

6 Lori Kido Lopez, "The Radical Act of 'Mommy Blogging': Redefining Motherhood through the Blogosphere," *New Media & Society* 11, no. 5: 729–747.

7 McCabe, "Mothercraft," 178.

8 While some of the vaccine resistance movements argue that vaccines are harmful, this was not the position the conservative groups adopted. They did not contend that the vaccine would physically harm a child; their contention was that vaccinating a child might indicate parents' permissive attitudes toward sexual activity.

9 Elisa J. Sobo, Arianna Huhn, Autumn Sannwald, and Lori Thurman, "Information Curation among Vaccine Cautious Parents: Web 2.0, Pinterest Thinking, and Pediatric Vaccination Choice," *Medical Anthropology* 35, no. 6 (2016): 529–546.

10 Not a pseudonym.

11 *Jay Gordon, MD FAAP*, https://web.archive.org/web/20080615005317/http://www.drjaygordon.com:80/development/index.asp, accessed May 29, 2008.

12 Jenny McCarthy, appearance on *Larry King Live*, April 8, 2008.

13 Jenny McCarthy and Jim Carrey, "Jenny McCarthy: My Son's Recovery from Autism," *CNN.com*, April 3, 2008, http://www.cnn.com/2008/US/04/02/mccarthy.autismtreatment/, accessed April 3, 2008.

14 McCarthy currently claims her son has been cured of autism. See McCarthy and Carrey, "Jenny McCarthy: My Son's Recovery from Autism."

15 "Educate before You Vaccinate," *GenerationRescue.org*. http://www.generationrescue.org/resources/vaccination, accessed July 8, 2014.

16 "Jenny McCarthy Body Count," https://web.archive.org/web/20110207105812/
    http://jennymccarthybodycount.com/Jenny_McCarthy_Body_Count/Home
    .html, accessed February 8, 2011.

17 Andrew J. Wakefield, Simon H. Murch, Andrew Anthony, John Linnell, D. M. Cas-
    son, Mohsin Malik, Mark Berelowitz, Amar P. Dhillon, Michael A. Thomson, and
    Peter Harvey, "Retracted: Ileal-lymphoid-Nodular Hyperplasia, Non-Specific Coli-
    tis, and Pervasive Developmental Disorder in Children," The Lancet 351, no. 9103
    (1998): 637–641.

18 Simon H. Murch, Andrew Anthony, David H. Casson, Mohsin Malik, Mark Bere-
    lowitz, Amar P. Dhillon, Michael A. Thomson, Alan Valentine, Susan E. Davies,
    and John A. Walker Smith, "Retraction of An Interpretation," The Lancet 363,
    no. 9411 (2004): 750.

19 The Editors, "Retraction—Ileal-lymphoid-Nodular Hyperplasia, Non-Specific
    Colitis, and Pervasive Developmental Disorder in Children," The Lancet 375,
    no. 9713 (2010): 445.

20 NHS Choices, "Ruling on Doctor in MMR Scare," NHS, January 29, 2010, http://
    www.nhs.uk/news/2010/01january/pages/mmr-vaccine-autism-scare-doctor.aspx,
    accessed July 4, 2017.

21 Stuart Blume, "Anti-Vaccination Movements and Their Interpretations," Social Sci-
    ence & Medicine 62, no. 3 (2006): 628–642; James Keith Colgrove, State of Immu-
    nity: The Politics of Vaccination in Twentieth-Century America (Berkeley: University
    of California Press, 2006); Jeffrey P. Baker, "The Pertussis Vaccine Controversy
    in Great Britain, 1974–1986," Vaccine 21, no. 25–26 (2003): 4003–4010; Susan L.
    Smith, "The Effective Use of Fear Appeals in Persuasive Immunization: An Analysis
    of National Immunization Intervention Messages," Journal of Applied Communica-
    tion Research 25, no. 4 (1997): 264–292.

22 Baker, "The Pertussis Vaccine Controversy in Great Britain."

23 Blume and Zanders, "Vaccine Independence, Local Competences and Globalisa-
    tion: Lessons from the History of Pertussis Vaccines," Social Science & Medicine 63,
    no. 7 (2006): 1825–1835.

24 National Vaccine Information Center, "About National Vaccine Information
    Center," National Vaccine Information Center, http://www.nvic.org/about.aspx,
    accessed July 4, 2017.

25 National Vaccine Information Center, "NVIC's Notable Accomplishments and
    History," National Vaccine Information Center, http://www.nvic.org/about/notable
    -accomplishments-and-history.aspx, accessed July 4, 2017.

26 Blume and Zanders, "Vaccine Independence, Local Competences and
    Globalisation."

27 Nicola P. Klein, Joan Bartlett, Ali Rowhani-Rahbar, Bruce Fireman, and Roger Bax-
    ter, "Waning Protection after Fifth Dose of Acellular Pertussis Vaccine in Children,"
    New England Journal of Medicine 367, no. 11 (2012): 1012–1019.

28 Anna Kirkland, "Credibility Battles in the Autism Litigation," Social Studies of Sci-
    ence 42, no. 2 (2012): 237–261.

29 S. Lochlann Jain, Malignant: How Cancer Becomes Us (Berkeley: University of
    California Press, 2013), 118.

30 Although Mary's description of the oral polio vaccine is not completely accurate,
    she is referring to the 2000 decision in the United States to switch back to the inac-
    tivated polio vaccine after growing concerns in the United States about oral polio

vaccine-related paralysis. See William Muraskin, *Polio Eradication and Its Discontents: An Historian's Journey through an International Public Health (Un)Civil War* (Himayatnagar, Hyderabad: Orient Blackswan, 2012), 13–14; and Stuart S. Blume, "Lock In, the State and Vaccine Development: Lessons from the History of the Polio Vaccines," *Research Policy* 34, no. 2 (2005): 164–170. The inexpensive oral polio vaccine is the preferred vaccine of the World Health Organization.

31 This absence in our discussions may illuminate why Gardasil is not like other vaccines. HPV is not a childhood contagion that needs to be contained in the same way that measles or chicken pox do. Thus, in some ways, Gardasil may also suffer from its identity as a vaccine. Because it was not presented as a sexual health prophylactic, it did not fit into parents' considerations of the needs of young adolescents.

Chapter 9—The "Tragically Underused" Vaccine

1 "NCI-Designated Cancer Centers Urge HPV Vaccination for the Prevention of Cancer," January 27, 2016, http://www.salk.edu/wp-content/uploads/2016/01/NCI_HPV_Consensus_Statement_012716.pdf, accessed January 31, 2016. See also Laurie McGinley, "Cancer Doctors Leading Campaign to Boost Use of HPV Vaccine," *Washington Post*, June 19, 2016.

2 President's Cancer Panel, *Accelerating HPV Vaccine Uptake: Urgency for Action to Prevent Cancer* (Bethesda, MD: U.S. Department of Health and Human Services, 2014), https://deainfo.nci.nih.gov/advisory/pcp/annualreports/hpv/PDF/PCP_Annual_Report_2012-2013.pdf, accessed September 13, 2016.

3 Centers for Disease Control, "Top 10 List for HPV #VaxSuccess," https://www.cdc.gov/hpv/downloads/top10-improving-practice.pdf, accessed October 18, 2016.

4 Betsy McKay, "New Approach to Promoting HPV Vaccinations," *Wall Street Journal*, October 17, 2016, http://www.wsj.com/articles/new-approach-to-promoting-hpv-vaccinations-1476727458, accessed October 18, 2016.

5 A 2017 article explored how patient advocacy organizations may be influenced by corporate and pharmaceutical contributions. The authors found that two-thirds of the sampled organizations had received some industry funding and that a third of those groups received more than 25 percent of their funds from industry. Susannah L. Rose, Janelle Highland, Matthew T. Karafa, and Steven Joffe, "Patient Advocacy Organizations, Industry Funding, and Conflicts of Interest," *JAMA Internal Medicine* 177, no. 3 (2017): 344–350.

6 See, for example, Joseph Dumit, *Drugs for Life: How Pharmaceutical Companies Define Our Health* (Durham, NC: Duke University Press, 2012); Meika Loe, *The Rise of Viagra: How the Little Blue Pill Changed Sex in America* (New York: New York University Press, 2004); and Michael J. Oldani, "Thick Prescriptions: Toward an Interpretation of Pharmaceutical Sales Practices," *Medical Anthropology Quarterly* 18, no. 3 (2004): 325–356.

7 I am thinking of Lorraine Daston's discussion of moral economies, especially in the sciences. She describes them as "a web of affect-saturated values that stand and function in well-defined relationship to one another . . . an organized system that displays certain regularities, regularities that are explicable but not always predictable in their detail. A moral economy is a balanced system of emotional forces, with

equilibrium points and constraints." Lorraine Daston, "The Moral Economy of Science," *Osiris*, 2nd ser., 10 (1995): 4.

8 Claire Dederer, "Pitching Protection, to Both Mothers and Daughters," *New York Times*, February 18, 2007.

9 Anna L. Beavis, Patti E. Gravitt, and Anne F. Rositch, "Hysterectomy-Corrected Cervical Cancer Mortality Rates Reveal a Larger Racial Disparity in the United States," *Cancer* 123, no. 6 (2017): 1044–1050.

10 George F. Sawaya and Karen Smith-McCune, "HPV Vaccination: More Answers, More Questions," *New England Journal of Medicine* 356, no. 19 (2007): 1991–1993.

11 I realize that qualifying the standard schedule with "more or less" does not actually mean following the standard schedule. Public health officials consider any deviation from the recommended schedule to be troubling.

12 Mandy A. Allison, Laura P. Hurley, Lauri Markowitz, Lori A. Crane, Michaela Brtnikova, Brenda L. Beaty, Megan Snow, Janine Cory, Shannon Stokley, and Jill Roark, "Primary Care Physicians' Perspectives about HPV Vaccine," *Pediatrics* 137, no. 2 (2016): e20152488; National Vaccine Advisory Committee, "Overcoming Barriers to Low HPV Vaccine Uptake in the United States: Recommendations from the National Vaccine Advisory Committee," *Public Health Reports* (January–February 2016): 17–25; National Cancer Institute, "NCI-Designated Cancer Centers Urge HPV Vaccination for the Prevention of Cancer," January 27, 2016, https://www.fredhutch.org/en/news/center-news/2016/01/cancer-centers-consensus-hpv-vaccine.html, accessed January 31, 2016; Shannon Stokley, Jenny Jeyarajah, David Yankey, Maria Cano, Julianne Gee, Jill Roark, R. C. Curtis, and Lauri Markowitz, "Human Papillomavirus Vaccination Coverage among Adolescents, 2007–2013, and Post-Licensure Vaccine Safety Monitoring, 2006–2014—United States," *Morbidity and Mortality Weekly Report* 63, no. 29 (2014): 623–633; Richard M. Grimes, Laura J. Benjamins, and Kendra L. Williams, "Counseling about the HPV Vaccine: Desexualize, Educate, and Advocate," *Journal of Pediatric and Adolescent Gynecology* 26, no. 4 (2013): 243–248; Patricia Jeudin, Elizabeth Liveright, Marcela G. del Carmen, and Rebecca B Perkins, "Race, Ethnicity and Income as Factors for HPV Vaccine Acceptance and Use," *Human Vaccines & Immunotherapeutics* 9, no. 7 (2013): 1413–1420.

13 Allison et al., "Primary Care Physicians' Perspectives about HPV Vaccine."

14 Laurie D. Elam-Evans, David Yankey, Jenny Jeyarajah, James A. Singleton, R. C. Curtis, Jessica MacNeil, and Susan Hariri, "National, Regional, State, and Selected Local Area Vaccination Coverage among Adolescents Aged 13–17 Years—United States, 2013," *Morbidity and Mortality Weekly Report* 63, no. 29 (2014): 627.

15 Ibid.

16 Ibid.

17 Associated Press, "Preteens Need Only Two HPV Shots—Not Three, Government Panel Says," *STAT*, October 19, 2016, https://www.statnews.com/2016/10/19/hpv-vaccine-preteens/, accessed October 20, 2016.

18 Statement at the Commonwealth Club meeting "HPV The Silent Killer—Prevention, Treatment, and Controversy," October 9, 2009.

19 Shalanda A. Bynum, Heather M. Brandt, Patricia A. Sharpe, Michelle S. Williams, and Jelani C. Kerr, "Working to Close the Gap: Identifying Predictors of HPV Uptake among Young African-American Women," *Journal of Health Care for the Poor and Underserved* 22, no. 2 (2011): 558.

20 Diane R. Brown and Caroline E. S. Harris, "Cervical Cancer Screening among Ethnically Diverse Black Women: Knowledge, Attitudes, Beliefs, and Practices," *Journal of the National Medical Association* 103, no. 8 (2011): 727.

21 Laurie McGinley, "Do the New Merck HPV Ads Guilt-Trip Parents or Tell Hard Truths? Both," *Washington Post*, August 11, 2016.

22 Wendy Sue Swanson, "HPV Vaccine Decreases HPV Infections!" *Seattle Children's Hospital Research Foundation*, March 1, 2016, http://seattlemamadoc .seattlechildrens.org/decreasing-rates-of-hpv/, accessed May 23, 2016.

Bibliography

"The AIDS Memorial Quilt." *The NAMES Project Foundation.* http://www.aidsquilt.org/about/the-aids-memorial-quilt. Accessed February 3, 2015.

"About Dr. Jay." *Dr. Jay Gordon*, drjaygordon.com. Accessed May 29, 2008.

"About Us." *Women in Government.* http://womeningovernment.org/. Accessed November 10, 2008.

Adams, Vincanne, Michelle Murphy, and Adele E. Clarke. "Anticipation: Technoscience, Life, Affect, Temporality." *Subjectivity* 28, no. 1 (2009): 246–265.

Advisory Committee on Immunization Practices. "Quadrivalent Human Papillomavirus Vaccine." *Morbidity and Mortality Weekly Report* 56 (2007): 1–24.

Allison, Mandy A., Laura P. Hurley, Lauri Markowitz, Lori A. Crane, Michaela Brtnikova, Brenda L. Beaty, Megan Snow, Janine Cory, Shannon Stokley, and Jill Roark. "Primary Care Physicians' Perspectives about HPV Vaccine." *Pediatrics* 137, no. 2 (2016): e20152488.

Anhang, Rebecca, Annekathryn Goodman, and Sue J. Goldie. "HPV Communication: Review of Existing Research and Recommendations for Patient Education." *CA: A Cancer Journal for Clinicians* 54, no. 5 (2004): 248–259.

Applbaum, Kalman. "Consumers Are Patients! Shared Decision-Making and Treatment Non-Compliance as Business Opportunity." *Transcultural Psychiatry* 46, no. 1 (2009): 107–130.

———. "Pharmaceutical Marketing and the Invention of the Medical Consumer." *PLoS Medicine* 3, no. 4 (2006): e189.

Applebaum, Michael. "Beverly J. Lybrand, Merck Vaccines." *Adweek*, October 8, 2007.

Arnold, Matthew. "MM&M All-Stars Company of the Year: Merck." *Medical Marketing & Media*, January 1, 2008.

Aronowitz, Robert. *Risky Medicine: Our Quest to Cure Fear and Uncertainty.* Chicago: University of Chicago Press, 2015.

Aronowitz, Robert A. "The Converged Experience of Risk and Disease." *Milbank Quarterly* 87, no. 2 (2009): 417–442.

Associated Press. "Preteens Need Only Two HPV Shots—Not Three, Government Panel Says." *STAT*, October 19, 2016. https://www.statnews.com/2016/10/19/hpv-vaccine-preteens/. Accessed October 20, 2016.

Baay, Marc F. D., Veronique Verhoeven, Lieve Peremans, Dirk Avonts, and Jan Baptist Vermorken. "General Practitioners' Perception of Risk Factors for Cervical Cancer Development: Consequences for Patient Education." *Patient Education and Counseling* 62, no. 2 (2006): 277–281.

Baer, Heather, Susan Allen, and Lundy Braun. "Knowledge of Human Papillomavirus Infection among Young Adult Men and Women: Implications for Health Education and Research." *Journal of Community Health* 25, no. 1 (2000): 67–78.

Baker, Jeffrey P. "The Pertussis Vaccine Controversy in Great Britain, 1974–1986." *Vaccine* 21, nos. 25–26 (2003): 4003–4010.

Baseman, Janet G., and Laura A. Koutsky. "The Epidemiology of Human Papillomavirus Infections." *Journal of Clinical Virology* 32 (2005): 16–24.

Beavis, Anna L., Patti E. Gravitt, and Anne F. Rositch. "Hysterectomy-Corrected Cervical Cancer Mortality Rates Reveal a Larger Racial Disparity in the United States." *Cancer* 123, no. 6 (2017): 1044–1050.

Beavis, Anna Louise, and Kimberly L. Levinson. "Preventing Cervical Cancer in the United States: Barriers and Resolutions for HPV Vaccination." *Frontiers in Oncology* 6 (2016): 1–9.

Beck, Julie. "The Different Stakes of Male and Female Birth Control." *The Atlantic*, November 1, 2016.

Behre, Hermann M., Michael Zitzmann, Richard A. Anderson, David J. Handelsman, Silvia W. Lestari, Robert I. McLachlan, M. Cristina Meriggiola, Man Mohan Misro, Gabriela Noe, and Frederick C. W. Wu. "Efficacy and Safety of an Injectable Combination Hormonal Contraceptive for Men." *Journal of Clinical Endocrinology & Metabolism* 101, no. 12 (2016): 4779–4788.

Belkin, Lisa. "Queen of the Mommy Bloggers." *New York Times*, February 23, 2011.

Berenson, Alex. "Merck Agrees to Pay $4.85 Billion in Vioxx Claims." *New York Times*, November 9, 2007.

Berg, Marc, and Paul Harterink. "Embodying the Patient: Records and Bodies in Early 20th Century US Medical Practice." *Body & Society* 10, no. 2–3 (2004): 13–41.

"A Bill to Prohibit Federal Funding or Other Assistance for Mandatory Human Papillomavirus (HPV) Vaccination Programs," HR 1153, 111th Congress, February 16, 2007, https://www.govtrack.us/congress/bills/111/hr3188/text, accessed July 20, 2007.

Black, Carla L., David Yankey, and Maureen Kolasa. "National, State, and Local Area Vaccination Coverage among Children Aged 19–35 Months—United States, 2012." *Morbidity and Mortality Weekly Report* 62, no. 36 (2013): 733–737.

Blume, S. S., and D. Rose. "Citizens as Users of Technology: An Exploratory Study of Vaccines and Vaccination." In *How Users Matter: The Co-Construction of Users and Technology*, edited by Nelly Oudshoorn and Trevor Pinch, 103–132. Cambridge, MA: MIT Press, 2005.

Blume, Stuart. "Anti-Vaccination Movements and Their Interpretations." *Social Science & Medicine* 62, no. 3 (2006): 628–642.

———. "Lock In, the State and Vaccine Development: Lessons from the History of the Polio Vaccines." *Research Policy* 34, no. 2 (2005): 159–173.

Blume, Stuart, and Mariska Zanders. "Vaccine Independence, Local Competences and Globalisation: Lessons from the History of Pertussis Vaccines." *Social Science & Medicine* 63, no. 7 (2006): 1825–1835.

Blumenthal, Ralph. "Texas Is First to Require Cancer Shots for Schoolgirls." *New York Times*, February 3, 2007.

Boronow, Richard C. "Death of the Papanicolaou Smear? A Tale of Three Reasons." *American Journal of Obstetrics and Gynecology* 179, no. 2 (1998): 391–396.

Bosch, F. Xavier, and Silvia De Sanjosé. "Human Papillomavirus and Cervical Cancer Burden and Assessment of Causality." *JNCI Monographs* 2003, no. 31 (2003): 3–13.

Brandt, Heather M., Donna H. McCree, Lisa L. Lindley, Patricia A. Sharpe, and Brent E. Hutto. "An Evaluation of Printed HPV Educational Materials." *Cancer Control* 12, suppl. 2 (2005): 103–106.

Braun, Lundy, Anne Fausto-Sterling, Duana Fullwiley, Evelynn M. Hammonds, Alondra Nelson, William Quivers, Susan M. Reverby, and Alexandra E. Shields. "Racial Categories in Medical Practice: How Useful Are They?" *PLoS Med* 4, no. 9 (2007): 1423–1428.

Briggs, Charles L. "Communicability, Racial Discourse, and Disease." *Annual Review of Anthropology* 34 (2005): 269–291.

Briggs, Laura. "The Race of Hysteria: 'Overcivilization' and the 'Savage' Woman in Late Nineteenth-Century Obstetrics and Gynecology." *American Quarterly* 52, no. 2 (2000): 246–273.

Brown, Diane R., and Caroline E. S. Harris. "Cervical Cancer Screening among Ethnically Diverse Black Women: Knowledge, Attitudes, Beliefs, and Practices." *Journal of the National Medical Association* 103, no. 8 (2011): 719–728.

Bynum, Shalanda A., Heather M. Brandt, Patricia A. Sharpe, Michelle S. Williams, and Jelani C. Kerr. "Working to Close the Gap: Identifying Predictors of HPV Vaccine Uptake among Young African American Women." *Journal of Health Care for the Poor and Underserved* 22, no. 2 (2011): 549–561.

California Department of Public Health Immunization Branch, "2014–2015 Kindergarten Immunization Assessment Results." www.cdph.ca.gov/programs/immunize/Documents/2014-15%20CA%20Kindergarten%20Immunization%20Assessment.pdf. Accessed March 15, 2015.

Callon, Michel, P. Lascoumes, and Y. Barthe. *Acting in An Uncertain World: An Essay on Technological Democracy*. Cambridge, MA: MIT Press, 2009.

Carlat, Daniel. "Dr. Drug Rep." *New York Times*, November 25, 2007.

Casper, Monica J., and Adele E. Clarke. "Making the Pap Smear into the 'Right Tool' for the Job: Cervical Cancer Screening in the USA, Circa 1940–95." *Social Studies of Science* 28, no. 2 (1998): 255–290.

Casper, Monica J., and Laura M. Carpenter. "Sex, Drugs, and Politics: The HPV Vaccine for Cervical Cancer." *Sociology of Health & Illness* 30, no. 6 (2008): 886–899.

Centers for Disease Control. "2013 Cancer Types Grouped by Race and Ethnicity." *Centers for Disease Control and Prevention*, https://nccd.cdc.gov/uscs/cancersbyraceandethnicity.aspx.

———. "Incidence, Prevalence, and Cost of Sexually Transmitted Diseases in the United States," *Centers for Disease Control and Prevention*, https://www.cdc.gov/std/stats/sti-estimates-fact-sheet-feb-2013.pdf. Accessed June 17, 2017.

———. "More Than 3 Million US Women at Risk for Alcohol-Exposed Pregnancy." *Centers for Disease Control and Prevention*, February 2, 2016. http://www.cdc.gov/media/releases/2016/p0202-alcoholexposed-pregnancy.html. Accessed October 24, 2016.

———. "STD Facts—Human Papillomavirus (HPV)." *Centers for Disease Control and Prevention*. http://www.cdc.gov/std/hpv/stdfact-hpv.htm. Accessed February 4, 2014.

———. "Top 10 List for HPV #VaxSuccess." https://www.cdc.gov/hpv/downloads/top10 -improving-practice.pdf. Accessed April 6, 2017.

"Cervical Cancer Facts and Stats." *The Training Center*, March 6, 2017. https://qap.sdsu.edu/ screening/cervicalcancer/facts.html. Accessed June 1, 2017.

"Chose to Know: Take Control of Your Cervical Cancer Risk with an HPV Test." TheHPVTest.com. http://web.archive.org/web/20060819040137/http://www .thehpvtest.com/index.html. Accessed November 14, 2008.

Clarke, Adele E., and Monica J. Casper. "From Simple Technology to Complex Arena: Classification of Pap Smears, 1917–90." *Medical Anthropology Quarterly* 10, no. 4 (1996): 601–623.

Clarke, Adele E., and Joan H. Fujimura. *The Right Tools for the Job: At Work in Twentieth-Century Life Sciences*. Princeton, NJ: Princeton University Press, 1992.

Clarke, Adele E., Janet K. Shim, Laura Mamo, Jennifer Ruth Fosket, and Jennifer R. Fishman. "Biomedicalization: Technoscientific Transformations of Health, Illness, and U.S. Biomedicine." *American Sociological Review* 68, no. 2 (2003): 161–194.

Colgrove, James Keith. "The Ethics and Politics of Compulsory HPV Vaccination." *New England Journal of Medicine* 355, no. 23 (2006): 2389–2391.

———. *State of Immunity: The Politics of Vaccination in Twentieth-Century America*. Berkeley: University of California Press, 2006.

Cooper, Diane, Margaret Hoffman, Henri Carrara, Lynn Rosenberg, Judy Kelly, Ilse Stander, Lynnette Denny, Anna-Lise Williamson, and Samuel Shapiro. "Determinants of Sexual Activity and Its Relation to Cervical Cancer Risk among South African Women." *BMC Public Health* 7, no. 1 (2007): 341.

Culp-Ressler, Tara. "Texas May Slash Cancer Screenings for Low-Income Women." *Think Progress*, January 29, 2015. https://thinkprogress.org/texas-may-slash-cancer-screenings -for-low-income-women-7289cd186c48 Accessed April 23, 2015.

Daley, Ellen M., Karen Kay M. Perrin, Cheryl Vamos, Candace Webb, Trish Mueller, Jennifer L. Packing-Ebuen, Holly L. Rayko, Mary McFarlane, and Robert J. McDermott. "HPV Knowledge among HPV+ Women." *American Journal of Health Behavior* 32, no. 5 (2008): 477–487.

Daston, Lorraine, "The Moral Economy of Science." *Osiris* 2nd Series, Vol. 10, (1995): 2–24.

Diekema, Douglas S. "Responding to Parental Refusals of Immunization of Children." *Pediatrics* 115, no. 5 (2005): e1696.

Digene Corporation. "Digene Consumer Ad Wins Industry Award for Best Product Launch." *PR Newswire*, November 17, 2005, http://www.prnewswire.com/news-releases/ digene-consumer-ad-wins-industry-award-for-best-product-launch-55703912.html. Accessed April 7, 2017.

Dimond, Rebecca, Andrew Bartlett, and Jamie Lewis. "What Binds Biosociality? The Collective Effervescence of the Parent-Led Conference." *Social Science & Medicine* (February 2015): 1–8.

Doan, Lynn. "Schools to Offer STD Vaccine." *Los Angeles Times*, July 24, 2006.

Donzelot, Jacques. *The Policing of Families*. New York: Pantheon, 1979.

D'Souza, Gypsyamber, Aimee R. Kreimer, Raphael Viscidi, Michael Pawlita, Carole Fakhry, Wayne M. Koch, William H. Westra, and Maura L Gillison. "Case—Control Study of Human Papillomavirus and Oropharyngeal Cancer." *New England Journal of Medicine* 356, no. 19 (2007): 1944–1956.

Dumit, Joseph. *Drugs for Life: How Pharmaceutical Companies Define Our Health*. Durham, NC: Duke University Press, 2012.

———. "Illnesses You Have to Fight to Get: Facts as Forces in Uncertain, Emergent Illnesses." *Social Science & Medicine* 62, no. 3 (2006): 577–590.

D'Urso, Jennifer, Melva Thompson-Robinson, and Steve Chandler. "HPV Knowledge and Behaviors of Black College Students at a Historically Black University." *Journal of American College Health* 56, no. 2 (2007): 159–163.

Editors. "Retraction—Ileal-Hyperplasia, Non-Specific Colitis, and Pervasive Developmental Disorder in Children." *The Lancet* 375, no. 9713 (2010): 445.

"Educate before You Vaccinate." *Generation Rescue*, 2013. http://www.generationrescue.org/resources/vaccination. Accessed July 8, 2014.

Eggen, Dan. "Rick Perry Reverses Himself, Calls HPV Vaccine Mandate a 'Mistake.'" *Washington Post*, September 13, 2011.

Ehrenreich, Barbara. "Slap on a Pink Ribbon and Call It a Day." *Salon.com*, December 2, 2009, http://www.salon.com/2009/12/02/womens_health_2/. Accessed June 29, 2011.

Elam-Evans, Laurie D., David Yankey, Jenny Jeyarajah, James A. Singleton, R. C. Curtis, Jessica MacNeil, and Susan Hariri. "National, Regional, State, and Selected Local Area Vaccination Coverage among Adolescents Aged 13–17 Years: United States, 2013." *Morbidity and Mortality Weekly Report* 63, no. 29 (2014): 625–633.

Elliott, Andrea M., Stewart C. Alexander, Craig A. Mescher, Deepika Mohan, and Amber E. Barnato. "Differences in Physicians' Verbal and Nonverbal Communication with Black and White Patients at the End of Life." *Journal of Pain and Symptom Management* 51, no. 1 (2016): 1–8.

Epstein, Steven. "The Construction of Lay Expertise: AIDS Activism and the Forging of Credibility in the Reform of Clinical Trials." *Science, Technology, & Human Values* 20, no. 4 (1995): 408–437.

Fischetti, Mark. "Too Many Children Go Unvaccinated." *Scientific American*, May 14, 2013.

Foucault, Michel. *The Foucault Reader*. New York: Pantheon, 1984.

———. "The Means of Correct Training." In *The Foucault Reader*, edited by Paul Rabinow, 188–205. New York: Pantheon, 1984.

Foulks, Margaret J. "The Papanicolaou Smear: Its Impact on the Promotion of Women's Health." *Journal of Obstetric, Gynecologic, & Neonatal Nursing* 27, no. 4 (1998): 367–373.

Fowler, Erika Franklin, Sarah E. Gollust, Amanda F. Dempsey, Paula M. Lantz, and Peter A. Ubel. "Issue Emergence, Evolution of Controversy, and Implications for Competitive Framing: The Case of the HPV Vaccine." *The International Journal of Press/Politics* 17, no. 2 (2012): 169–189.

Fox, Nick J., and Katie J. Ward. "Pharma in the Bedroom . . . and the Kitchen: The Pharmaceuticalisation of Daily Life." *Sociology of Health & Illness* 30, no. 6 (2008): 856–868.

Franco, Eduardo L., Salaheddin M. Mahmud, Joseph Tota, Alex Ferenczy, and François Coutlée. "The Expected Impact of HPV Vaccination on the Accuracy of Cervical Cancer Screening: The Need for a Paradigm Change." *Archives of Medical Research* 40, no. 6 (2009): 478–485.

Freeman, Harold P. "Why Black Women Die of Cancer." *New York Times*, March 13, 2014.

Freeman, Harold P., and Barbara K. Wingrove. *Excess Cervical Cancer Mortality: A Marker for Low Access to Health Care in Poor Communities: An Analysis*. Rockville, MD: National Cancer Institute, Center to Reduce Cancer Health Disparities, 2005.

Friedman, Allison L., and Hilda Shepeard. "Exploring the Knowledge, Attitudes, Beliefs, and Communication Preferences of the General Public Regarding HPV Findings from CDC

Focus Group Research and Implications for Practice." *Health Education & Behavior* 34, no. 3 (2007): 471–485.

Fullilove, Mindy Thompson. "Comment: Abandoning 'Race' as a Variable in Public Health Research: An Idea Whose Time Has Come." *American Journal of Public Health* 88, no. 9 (1998): 1297–1298.

"Gardasil: What Is Cervical Cancer?" Gardasil.com. http://www.gardasil.com/hpv/human -papillomavirus/cervical-cancer/index.html. Accessed December 29, 2009.

"Gardasil Campaign Taps Public Fear of Cancer." *Pharmaceutical Executive*, November 29, 2006.

Gargano, J. W., Elizabeth R. Unger, Gui Liu, Martin Steinau, Elissa Meites, Eileen Dunne and Lauri E Markowitz. "Prevalence of Genital Human Papillomavirus in Males, United States, 2013–2014." *Journal of Infectious Diseases* 215, no 7 (2017): 1070–1079.

Gibbs, Nancy. "Defusing the War over the 'Promiscuity' Vaccine." *Time*, June 21, 2006.

Gillison, Maura L., Tatevik Broutian, Robert K. L. Pickard, Zhen-yue Tong, Weihong Xiao, Lisa Kahle, Barry I. Graubard, and Anil K. Chaturvedi. "Prevalence of Oral HPV Infection in the United States, 2009–2010." *JAMA* 307, no. 7 (2012): 693–703.

Gillison, Maura L., Wayne M. Koch, Randolph B. Capone, Michael Spafford, William H. Westra, Li Wu, Marianna L. Zahurak, Richard W. Daniel, Michael Viglione, and David E. Symer. "Evidence for a Causal Association Between Human Papillomavirus and a Subset of Head and Neck Cancers." *Journal of the National Cancer Institute* 92, no. 9 (2000): 709–720.

Ginsburg, Ophira, Freddie Bray, Michel P. Coleman, Verna Vanderpuye, Alexandru Eniu, S. Rani Kotha, Malabika Sarker, et al. "The Global Burden of Women's Cancers: A Grand Challenge in Global Health." *The Lancet* 389, no. 10071 (2016): 847–860.

Gladwell, Malcolm. "John Rock's Error." *New Yorker*, March 13, 2000.

Griffiths, Malcolm. "Nuns, Virgins, and Spinsters: Rigoni-Stern and Cervical Cancer Revisited." *BJOG: An International Journal of Obstetrics & Gynaecology* 98, no. 8 (1991): 797–802.

Grimes, Richard M., Laura J. Benjamins, and Kendra L. Williams. "Counseling about the HPV Vaccine: Desexualize, Educate, and Advocate." *Journal of Pediatric and Adolescent Gynecology* 26, no. 4 (2013): 243–248.

Groopman, Jerome. "Contagion: Papilloma Virus." *New Yorker*, September 13, 1999.

Haddix, Ann. "Criteria for Vaccination Requirements for U.S. Immigration Purposes." *Federal Register* 74, no. 218 (2009).

Harris, Gardiner. "U.S. Approves Cervical Cancer Vaccine." *New York Times*, June 8, 2006.

Hartzband, Pamela, and Jerome Groopman. "The New Language of Medicine." *New England Journal of Medicine* 365 (2011): 1372–1373.

Hendricks, Melissa. "HPV Vaccine: Who Chooses?" *Los Angeles Times*, February 5, 2007.

Henry, Kevin A., Antoinette M. Stroup, Echo L. Warner, and Deanna Kepka. "Geographic Factors and Human Papillomavirus (HPV) Vaccination Initiation among Adolescent Girls in the United States." *Cancer Epidemiology Biomarkers & Prevention* 25, no. 2 (2016): 309–317.

Herskovits, Beth. "Brand of the Year." *Pharmaceutical Executive*, February 1, 2007.

Hodge, James G., Jr., and Lawrence O. Gostin. *School Vaccination Requirements: Legal and Social Perspectives*. Denver: National Conference of State Legislatures, 2002.

Hogarth, Stuart, Michael M. Hopkins, and Victor Rodriguez. "A Molecular Monopoly? HPV Testing, the Pap Smear and the Molecularisation of Cervical Cancer Screening in the USA." *Sociology of Health & Illness* 34, no. 2 (2012): 234–250.

Howson, Alexandra. "Locating Uncertainties in Cervical Screening." *Health, Risk & Society* 3, no 2 (2001): 167–179.

———. "Surveillance, Knowledge and Risk: The Embodied Experience of Cervical Screening." *Health* 2, no. 2 (1998): 195–215.

———. "Watching You—Watching Me: Visualising Techniques and the Cervix." *Women's Studies International Forum* 24, no. 1 (2001): 97–109.

"HPV Vaccine and State Legislatures." *National Conference of State Legislatures*, April 4, 2017, http://www.ncsl.org/research/health/hpv-vaccine-state-legislation-and-statutes .aspx. Accessed April 7, 2017.

Hunt, Linda M., Nicole D. Truesdell, and Meta J. Kreiner. "Genes, Race, and Culture in Clinical Care." *Medical Anthropology Quarterly* 27, no. 2 (2013): 253–271.

International Agency for Research on Cancer. "Globocan 2012: Estimated Cancer Incidence, Mortality and Prevention Worldwide." *International Agency for Research on Cancer.* http://globocan.iarc.fr/Pages/fact_sheets_cancer.aspx. Accessed November 3, 2016.

Jain, Nidhi, Gary L. Euler, Abigail Shefer, Pengjun Lu, David Yankey, and Lauri Markowitz. "Human Papillomavirus (HPV) Awareness and Vaccination Initiation among Women in the United States, National Immunization Survey—Adult 2007." *Preventive Medicine* 48, no. 5 (2009): 426–431.

Jain, Sarah Lochlann. "Cancer Butch." *Cultural Anthropology* 22, no. 4 (2007): 501–538.

———. *Malignant: How Cancer Becomes Us.* Berkeley: University of California Press, 2013.

Jasanoff, Sheila. "Science and Citizenship: A New Synergy." *Science and Public Policy* 31, no. 2 (2004): 90–94.

Jemal, Ahmedin, Freddie Bray, Melissa M. Center, Jacques Ferlay, Elizabeth Ward, and David Forman. "Global Cancer Statistics." *CA: A Cancer Journal for Clinicians* 61, no. 2 (2011): 69–90.

"Jenny McCarthy Body Count." https://web.archive.org/web/20110207105812/http:// jennymccarthybodycount.com/Jenny_McCarthy_Body_Count/Home.html. Accessed February 8, 2011.

Jeudin, Patricia, Elizabeth Liveright, Marcela G. del Carmen, and Rebecca B. Perkins. "Race, Ethnicity and Income as Factors for HPV Vaccine Acceptance and Use." *Human Vaccines & Immunotherapeutics* 9, no. 7 (2013): 1413–1420.

Kapsalis, Terri. *Public Privates: Performing Gynecology from Both Ends of the Speculum.* Durham, NC: Duke University Press, 1997.

Kaufman, Sharon R. "Regarding the Rise in Autism: Vaccine Safety Doubt, Conditions of Inquiry, and the Shape of Freedom." *Ethos* 38, no. 1 (2010): 8–32.

Kavanagh, Anne M., and Dorothy H. Broom. "Embodied Risk: My Body, Myself?" *Social Science & Medicine* 46, no. 3 (1998): 437–444.

King, Samantha. "Pink Ribbons Inc.: Breast Cancer Activism and the Politics of Philanthropy." *International Journal of Qualitative Studies in Education* 17, no. 4 (2004): 473–492.

Kirkland, Anna. "Credibility Battles in the Autism Litigation." *Social Studies of Science* 42, no. 2 (2012): 237–261.

———. "The Legitimacy of Vaccine Critics: What Is Left After the Autism Hypothesis?" *Journal of Health Politics, Policy and Law* 37, no. 1 (2012): 69–97.

Klawiter, Maren. "Racing for the Cure, Walking Women, and Toxic Touring: Mapping Cultures of Action within the Bay Area Terrain of Breast Cancer." *Social Problems* 46, no. 1 (1999): 104–126.

———. "Risk, Prevention and the Breast Cancer Continuum: The NCI, the FDA, Health Activism and the Pharmaceutical Industry." *History and Technology* 18, no. 4 (2002): 309–353.

Klein, Nicola P., Joan Bartlett, Ali Rowhani-Rahbar, Bruce Fireman, and Roger Baxter. "Waning Protection after Fifth Dose of Acellular Pertussis Vaccine in Children." *New England Journal of Medicine* 367, no. 11 (2012): 1012–1019.

Klug, Stefanie J., Meike Hukelmann, and Maria Blettner. "Knowledge about Infection with Human Papillomavirus: A Systematic Review." *Preventive Medicine* 46, no. 2 (2008): 87–98.

Kolker, Emily S. "Framing as a Cultural Resource in Health Social Movements: Funding Activism and the Breast Cancer Movement in the US 1990—1993." *Sociology of Health & Illness* 26, no. 6 (2004): 820–844.

Krieger, Lisa M., and Jessica Calefati. "Measles Outbreak: Vaccination Exemption Would End under Proposed California Law." *San Jose Mercury News*, February 5, 2015.

Laqueur, Thomas Walter. *Making Sex: Body and Gender from the Greeks to Freud.* Cambridge, MA: Harvard University Press, 1990.

Leach, Melissa, and James Fairhead. *Vaccine Anxieties: Global Science, Child Health and Society.* Abingdon: Earthscan, 2007.

Lehoux, Pascale, and Stuart Blume. "Technology Assessment and the Sociopolitics of Health Technologies." *Journal of Health Politics, Policy and Law* 25, no. 6 (2000): 1083–1120.

Lipphardt, Veronika, and Jörg Niewöhner. "Producing Difference in an Age of Biosociality: Biohistorical Narratives, Standardisation and Resistance as Translations." *Science, Technology & Innovation Studies* 3, no. 1 (2007): 45–65.

Lock, Margaret. "The Tempering of Medical Anthropology: Troubling Natural Categories." *Medical Anthropology Quarterly* 15, no. 4 (2001): 478–492.

Loe, Meika. *The Rise of Viagra: How the Little Blue Pill Changed Sex in America.* New York: New York University Press, 2004.

Longoria, Thalia. "Human Papillomavirus Vaccination Requirement for Immigrants Raises Concerns." *Dallas Morning News*, September 27, 2008.

Lopez, Lori Kido. "The Radical Act of 'Mommy Blogging': Redefining Motherhood through the Blogosphere." *New Media & Society* 11, no. 5: 729–747.

Lupton, Deborah. "Risk and Emotion: Towards an Alternative Theoretical Perspective." *Health, Risk & Society* 15, no. 8 (2013): 634–647.

Luque, John S., Heide Castañeda, Dinorah Martinez Tyson, Natalia Vargas, Sara Proctor, and Cathy D. Meade. "HPV Awareness among Latina Immigrants and Anglo-American Women in the Southern United States: Cultural Models of Cervical Cancer Risk Factors and Beliefs." *NAPA Bulletin* 34, no. 1 (2010): 84–104.

Maher, Bill. "Christians Crusade against Cancer Vaccine." *Salon.com*, March 2, 2007. http://www.salon.com/2007/03/02/hpv_7/. Accessed March 4, 2007.

Mamo, Laura, Amber Nelson, and Aleia Clark. "Producing and Protecting Risky Girlhoods." In *Three Shots at Prevention*, edited by Keith Wailoo, Julie Livingston, Steven Epstein, and Robert Aronowitz, 121–145. Johns Hopkins University Press, 2010.

Mamo, Laura, and Steven Epstein. "The Pharmaceuticalization of Sexual Risk: Vaccine Development and the New Politics of Cancer Prevention." *Social Science & Medicine* 101 (2014): 155–165.

Markowitz, Lauri E., Gui Liu, Susan Hariri, Martin Steinau, Eileen F. Dunne, and Elizabeth R. Unger. "Prevalence of HPV after Introduction of the Vaccination Program in the United States." *Pediatrics* 137, no. 2 (2016). http://pediatrics.aappublications.org/content/pediatrics/early/2016/02/19/peds.2015-1968.full.pdf. Accessed August 17, 2017.

Marlow, Laura A. V., Gregory D. Zimet, Kirsten J. McCaffery, Remo Ostini, and Jo Waller. "Knowledge of Human Papillomavirus (HPV) and HPV Vaccination: An International Comparison." *Vaccine* 31, no. 5 (2013): 763–769.

Martin, Emily. "The Egg and the Sperm: How Science Has Constructed a Romance Based on Stereotypical Male-Female Roles." *Signs* 16, no. 3 (1991): 485–501.

———. *The Woman in the Body: A Cultural Analysis of Reproduction.* Boston: Beacon Press, 2001.

Massad, L. Stewart, Mark H. Einstein, Warner K. Huh, Hormuzd A. Katki, Walter K. Kinney, Mark Schiffman, Diane Solomon, Nicolas Wentzensen, and Herschel W. Lawson. "2012 Updated Consensus Guidelines for the Management of Abnormal Cervical Cancer Screening Tests and Cancer Precursors." *Obstetrics & Gynecology* 121, no. 4 (2013): 829–846.

Mayhew, Allison, Tanya L. Kowalczyk Mullins, Lili Ding, Susan L. Rosenthal, Gregory D. Zimet, Charlene Morrow, and Jessica A. Kahn. "Risk Perceptions and Subsequent Sexual Behaviors after HPV Vaccination in Adolescents." *Pediatrics* 133, no. 3 (2014): 404–411.

Mays, Rose M., Gregory D. Zimet, Yvette Winston, Romina Kee, James Dickes, and Ling Su. "Human Papillomavirus, Genital Warts, Pap Smears, and Cervical Cancer: Knowledge and Beliefs of Adolescent and Adult Women." *Health Care for Women International* 21, no. 5 (2000): 361–374.

McCabe, Katharine. "Mothercraft: Birth Work and the Making of Neoliberal Mothers." *Social Science & Medicine* 162 (2016): 177–184.

McCarthy, Jenny, and Jim Carrey. "Jenny McCarthy: My Son's Recovery from Autism." *CNN.com*, April 3, 2008, http://www.cnn.com/2008/US/04/02/mccarthy .autsimtreatment/. Accessed April 3, 2008.

McGinley, Laurie. "Cancer Doctors Leading Campaign to Boost Use of HPV Vaccine." *Washington Post*, June 19, 2016.

———. "CDC Now Recommends Just Two HPV Vaccine Doses for Preteens." *Washington Post*, October 19, 2016.

———. "Do the New Merck HPV Ads Guilt-Trip Parents or Tell Hard Truths? Both." *Washington Post*, August 11, 2016.

McKay, Betsy. "New Approach to Promoting HPV Vaccinations." *Wall Street Journal*, October 17, 2016.

McKinley, Jesse. "Lawmaker Ends Effort to Make Spanking a Crime." *New York Times*, February 23, 2007.

McNeil, Donald G., Jr. "How a Vaccine Search Ended in Triumph." *New York Times*, August 29, 2006.

Mello, Michelle M., Sara Abiola, and James Colgrove. "Pharmaceutical Companies' Role in State Vaccination Policymaking: The Case of Human Papillomavirus Vaccination." *American Journal of Public Health* 102, no. 5 (2012): 893–898.

Michalas, Stylianos P. "The Pap Test: George N. Papanicolaou (1883–1962): A Screening Test for the Prevention of Cancer of Uterine Cervix." *European Journal of Obstetrics & Gynecology and Reproductive Biology* 90, no. 2 (2000): 135–138.

Mishra, Amrita, and Janice E. Graham. "Risk, Choice and the 'Girl Vaccine': Unpacking Human Papillomavirus (HPV) Immunisation." *Health, Risk & Society* 14, no. 1 (2012): 57–69.

Monk-Turner, Elizabeth, Kristy Wren, Leanne McGill, Chris Matthiae, Stephan Brown, and Derrick Brooks. "Who Is Gazing at Whom? A Look at How Sex Is Used in Magazine Advertisements." *Journal of Gender Studies* 17, no. 3 (2008): 201–209.

Morrison, Aimée. "Autobiography in Real Time: A Genre Analysis of Personal Mommy Blogging." *Cyberpsychology: Journal of Psychosocial Research on Cyberspace* 42, no. 2 (2015): Article 5.

Moynihan, Ray, Iona Heath, and David Henry. "Selling Sickness: The Pharmaceutical Industry and Disease Mongering. Commentary: Medicalisation of Risk Factors." *BMJ* 324, no. 7342 (2002): 886–891.

Mukherjee, Siddhartha. *The Emperor of All Maladies: A Biography of Cancer*. New York: Simon and Schuster, 2010.

Muñoz, Nubia, Xavier Castellsagué, Amy Berrington de González, and Lutz Gissmann. "HPV in the Etiology of Human Cancer." *Vaccine* 24 (2006): S1–S10.

Muñoz, Nubia, F. Xavier Bosch, Silvia de Sanjosé, Rolando Herrero, Xavier Castellsagué, Keerti V. Shah, Peter J. F. Snijders, and Chris J. L. M. Meijer. "Epidemiologic Classification of Human Papillomavirus Types Associated with Cervical Cancer." *New England Journal of Medicine* 348, no. 6 (2003): 518–527.

Muraskin, William A. *Polio Eradication and Its Discontents: An Historian's Journey through an International Public Health (Un)Civil War*. Himayatnagar, Hyderabad: Orient Blackswan, 2012.

Murch, Simon H., Andrew Anthony, David H. Casson, Mohsin Malik, Mark Berelowitz, Amar P. Dhillon, Michael A. Thomson, Alan Valentine, Susan E. Davies, and John A. Walker Smith. "Retraction of an Interpretation." *Lancet* 363, no. 9411 (2004): 750.

Murphy, Michelle. *Seizing the Means of Reproduction: Entanglements of Feminism, Health, and Technoscience*. Durham, NC: Duke University Press, 2012.

Musselwhite, L. W., C. M. Oliveira, T. Kwaramba, N. de Paula Pantano, J. S. Smith, J. H. Fregnani, R. M. Reis, E. Mauad, F. L. Vazquez, and A. Longatto-Filho. "Racial/Ethnic Disparities in Cervical Cancer Screening and Outcomes." *Acta Cytologica* 60, no. 6 (2016): 518–526.

National Cancer Institute. "Cancer Disparities." *National Cancer Institute*, October 21, 2016. https://www.cancer.gov/about-cancer/understanding/disparities. Accessed January 17, 2017.

———. "Cancer Health Disparities—National Cancer Institute." *National Cancer Institute*, March 11, 2008. http://www.cancer.gov/cancertopics/factsheet/disparities/cancer-health -disparities. Accessed February 6, 2014.

———. "Cancer Stat Facts: Cancer of the Cervix Uteri." *National Cancer Institute: Surveillance, Epidemiology, and End Results Program*. http://seer.cancer.gov/statfacts/html/ cervix.html. Accessed April 6, 2014.

———. "NCI-Designated Cancer Centers Urge HPV Vaccination for the Prevention of Cancer." January 27, 2016. https://www.fredhutch.org/en/news/center-news/2016/01/ cancer-centers-consensus-hpv-vaccine.html. Accessed January 31, 2016.

National Cancer Institute-Designated Cancer Centers. "NCI-designated Cancer Centers Urge HPV Vaccination for the Prevention of Cancer." January 27, 2016.

NHS Choices. "Ruling on Doctor in MMR Scare." *NHS* January 29, 2010. http://www .nhs.uk/news/2010/01january/pages/mmr-vaccine-autism-scare-doctor.aspx. Accessed July 4, 2017.

National Vaccine Advisory Committee. "Overcoming Barriers to Low HPV Vaccine Uptake in the United States: Recommendations from the National Vaccine Advisory Committee." *Public Health Reports* (January–February 2016): 17–25.

National Vaccine Information Center. "About National Vaccine Information Center." http://www.nvic.org/about.aspx. Accessed July 4, 2017.

National Vaccine Information Center. "NVIC's Notable Accomplishments and History." *National Vaccine Information Center*. http://www.nvic.org/about/notable-accomplishments-and-history.aspx. Accessed July 4, 2017.

Novas, Carlos, and Nikolas Rose. "Genetic Risk and the Birth of the Somatic Individual." *Economy and Society* 29, no. 4 (2000): 485–513.

Offit, Paul A. "Let's Not Talk about Sex." *New York Times*, August 19, 2014.

Oldani, Michael J. "Thick Prescriptions: Toward an Interpretation of Pharmaceutical Sales Practices." *Medical Anthropology Quarterly* 18, no. 3 (2004): 325–356.

Oudshoorn, Nelly. "Drugs for Healthy People: The Culture of Testing Hormonal Contraceptives for Women and Men." *Clio Medica* 66 (2002): 123–140.

———. *The Male Pill: A Biography of a Technology in the Making*. Durham, NC: Duke University Press, 2003.

———. "On Masculinities, Technologies, and Pain: The Testing of Male Contraceptives in the Clinic and the Media." *Science, Technology & Human Values* 24, no. 2 (1999): 265–289.

Perry, Rick. "Statement of Gov. Rick Perry on HPV Vaccine Executive Order." *La Prensa* 13, no. 22 (2007): 18.

Petryna, Adriana, Andrew Lakoff, and Arthur Kleinman. *Global Pharmaceuticals: Ethics, Markets, Practices*. Durham, NC: Duke University Press, 2006.

Pitts, Marian, and Tracy Clarke. "Human Papillomavirus Infections and Risks of Cervical Cancer: What Do Women Know?" *Health Education Research* 17, no. 6 (2002): 706–714.

Pollack, Andrew. "F.D.A. Panel Recommends Replacement for the Pap Test." *New York Times*, March 12, 2014.

Pollack, Andrew, and Stephanie Saul. "Merck to Halt Lobbying for Vaccine for Girls." *New York Times*, February 21, 2007.

Pollitt, Katha. "Virginity or Death!" *The Nation*, May 30, 2005.

President's Cancer Panel. *Accelerating HPV Vaccine Uptake: Urgency for Action to Prevent Cancer*. Bethesda, MD: U.S. Department of Health and Human Services, 2014. https://deainfo.nci.nih.gov/advisory/pcp/annualReports/HPV/PDF/PCP_Annual_Report_2012-2013.pdf. Accessed September 13, 2016.

Pruitt, Sandi L., Patricia A. Parker, Susan K. Peterson, Tao Le, Michele Follen, and Karen Basen-Engquist. "Knowledge of Cervical Dysplasia and Human Papillomavirus Among Women Seen in a Colposcopy Clinic." *Gynecologic Oncology* 99, no. 3 (2005): S236–S244.

"Public Hearing on HPV Vaccine Went until Midnight." *KXAN.com*. February 20, 2007. Accessed February 21, 2007.

Ramsey, Lydia. "A Shocking New Ad Is Shaming Parents for Not Giving Their Children This Unpopular Vaccine." *Business Insider*, July 15, 2016.

Reventlow, Susanne Dalsgaard, Lotte Hvas, and Kirsti Malterud. "Making the Invisible Body Visible: Bone Scans, Osteoporosis and Women's Bodily Experiences." *Social Science & Medicine* 62, no. 11 (2006): 2720–2731.

Richart, Ralph M., and Thomas C. Wright. "Controversies in the Management of Low-Grade Cervical Intraepithelial Neoplasia." *Cancer* 71, no. 4 (supplement) (1993): 1413–1421.

Robertson, Ann. "Biotechnology, Political Rationality and Discourses on Health Risk." *Health*: 5, no. 3 (2001): 293–309.

Rose, Nikolas, and Carlos Novas. "Biological Citizenship." In *Global Assemblages: Technology, Politics, and Ethics as Anthropological Problems*, edited by Aihwa Ong and Stephen J. Collier, 439–463. Oxford: Blackwell Publishing, 2005.

Rose, Susannah L., Janelle Highland, Matthew T. Karafa, and Steven Joffe. "Patient Advocacy Organizations, Industry Funding, and Conflicts of Interest." *JAMA Internal Medicine* 177, no. 3 (2017): 344–350.

Rositch, Anne F., Rebecca G. Nowak, and Patti E. Gravitt. "Increased Age and Race-Specific Incidence of Cervical Cancer after Correction for Hysterectomy Prevalence in the United States from 2000 to 2009." *Cancer* 120, no. 13 (2014): 2032–2038.

Sagonowsky, Eric. "GSK Exits U.S. Market with Its HPV Vaccine Cervarix." *Fierce Pharma*, October 21, 2016. http://www.fiercepharma.com/pharma/gsk-exits-u-s-market-its-hpv -vaccine-cervarix. Accessed November 1, 2016.

Salit, Richard. "HPV Vaccination Rate for R.I. Seventh Graders 'Extremely Encouraging.'" *Providence Journal*, November 19, 2015.

Salmon, Daniel A., Stephen P. Teret, C. Raina MacIntyre, David Salisbury, Margaret A. Burgess, and Neal A. Halsey. "Compulsory Vaccination and Conscientious or Philosophical Exemptions: Past, Present, and Future." *The Lancet* 367, no. 9508 (2006): 436–442.

Samarasekera, Udani, and Richard Horton. "Women's Cancers: Shining a Light on a Neglected Health Inequity." *The Lancet* 389, no. 10071 (2016): 771–773.

Sandelowski, Margarete. "'This Most Dangerous Instrument:' Propriety, Power, and the Vaginal Speculum." *Journal of Obstetric, Gynecologic & Neonatal Nursing* 29, no. 1 (2000): 73–82.

Sandri, Maria T., Paola Lentati, Elvira Benini, Patrizia Dell'Orto, Laura Zorzino, Francesca M Carozzi, Patrick Maisonneuve, Rita Passerini, Michela Salvatici, and Chiara Casadio. "Comparison of the Digene HC2 Assay and the Roche AMPLICOR Human Papillomavirus (HPV) Test for Detection of High-risk HPV Genotypes in Cervical Samples." *Journal of Clinical Microbiology* 44, no. 6 (2006): 2141–2146.

Saul, Stephanie. "Merck Wrote Drug Studies for Doctors." *New York Times*, April 16, 2008.

Sawaya, George F., and Karen Smith-McCune. "Cervical Cancer Screening." *Obstetrics & Gynecology* 127, no. 3 (2016): 465–466.

———. "HPV Vaccination: More Answers, More Questions." *New England Journal of Medicine* 356, no. 19 (2007): 1991–1993.

Scharff, Darcell P., Katherine J. Mathews, Pamela Jackson, Jonathan Hoffsuemmer, Emeobong Martin, and Dorothy Edwards. "More Than Tuskegee: Understanding Mistrust about Research Participation." *Journal of Health Care for the Poor and Underserved* 21, no. 3 (2010): 879–897.

Schwartz, J. L., A. L. Caplan, R. R. Faden, and J. Sugarman. "Lessons from the Failure of Human Papillomavirus Vaccine State Requirements." *Clinical Pharmacology & Therapeutics* 82, no. 6 (2007): 760–763.

Selleck, Laurie Gilmore. "Pretty in Pink: The Susan G. Komen Network and the Branding of the Breast Cancer Cause." *Nordic Journal of English Studies* 9, no. 3 (2010): 119–138.

Siegel, Rebecca L., Kimberly D. Miller, and Ahmedin Jemal. "Cancer Statistics, 2016." *CA: A Cancer Journal for Clinicians* 66, no. 1 (2016): 7–30.

Siers-Poisson, Judith. "Women in Government, Merck's Trojan Horse: Part Three in a Series on the Politics and PR of Cervical Cancer." *Alternet*, July 17, 2007. http://www.alternet .org/story/56679/women_in_government,_merck's_trojan_horse%3A_part_three_in_a _series_on_the_politics_and_pr_of_cervical_cancer. Accessed November 9, 2008.

Silberner, Joanne. "FDA to Review Vaccine for Cancer-Causing Virus." *NPR*, May 18, 2006. http://www.npr.org/templates/story/story.php?storyId=5413896. Accessed May 18, 2006.

Silverman, Ed. "Drug Firms Still Abuse Citizen Petitions, FDA Tells Congress." *STAT*, August 22, 2016. https://www.statnews.com/pharmalot/2016/08/22/fda-generics -citizen-petition/. Accessed October 31, 2016.

———. "Pharmalot, Pharmalittle: Was the FDA Commissioner Paid by Drug Makers Last Year?" *STAT*, July 5, 2016. https://www.statnews.com/pharmalot/2016/07/05/robert -califf-fda-generics-teva/. Accessed February 1, 2017.

Singh, Gopal K. "Rural-Urban Trends and Patterns in Cervical Cancer Mortality, Incidence, Stage, and Survival in the United States, 1950–2008." *Journal of Community Health* 37, no. 1 (2012): 217–223.

Skloot, Rebecca. *The Immortal Life of Henrietta Lacks*. New York: Broadway Books, 2010.

Smith, Aaron. "Street Divided over Numbers from Big Pharma." *CNN Money*, April 20, 2007, http://money.cnn.com/2007/04/19/news/companies/drug_wrap/. Accessed April 19, 2007.

Smith, Susan L. "The Effective Use of Fear Appeals in Persuasive Immunization: An Analysis of National Immunization Intervention Messages." *Journal of Applied Communication Research* 25, no. 4 (1997): 264–292.

Sobo, Elisa J., Arianna Huhn, Autumn Sannwald, and Lori Thurman. "Information Curation among Vaccine Cautious Parents: Web 2.0, Pinterest Thinking, and Pediatric Vaccination Choice." *Medical Anthropology* 35, no. 6 (2016): 529–546.

Sontag, Susan. Illness as Metaphor *and* AIDS and Its Metaphors. New York: Macmillan, 2001.

Specter, Michael. "Reporter at Large—Political Science." *New Yorker*, March 13, 2006.

Steenhuysen, Julie. "Merck Cancer Vaccine Faces Christian Right Scrutiny." *Reuters*, May 22, 2006.

Stein, Rob. "Specialists Split over HPV Test's Role in Cancer Screening." *Shots: Health News from NPR*, January 8, 2015. http://www.npr.org/blogs/health/2015/01/08/375619687/ specialists-split-over-hpv-tests-role-in-cancer-screening. Accessed January 8, 2015.

Stokley, Shannon, Jenny Jeyarajah, David Yankey, Maria Cano, Julianne Gee, Jill Roark, R. C. Curtis, and Lauri Markowitz. "Human Papillomavirus Vaccination Coverage among Adolescents, 2007–2013, and Postlicensure Vaccine Safety Monitoring, 2006–2014 United States." *Morbidity and Mortality Weekly Report* 63, no. 29 (2014): 620–624.

Streefland, Pieter, A. M. R. Chowdhury, and Pilar Ramos-Jimenez. "Patterns of Vaccination Acceptance." *Social Science & Medicine* 49, no. 12 (1999): 1705–1716.

Sufrin, Carolyn B., and Joseph S. Ross. "Pharmaceutical Industry Marketing: Understanding Its Impact on Women's Health." *Obstetrical & Gynecological Survey* 63, no. 9 (2008): 585–596.

Swanson, Wendy Sue. "HPV Vaccine Decreases HPV Infections!" *Seattle Children's Hospital Research Foundation*, March 1, 2016. http://seattlemamadoc.seattlechildrens.org/ decreasing-rates-of-hpv/. Accessed March 5, 2016.

Tan, Thanh. "31 Days, 31 Ways: Family Planning Funding Slashed." *Texas Tribune*, August 15, 2011. https://www.texastribune.org/2011/08/15/day-15/. Accessed April 25, 2015.

Tavernise, Sabrina. "Rise in Early Cervical Cancer Detection Is Linked to Affordable Care Act." *New York Times*, November 24, 2015.

Taylor, Janelle S. "Surfacing the Body Interior." *Annual Review of Anthropology* 34 (2005): 741–756.

Teixeira, Luiz Antonio, and Ilana Löwy. "Imperfect Tools for a Difficult Job: Colposcopy, 'Colpocytology,' and Screening for Cervical Cancer in Brazil." *Social Studies of Science* 41, no. 4 (2011): 585–608.

Tiefer, Leonore. "Female Sexual Dysfunction: A Case Study of Disease Mongering and Activist Resistance." *PLoS Medicine* 3, no. 4 (2006): e178.

Tiro, Jasmin A., Helen I. Meissner, Sarah Kobrin, and Veronica Chollette. "What Do Women in the US Know about Human Papillomavirus and Cervical Cancer?" *Cancer Epidemiology Biomarkers & Prevention* 16, no. 2 (2007): 288–294.

Todorova, Irina. "Introduction to the Special Section: Cross-Cultural Beliefs, Attitudes, and Dilemmas about Vaccination." *International Journal of Behavioral Medicine* 21, no. 1 (2014): 1.

Tolbert, Pamela S., and Lynne G. Zucker. "The Institutionalization of Institutional Theory." In *Handbook of Organization Studies*, edited by S. Clegg, C. Hardy, and W. Nord, 175–190. London: Sage.

Towghi, Fouzieyha. "The Biopolitics of Reproductive Technologies beyond the Clinic: Localizing HPV Vaccines in India." *Medical Anthropology* 32, no. 4 (2013): 325–342.

U.S. Food and Drug Administration. "Fast Track." *U.S. Food and Drug Administration.* http://www.fda.gov/forconsumers/byaudience/forpatientadvocates/speedingaccesstoimportantnewtherapies/ucm128291.html. Accessed February 10, 2014.

———. "FDA Approves First Human Papillomavirus Test for Primary Cervical Cancer Screening." *U.S. Food and Drug Administration*, April 24, 2014. http://www.fda.gov/NewsEvents/Newsroom/PressAnnouncements/ucm394773.htm. Accessed January 19, 2015.

Vaccines and Related Biological Products Advisory Committee minutes. Food and Drug Administration, Center for Biologics Evaluation and Research, May 18, 2006. https://www.fda.gov/OHRMS/DOCKETS/ac/06/transcripts/2006-4222t1.pdf. Accessed October 12, 2008.

van Kammen, Jessika. "Representing Users' Bodies: The Gendered Development of Anti-Fertility Vaccines." *Science, Technology & Human Values* 24, no. 3 (1999): 307–337.

Victor, Daniel. "C.D.C. Defends Advice to Women on Drinking and Pregnancy." *New York Times*, February 5, 2016.

Viens, Laura J., Jane Henley, Meg Watson, Lauri E. Markowitz, Cheryll C. Thomas, Trevor D. Thompson, Hilda Razzaghi, and Mona Saraiya. "Human Papillomavirus—Associated Cancers—United States, 2008–2012." *Morbidity and Mortality Weekly Report* 65 (2016): 661–666.

Vuckovic, Nancy, and Mark Nichter. "Changing Patterns of Pharmaceutical Practice in the United States." *Social Science & Medicine* 44, no. 9 (1997): 1285–1302.

Wailoo, Keith, Julie Livingston, Steven E. Epstein, and Robert Aronowitz. *Three Shots at Prevention: The HPV Vaccine and the Politics of Medicine's Simple Solutions*. Baltimore, MD: Johns Hopkins University Press, 2010.

Wakefield, Andrew J., Simon H. Murch, Andrew Anthony, John Linnell, D. M. Casson, Mohsin Malik, Mark Berelowitz, Amar P. Dhillon, Michael A. Thomson, and Peter Harvey. "Retracted: Ileal-Lymphoid-Nodular Hyperplasia, Non-Specific Colitis, and Pervasive Developmental Disorder in Children." *The Lancet* 351, no. 9103 (1998): 637–641.

Waller, J., K. McCaffery, S. Forrest, A. Szarewski, L. Cadman, and J. Wardle. "Awareness of Human Papillomavirus among Women Attending a Well Woman Clinic." *Sexually Transmitted Infections* 79, no. 4 (2003): 320–322.

Washington, Harriet A. *Medical Apartheid: The Dark History of Medical Experimentation on Black Americans from Colonial Times to the Present*. New York: Doubleday Books, 2006.

Whyte, Susan Reynolds. "Health Identities and Subjectivities." *Medical Anthropology Quarterly* 23, no. 1 (2009): 6–15.

Whyte, Susan Reynolds, Sjaak Van der Geest, and Anita Hardon. *Social Lives of Medicines*. Cambridge: Cambridge University Press, 2002.

Williams, Simon J., Paul Martin, and Jonathan Gabe. "The Pharmaceuticalisation of Society? A Framework for Analysis." *Sociology of Health & Illness* 33, no. 5 (2011): 710–725.

Willig, Carla. "Cancer Diagnosis as Discursive Capture: Phenomenological Repercussions of Being Positioned within Dominant Constructions of Cancer." *Social Science & Medicine* 73, no. 6 (2011): 897–903.

Willon, Phil, and Melanie Mason. "California Gov. Jerry Brown Signs New Vaccination Law, One of Nation's Toughest." *Los Angeles Times*. June 30, 2015. http://www.latimes.com/local/political/la-me-ln-governor-signs-tough-new-vaccination-law-20150630-story.html, accessed August 15, 2017.

Wilson, Duff. "Merck to Pay $950 Million Over Vioxx." *New York Times*, November 22, 2011.

Winer, Rachel L., James P. Hughes, Qinghua Feng, Sandra O'Reilly, Nancy B. Kiviat, King K. Holmes, and Laura A. Koutsky. "Condom Use and the Risk of Genital Human Papillomavirus Infection in Young Women." *New England Journal of Medicine* 354, no. 25 (2006): 2645–2654.

Wolinsky, Howard. "Disease Mongering and Drug Marketing." *EMBO Reports* 6, no. 7 (2005): 612–614.

Wynn, Lisa L., and James Trussell. "The Social Life of Emergency Contraception in the United States: Disciplining Pharmaceutical Use, Disciplining Sexuality, and Constructing Zygotic Bodies." *Medical Anthropology Quarterly* 20, no. 3 (2006): 297–320.

Yaqub, Ohid, Sophie Castle-Clarke, Nick Sevdalis, and Joanna Chataway. "Attitudes to Vaccination: A Critical Review." *Social Science & Medicine* 112 (2014): 1–11.

Zald, Mayer N., and Patricia Denton. "From Evangelism to General Service: The Transformation of the YMCA." *Administrative Science Quarterly* 9, no. 2 (1963): 214–234.

Zapler, Mike. "Local Assemblywoman Drops Cervical Cancer Bill." *Palo Alto Daily News*, February 2, 2007.

Zilber, Tammar B. "Institutionalization as an Interplay between Actions, Meanings, and Actors: The Case of a Rape Crisis Center in Israel." *Academy of Management Journal* 45, no. 1 (2002): 234–254.

Zimet, Gregory D., Zeev Rosberger, William A. Fisher, Samara Perez, and Nathan W. Stupiansky. "Beliefs, Behaviors and HPV Vaccine: Correcting the Myths and the Misinformation." *Preventive Medicine* 57, no. 5 (2013): 414–418.

Zola, Irving Kenneth. "Medicine as an Institution of Social Control." *Sociological Review* 20, no. 4 (1972): 487–504.

zur Hausen, Harald. "Oncogenic Herpes Viruses." *Biochimica et Biophysica Acta (BBA) Reviews on Cancer* 417, no. 1 (1975): 25–53.

———. "The Role of Viruses in Human Tumors." *Advances in Cancer Research* 33 (1980): 77–107.

———. "Human Genital Cancer: Synergism Between Two Virus Infections or Synergism Between a Virus Infection and Initiating Events?" *The Lancet*, December 18, 1982: 1370–1372.

Index

About the Author

S. D. Gottlieb is a medical anthropologist whose work has been published in *Medical Anthropology Quarterly*, *BioSocieties*, and an edited volume about biomedical resistances. Funded by the National Science Foundation and the Wenner-Gren Foundation, her research explores patient advocacies in response to new medical technologies. She has taught at California State University, East Bay, and was a visiting scholar at the Center for Science, Technology, Medicine, and Society at the University of California, Berkeley.

CPSIA information can be obtained
at www.ICGtesting.com
Printed in the USA
LVOW03s0625081117
555436LV00001B/1/P